ON
ASSIGNMENT

ON
ASSIGNMENT

Memoir of a **National Geographic Filmmaker**

JAMES R. LARISON

CHICAGO
REVIEW
PRESS

Published by Chicago Review Press Incorporated
814 North Franklin Street
Chicago, Illinois 60610
ISBN 978-1-64160-520-5

Library of Congress Control Number: 2021942406

Typesetting: Nord Compo
Unless otherwise indicated, all images are from the author's collection

Printed in the United States of America
5 4 3 2 1

In memory of a brilliant, thoughtful friend
taken from us too soon.

Donald M. Cooper

Associate Director and Acting Director
Educational Films Division
National Geographic Society

CONTENTS

Author's Note   ix
Prologue   xi

Part I: Coming into the Wild

  1. Lake Timagami   3
  2. Breaking Trail   9
  3. Egegik, Alaska   19
  4. The Flying Coffin   32
  5. Rescue and Recovery   36
  6. The Conversation   41

Part II: On Assignment

  7. That Big Break   49
  8. Our First Assignment   62
  9. The Cayman Trench   83
 10. Hart Mountain   98
 11. A Living Ocean   113
 12. Tiger Shark!   127

Part III: Love of Wilderness

 13. The Unforgiving World of Ice   137
 14. Robson Glacier   151

Part IV: Advocacy

15. *The Living Earth*   167
16. Old Growth   178
17. *Ancient Forests*   196
18. *Diversity of Life*   204
19. Palau   216
20. Egegik Revisited   231

Part V: Wounds That Will Not Heal

21. A World of Wounds   243

Epilogue: How Films Were Made   247

Acknowledgments   251
The Films of James and Elaine Larison   253
About the Author   255

AUTHOR'S NOTE

THIS MEMOIR SPANS MORE THAN sixty years. To make it more readable, I have taken the liberty of collapsing time and occasionally bringing events that may have happened at separate locations together for the sake of clarity and brevity. Otherwise, this memoir captures events and people as best I can remember them.

I have changed and omitted some names to protect people and their privacy.

I make no apologies for my defense of nature, wildlife, and intact healthy ecosystems. I am an ecologist. I believe the future of the entire planetary biological system, which includes human beings, depends on the preservation and conservation of wild lands and wildlife.

I hope this book will inspire its readers to look to nature for peace of mind.

PROLOGUE

ONE INCH AT A TIME, I crawled on my belly into an underground cave cradling my Arriflex motion picture camera. There was not enough head room in the cave to turn over let alone sit up. Snakes—thousands of them—carpeted the cave floor. The only sound came from the snakes themselves as countless individuals slid over top of one another in a continual roiling mass of writhing, scale-covered bodies. The snakes had no interest in me. The males were trying to mate with the females. The females were trying to escape the craziness. I was just trying not to panic. Gently, I pushed the snakes to the side as I struggled to move deeper into the dark. But the snakes were implacable, and soon they began crawling over top of me, through my clothes, and under my armpits. I could feel an especially big one starting up the inside of my left pant leg headed— who knows where. The deeper I went into the cave, the more the walls and snakes seemed to close in on me. I was on the verge of a full-blown panic attack, but if I panicked and had to suddenly get out, I would have had to shimmy feetfirst, back the way I came in.

You might ask, what was a person who harbors an irrational fear of snakes and another, perhaps not-so-irrational, fear of closed-in spaces doing in a tiny cave in springtime when snakes like to breed by the tens of thousands in these tight underground spaces?

That would be a *good question*. Many of the things I did in those days a normal person might consider reckless, but I did them because

I cared more about the footage I might obtain and the film I wanted to make than I did about the panic welling up inside of me. I came to film red-sided garter snakes coming out of hibernation for the National Geographic Society, and I was not going to leave until I got that footage, no matter how many snakes crawled inside my pants.

For nearly two decades, my wife Elaine and I worked for the Television and Educational Films Division of the National Geographic Society. It was the best job in the world, even when underground in a snake pit. Every assignment—and there were nearly one hundred of them—came with its own set of challenges. Underground a snake pit in Manitoba one day, and not a year later, I was in a frozen northern Wisconsin lake photographing a mud minnow that breathed air from tiny bubbles trapped on the underside of a sheet of ice two feet thick. Other times, Elaine and I would willingly strap ourselves to the side of a mountain with an eleven-millimeter rope affixed to a single ice screw, a thousand feet of mostly air beneath our feet. Then, before you knew it, we would be bathing in the warm waters of the South Pacific with a two-thousand pound, twenty-foot manta ray gliding silently overhead.

We went to these places and we did these things because we wanted to share our love of wilderness with others. I thought if I could just show enough people what was out there, if I could use my skill as a filmmaker to capture the essence of wilderness, if I could make others feel nature the way I felt it, they too would believe in the importance of wild places. They too would want to save as much wilderness as possible. Yes, there were risks and there were challenges, but these were the choices Elaine and I had to make every day of our lives, just to do this spectacularly rewarding job.

In a continual struggle to maintain a reasonably normal family life, we took our two young sons with us most everywhere we went. John and Ted spent two years on a desert mountain in eastern Oregon, six months snorkeling on the Great Barrier Reef, and most of one summer living with bears in Alaska. They learned to scuba dive in Palau, map the stars in the sky above Bora-Bora, and climb ice on Athabasca Glacier in Alberta.

Not surprisingly, when they came home from one of their many long trips, our sons wanted to share their experiences with classmates.

One time we got a call from our oldest son's teacher, who told Elaine we needed to do something about our son telling such tall tales. "So, what exactly did John say?" Elaine respectfully asked. The teacher repeated John's story about a blue-ringed octopus—one of the most poisonous animals in the world—coming to within a few inches of his dive mask. Elaine simply asked, "Did you ever consider that he might be telling the truth?"

Our lives were different, always challenging, and often dangerous. A lot of people have had trouble wrapping their minds around what we did; a few of my best friends have even told me I was crazy to dive with man-eating sharks, hang on the outside of helicopters, and climb vertical ice, but when I look back at the break points in our lives, it occurs to me that we never really considered any other options. We wanted so badly to do this job and make a difference in the struggle to preserve the environment. For us, there was only one choice, to eagerly accept that next assignment and break our own trail in pursuit of those priceless National Geographic images, and to tell the story of wilderness.

PART I

COMING
INTO THE WILD

1

LAKE TIMAGAMI

With little more than a seventeen-foot wood-and-canvas canoe, two paddles, and a youthful certainty that all would end well, we launched our marriage from a gravel bar at the eastern end of Lake Timagami (now Temagami) and cut our own path into a largely undisturbed Canadian wilderness. It was the summer of 1967, and Elaine and I were on our honeymoon, just two eighteen-year-old kids with vivid dreams and insufficient experience. Elaine took the bow of our canoe, using her paddle to set a four-count rhythm while I sat in the stern using a J-stroke to provide power and direction. Of course it couldn't last, but our lives began smoothly enough with our canoe gliding effortlessly across glassy, still, and deep waters. In those endlessly quiet moments, the wilderness spoke to us in a language of its own. As we listened, the bonds between the three of us grew, and I came to understand that one could do far worse than to build a marriage in a place of such beauty, harmony, and elegance.

Together, we slid across the mirrorlike surface of the lake, our own images reflecting back at us, everything tinted in a surreal golden glow. Each time Elaine would pull her paddle through the water and retrieve it in preparation for the next stroke, a glistening sheet of water would slide down the paddle blade and drain hypnotically back to the lake. Driven by a light cool breeze, a constant procession of parallel ripples slid across the watery expanse, each in its turn coming to lap gently against the bow of our Old Town canoe. The hollow slapping sound drifted away and came back seconds later as rhythmic echoes from a distant shore. It was peaceful and quiet and we were deliriously happy together.

Just before the sun set that first evening, Elaine and I landed miles from the nearest road on a tiny island with no name, pitched our tent beneath an ancient white pine, and crawled into our zip-together sleeping bags. "Are you happy?" I whispered. Her bright eyes beamed back her unmistakable answer. We spent that first night together locked in an embrace, talking and planning our lives.

Elaine fell asleep first, but I was too excited. The wilderness spoke and I eagerly listened. There was the sound of water lapping gently against a pebble-strewn beach. Drifting above was the unmistakable rustling of an aspen responding to the delicate breath of air coming off the lake. Through the open tent flap, I could see fragile fingers of fog rising silently from the water's surface, drifting into the black night, backlit by the faint blue glow of a quarter moon. Overhead, a squadron of little brown bats slashed through the sky, feasting on an ample supply of mosquitoes. And, one by one, bullfrogs began to sound off.

Elaine's warmth radiated through our sleeping bag. Her eyes fluttered beneath delicate lids. Wherever her mind had taken her, she seemed happy. Her straight dark hair flowed over her neck and across our sleeping bag, tickling the stubble on my chin. I wrapped one single curl around my index finger and promised never to forget this moment nor take this woman for granted. For more than fifty years, I have worked to keep that promise.

Just as everything seemed to be quieting down for the night, the silence was broken by a distant haunting sound—a long, slow, mournful wail. At first it sounded like a lonely timber wolf howling into the night. Then, as the wail echoed over the water, it began to sound more like a woman crying in anguish. From farther down the lake, a second cry answered the first, and both calls seemed to chase each other across the water's surface until they topped the shoreline trees then vanished, leaving behind only echoes.

With the sound still heavy in the air, Elaine woke from a deep sleep, bolted out of our sleeping bag, landed on her feet in the middle of our tent, and screamed, "Wolf! Jim, wolves!"

Elaine had grown up in upstate New York, the daughter of a dairy farmer who desperately wanted a son to help with the chores but got four girls instead. So, it fell to his eldest daughter to join him in the barn to milk the cows, to carry fifty-pound milk pails, and to work on weekends tossing hay bales into the loft. Later, Elaine would follow along behind her dad in the woods hunting rabbits by day and raccoon by night. By her eighth birthday, she was also helping her mom raise her younger sisters and cooking for all the hired hands who came to help with the fall harvest. Elaine was strong, never seeming to tire or disappoint.

Many of Elaine's friends had told her that an eighteen-year-old is too young to get married, but she had grown up fast. Her mom and dad had reluctantly given their consent but were visibly anxious. Her dad had been sent to North Africa and then Italy during World War II and had seen so much loss that he was afraid to let his daughter out of his sight. On one of our many long walks before we were married, Elaine had told me she felt overprotected as a child. She did not know how to swim and once told me, "I am not allowed to wade in the lake deeper than my ankles." She had internalized some of her parents' fears but was also frustrated by the limits her parents had set for her and was eager to push back some of those boundaries. On the night before our wedding, with her eyes on fire with excitement, Elaine had said, "This marriage is going to be a very big adventure."

While she may have been eager for that adventure to begin, it was also true that she had never before spent a night outside her family farmhouse, let alone in the middle of a Canadian wilderness. Now, she was bravely canoeing across water that could easily kill her, should she accidentally fall in, surrounded by things she didn't fully understand, sharing a sleeping bag with someone she hardly knew. Understandably, Elaine was just a little bit on edge.

I was trying to be a good husband without really knowing a thing about it. My wife was frightened, so I took her hand and gently guided her back down into our sleeping bag, wrapped my arm over top of her head, and quietly whispered, "Don't worry, it's not a wolf. It's just a couple of lonely loons trying to find each other in the fog."

Truth be told, I was not much more worldly or experienced than Elaine was. I had grown up less than a mile down the road from her family farm, one of four boys who lived in an uninsulated house with coal heat and hand-me-down clothes. When I was just a toddler my father declared bankruptcy trying to make it with a tiny community grocery and never fully recovered. His failure would hang like a blanket over top of all of us for years to come. My mom worked first as a waitress and later as a secretary to help pick up the financial slack. We boys, without really knowing it, grew up rural poor.

Despite the financial limitations my father faced, he had what, at the time, was a very unusual idea. He wanted to show his boys the western national parks. So, in the summer of 1956, long before there was a viable airline industry and even before the interstate highway system would be built, he packed four boys, two adult parents, and a grandmother into a beat-up four-door Plymouth sedan—top speed fifty-five miles per hour—and began winding his way from tiny town to tiny town on unimproved two-lane roads, nursing that old car west.

Everything we owned was tightly packed in a tarp on top of the sedan. To save money, we all slept in that impossibly small car. My bed was the footwell behind the driver's seat. During the days we hiked the trails of Glacier, Yellowstone, and the Grand Canyon, visiting places with romantic names like Grinnell Glacier, Iceberg Lake, and the Firehole River. Evenings, we sat around campfires, listening to park naturalists describe the wonders of wilderness, and when the sun came up, we would see those wonders for ourselves.

That summer trip lit a fire in me, a fire that would change my life forever. Even then, I knew I would spend the rest of my life exploring wilderness, climbing mountains, and sleeping under the stars. I had only to find a way to make this improbable dream come true.

When we returned to our home that fall, I discovered the Boy Scouts of America and began attending summer camps where counselors taught me to swim and camp; they gave me merit badges for paddling a canoe, purifying drinking water, starting fires, and mending wounds. I was not a big boy: too small to play football, too short to dunk a basketball, too slow to compete on the track. So, I jumped headlong into Cayuga Lake and soon earned Red Cross lifesaving certification.

At seventeen, I was hired as a swimming instructor and the head lifeguard of Myers Park on Cayuga Lake, where one day I saved the life of a man who weighed twice as much as I did. He had slipped beneath the water without so much as a cry for help. I dove headfirst off the top of the lifeguard stand and pulled the man back to the surface moments before he would have been lost. As you might expect, I was pretty proud of myself, and that might have been the moment when I began thinking I must be invincible.

Elaine and I woke just before dawn on our second Timagami morning to the sound of our flapping tent. A stiff breeze had come up during the night and it was decidedly cooler. Whitecaps streaked across the lake beneath a mottled gray sky. We slipped out of our sleeping bag, pulled on pitifully inadequate cotton clothing, and started breaking camp. I fought with a few wooden matches and a pile of damp wood and finally started a smoky fire. Elaine made our first breakfast of oatmeal while I used my meager cooking skills to burn some toast over an open flame. Elaine just looked at me amused and said, "Why don't you let me handle that?"

After breaking camp, we launched our canoe into a stiff headwind and began fighting for inches. We had to cross a mile and a half of open, windswept water before we could proceed up the lee side of the lake. The day before, we had faced only ripples on a peaceful body of water. Now waves crashed over the bow, soaking our jeans and shoes, threatening our wholly inadequate food stores. Neither of us was very big, but we were both "country strong." We drove our paddles into the lake and fought our way toward the far shore. By the time we reached the other side of the lake, our canoe was nearly swamped.

It was the beginning of a tough few days and a glimpse of our futures. We would spend much of the next week in the rain, fighting headwinds, bailing water out of the bottom of our canoe, chilled to the core. Nature was, of course, just being itself—wild and unpredictable—and we were being reminded of the double meaning of that word, *wild*.

A week later, when we finally came back to that same gravel bar where we had launched our marriage, we knew that whatever we did in life from that day forward, we were going to be doing it together. I thought nothing would ever interfere with our growing affection for each other or for wilderness.

2

BREAKING TRAIL

WE WERE INSEPARABLE, REALLY. Every chance we got, we would pack up and go camping, hiking, or climbing together. The more I learned about ecology and wildlife from books and professors, the more I wanted to be in its presence. One day, I heard the mountains calling and could no longer resist. A single photograph in *National Geographic* is all it took, a mountain beaver swimming in a pond beneath a snow-covered mountain peak. That very evening, I asked Elaine if she wanted to try something new. Without hesitation, she responded, "Always."

At the end of March, when the ice on the lake outside our tiny apartment was just beginning to break up, we assembled all our heaviest clothes, threw them into the back of our Plymouth Barracuda, and headed west, knowing full well the mountains would still be locked in snow. Problem was, as college students, we had no money and even less time. To make things work, we took turns driving night and day, crossing the continent, sleeping in shifts, eating peanut butter on white bread as we drove. We were determined to explore something new to us—a winter wilderness—and we had only ten days of spring break to do it.

Bone-tired on Sunday afternoon, after a twenty-six-hour drive, we arrived and parked our car at one end of a snow-covered field just outside the small mountain town of Banff. At the time, Banff was just a little town with a Royal Canadian Mounted Police outpost, an old hotel with a hot spring, and a Greyhound bus stop. Hardy souls who wanted to climb mountains came in summer, but in winter it was very nearly a ghost town. Outside, the wind howled and blew snow in gusts that shook our car and penetrated the doors. Our moist breath condensed on the inside of the windows and froze while we waited and shivered.

By prior arrangement, the bush pilot who would deliver us into the backcountry arrived just after one in the afternoon. Flying conditions that day, he said, were marginal. A hand-sewn set of red ribbons, pretending to be a wind sock, streamed straight out, pointing almost due west. The wind chill hovered around zero. We wore almost everything we owned, but it was not enough. With chattering teeth, I told the pilot we wanted to be dropped off on a frozen lake about forty miles south and east of Banff in a remote wilderness park known as Mount Assiniboine.

Toby Burkes and his wife Jan had recommended this park to us. Toby was a backcountry ranger who worked for Banff National Park, and he loved wilderness. His love of the wild was infectious. I think he saw a kindred spirit in me and wanted to give me the opportunity to see the backcountry as he saw it. He had used his influence to get a pilot and airplane to help us make the hop over the mountains to the park, all the while assuring us we would be alone once we got over the mountain range. "There are no roads into Assiniboine. Almost no one goes there in winter."

"Perfect," I said.

After briefing us on what to expect and before sending us on our way, he had simply asked, "Are you prepared for that?"

"Sure. You bet." But Elaine and I were just kids, innocent and ignorant, fearless but clueless. What did we really know about wilderness, about snow, or about the dangerous mountain conditions we would face? And when did ignorance ever stop a twenty-four-year-old from following his heart? We were headed in harm's way, and no one could convince us not to go.

"Can you take us there?" I asked the pilot. He just looked at me as if he must not have heard me correctly. I nodded my head as if to say,

Yes, I know what I'm asking. But, of course, I did not, and the pilot knew it. He shrugged and asked, "When do you want me to pick you up?"

"We don't want to be picked up," Elaine said. "We're going to snow-shoe out." Slowly and deliberately, the pilot shifted his eyes from me to Elaine and then back again. He glanced down at our pitifully inadequate gear, shrugged his shoulders, and muttered, "*Crazy kids.*"

Turning back to his instrument panel, he opened the left-door window, stuck his head out into the cold, and yelled, "CONTACT!" The De Havilland DHC-3 Turbo Otter instantly sprang to life as the starter whined and kicked the propeller over. In a split second, the engine caught, spun up to speed, and the noise level rose until we could no longer hear each other's yells. Elaine slipped her headset over her wool hat to protect her ears and flashed me one of her infectious smiles. Her expression said it all; she was ready for the adventure to begin. I turned to the pilot and pointed forward as if to say *Charge!* And that is exactly what he did. He spun the airplane around in a tight half circle and immediately pushed the throttles to the post. Nine cylinders and six hundred horses drove us back into our seats. A cone-shaped hurricane of snow, torn from the ground beneath us, extended more than two hundred feet behind the accelerating airplane. My backbone tingled with excitement and anticipation. I was stoked!

We lifted off and left the snow-covered field and the tiny mountain town behind. Once airborne, our pilot backed off on the throttles, banked his brightly painted orange aircraft left, and flew directly at the face of Mount Rundle. When he got to within a half mile of the massive rock wall, we banked hard to the left and began hugging the mountain's northeast face. With storm clouds just over our heads and a fierce headwind, we flew down the length of the Bow Valley. Periodic downdrafts slapped the wings above our heads, each punching the airplane toward the ground. When the airplane dropped, we were all thrown upward. Our seat belts kept us from slamming into the ceiling, but the airplane was taking a beating and our gear was being bounced from side to side in the back of the plane. Elaine looked pale from the turbulence but was just as excited to be on our way as I was.

We flew over the dirt streets of a tiny mining town named Canmore, then headed into the backcountry skimming over top of Goat Creek and then the flat, snow-covered expanse of Spray Lake. Off the left wingtip, I saw a pack of six wolves silhouetted against the white snow, hunting its way along the dense forest on the east side of the lake. I pointed to the pack, and Elaine lit up with excitement. She yelled over the screaming engine, "Wilderness!"

As we came to the head of the valley, our pilot took another hard-right turn and began climbing in earnest. The massive rise in the ground known as Assiniboine Pass loomed ahead. The De Havilland skimmed past the solid rock wall of Wonder Mountain's north side, gained a little more altitude, and cleared the forested pass with just a hundred feet to spare. A thick snow cloud towered above us, preventing our pilot from climbing higher. He artfully directed his airplane to skim between the pass below and the white cloud mass above. The tops of the mountains were lost in storm clouds, and soon we were in the white world of snow. Our pilot powered forward, flying by the seat of his pants and years of experience.

Before long, everything below us and everything above us was white. This was a place unlike anything I had ever seen before. Pure, untouched, and challenging. The tingling in my spine spread to my legs and up into my neck.

Three short minutes later, we slid over the last of the few lonely treetops sticking out from a snow-covered ridge. Our pilot reached down, slid the throttle back, and deployed flaps, preparing to land. In the distance, visible through the rapidly spinning prop, three forlorn trees stood in a straight line, each about a hundred yards apart, each about the size of someone's Christmas tree. They seemed to have been planted in the snow in the middle of the lake to give the pilot some sense of depth perception or to mark a place to land.

Our pilot pointed at the trees and said, "The lake." He cut power, cranked the trim wheel forward, causing the nose of the aircraft to slide down. The airplane's skis touched the snow in the middle of Lake Magog and our pilot throttled back. The skis dug into the soft, powdery blanket of snow, and we came to a quicker-than-expected stop.

"I have to get out of here before this storm closes in, so hurry with your gear." The pilot stayed at his controls while Elaine and I threw our supplies out the main door, then unceremoniously the pilot glanced over his left shoulder and shouted above the rapidly building roar of his engine, "Good luck." He slammed the door shut, pushed the throttles forward, driving a torrent of snow and ice into our faces.

The Turbo-Otter accelerated down the lake, lifted into the sky, and promptly disappeared into the white nothingness of a gathering storm, taking the last evidence of civilization with it. I strained to hear the last faint engine noise as if trying to hold on to something familiar. Elaine too stared into the white clouds, not quite believing that our final link to the outside world was severed. We were alone—really alone—and perhaps for the first time in my life, I felt a twinge of fear and imagined the mountains were silently staring down at us amused, all the while preparing to swallow us whole. I looked at Elaine, and she looked back through her dark ski goggles. She must have been wondering if, this time, we had pushed too far.

"What now?" she asked.

We were, by this time, in a near whiteout. Just barely visible over my left shoulder was a tree line that marked the edge of the lake. Mount Assiniboine, Sunburst, Wonder Mountain, all the landmarks I had been expecting to see, were shrouded in snow clouds, invisible to us as we stood in the middle of Lake Magog. The only thing I knew for certain was we had better make a few good decisions and fast—otherwise someone was going to be finding our cold, dead bodies after the snow melted in the spring.

From the top pocket of my pack, I pulled a laminated map of the mountains and studied it one more time. I placed my compass across the surface of the map, lined it up with the needle pointing north along parallel grid lines, and adjusted my feet to face seventy degrees east. I turned to Elaine. "That way."

Our short stay on that snow-covered lake was exacting a fierce toll on our bodies. Cold cut its merciless way through all that we wore, sucking the heat from our arms and legs and core. Elaine pulled her hood over her head, bent over, and strapped on her catgut and wood snowshoes. I hefted her pack so that she could slip her arms through the straps. I brushed two inches of fresh snow from the top of my pack, swung it in a half-circle around behind my back, and punched my arms through the straps, then buckled the waist belt. Elaine handed me my bamboo ski poles, and we headed off on an azimuth of seventy degrees.

I took the lead, laboriously breaking trail. Twenty inches of new, fluffy snow lay on top of at least ten feet of hard packed snow, and somewhere below that was a solid frozen lake. Like a buffalo in winter, I plowed through the blanket of snow, crossing the lake one laborious step at a time. Before long, we were both soaked with sweat. A solid chunk of ice formed on my scarf where my wet breath met the frigid mountain air. Elaine's hair was frozen in two vertical icicles running down on either side of her face. Within just a few minutes, the muscles around my hips began screaming at me. I was asking something from them they had never given before. I felt as if a thousand needles were taking turns punching holes into my exposed cheeks. We were wearing cotton pants that were rapidly collecting snow.

By the time we reached the far shoreline, the temperature was cratering. We climbed from the lake surface up through a dense spruce forest. Elaine brushed the underside of a snow-laden limb, and forty pounds of cold snow silently collapsed across the top of her head. She looked like a polar bear with steam rising from her overheated head and shoulders. I brushed as much of the snow off her shoulders as possible to keep it from melting in place. We continued to struggle up a steep hill, finally breaking out of the trees into an open space only to be hit in the face with a harsh, cold north wind. The open area was blanketed with at least twelve feet of featureless snow. Hard, frozen chunks of sleet blew horizontally across the ridge, lashing any exposed skin.

"Where is it?" Elaine asked.

"I have no idea."

Toby had told us about a fifty-year-old cabin on the northeast shore of Lake Magog at the base of Mount Assiniboine. "Backcountry rangers occasionally use this cabin in summer when they are out patrolling the park," he said. "It would be an ideal shelter for you when you reach Assiniboine." Toby had put a tiny black dot on my map to show the cabin's location. But now we stood on what I thought was that spot only to find no sign of any cabin.

"Are we in the right place?" Elaine yelled.

"I think so." But the mountains were all lost in the storm. Even if we had wanted, there was no way of taking a compass bearing on any physical features. There were no features visible from where we stood. An endless blanket of white, punctuated by a few treetops protruding above the deep snow, was all we could see. I looked at my map, but without a known reference point, the map was almost useless. I spun around and could still see the lake edge below us. After some hard looking, I spotted the faintest trace of a long, thin depression in the snow. "That might be Wonder Creek," I offered, but my voice betrayed my lack of confidence. "The cabin is supposed to be within a hundred feet of that stream." I brushed the accumulating snow from my goggles and from the map, then studied the meadow.

"There," I yelled above the wind's roar. "I think that might be the cabin."

"Where?"

"That hump," I exclaimed.

If there was a cabin in this meadow, it too would be buried beneath twelve feet of snow. A hump might be the only evidence. Elaine asked to look at the map, and I showed her why that hump might be what we were looking for. She slowly moved her head back and forth and asked, "Are you sure?"

"No, not really," I admitted. "But it's all we have to go on."

I took hold of Elaine's shoulder, turned her around, and withdrew a collapsible shovel from the back of her pack. It was a risk. What if the hump was nothing more than a big rock or a buried tree? We couldn't tell for sure. I wasn't sure exactly where to dig, but if I had built this cabin, I would have placed the doorway facing outward toward the meadow and the back of the cabin against the woods. I hoped I was right, because we were cold and wet. I could ill afford to be wrong.

About five feet down, I struck a hard wood surface, cleared a small patch of snow away, revealing what looked like the roof of a small cabin. Elaine said, "Thank God!" She was beginning to shake. I worried she might become hypothermic. "Come take over digging. You need to keep warm. The work will help."

While Elaine took the shovel, I climbed back up on top of the hump and began using my hands to search for the flue from the cabin's stove.

I was by then up to my rear in snow, getting wetter by the minute. I could no longer see Elaine, but periodically a shovelful of snow streaked into the air above the tunnel she was excavating. I knew she was all right.

"I've got it," she yelled. We both kept digging. When the flue was free of snow, I rolled down off the hump to find Elaine clearing away the last of the snow from in front of a handmade wooden door. I slid down the tunnel Elaine had dug and pried the door open. As we stumbled into the dark cabin beneath the snow, Elaine began stomping her feet to pound the snow from her boots and legs. When my eyes finally adjusted to the dark, I could see a pile of dry wood stacked beside the stove, and we knew that we would survive the night. Some thoughtful person had left both dry wood and kindling inside the cabin sometime before the snow began to fall. It would be the difference between surviving and not.

While Elaine dug a few candles from her pack, I struck a wooden match and lit a fire in the stove. Within a few minutes, that cheap iron box began to warm, and the inside walls of the cabin began to shed their frost lining. Firelight escaped through a few holes rusted through the walls of the stove and danced against the dark cabin walls. Elaine peeled off her wet clothes and searched around for some dry things to get into. I pulled half of our sleeping bag out of my pack and covered her shoulders. By then, the stove was sucking air from the cold cabin, turning red. We were safe, finally safe.

A half hour later, Elaine went outside and filled our cook pot with snow to melt on the stove while I broke out our stove and fuel bottle. I put the two together and pumped white gas into the burn chamber. My hands were still numb from the cold, but when I struck a match, the stove took off like a blowtorch, roaring in the silent, dark cabin. In five minutes, we had boiling water and a few minutes later, hot tea. After a few sips, I could see color returning to Elaine's face. I worked fast to pump heat into our bodies. Before long, all was well. With the roar of the stove and the cracking and popping of burning wood, we felt safe. I zipped our down sleeping bags together. Soon, we were just two bears buried in our winter cave, drifting off in a state of torpor.

When daylight broke over the eastern ridgeline of Wonder Pass, I crawled out of our winter hiding place to embrace my first high-country wilderness winter dawn. The moment I poked my head out from under the snow, I knew I had found what I had been looking for my whole life.

During the night, the sky had cleared and the temperature had dropped dramatically. Warm yellow light streamed across the snow's surface, sparkling brilliantly through feather-like crystals of ice. Spruce needles and larch branches were adorned with hoarfrost. I came back down into the cabin overwhelmed. I suddenly realized I did not have the vocabulary to describe the beauty of this place, a wilderness unlike anything I had ever seen or even imagined.

"Elaine, you have to see this." She threw on her coat, climbed up to the surface of the snow, and stood silently, taking it all in. In front of the cabin, Wonder Peak stood completely covered in a thick blanket of snow, a magnificent mound of unbroken whiteness several thousand feet high. Behind the cabin, Mount Assiniboine towered above everything, making Mount Wonder look like a mere foothill. Yellow light struck Assiniboine's eastern flank, reflected off a massive hanging glacier. Its western face was still hiding in the dark, covered in blue ice and wind-scoured bare rock. This was the most impressive single mountain I had ever seen—a three-sided, so-called Canadian Matterhorn. A fragile wisp of a supercooled cloud had formed on the mountain's lee side, trailing off to the west. Across the lake, Sunburst Peaks caught much of the early morning light and reflected it back as heat.

After breakfast, we cut our first trail through virgin snow and sur-face hoar ice to the top of Wonder Pass, peeling clothes as we climbed. We were so excited we scarcely noticed the subzero temperature. The air was freezing, but with the exercise and sunlight, it seemed warm. We stopped along the way to plaster our noses with white zinc oxide to protect them from the blazing sun. All the way up, I broke trail and came to appreciate being out in front. I liked stepping out on clean, untracked snow, leading the way, making the decisions. Having an entire empty mountain in front of me that morning was intoxicating.

"I love this place," Elaine whispered in my ear. I pulled her balaclava down from her lips and gave her a delicate kiss. Her grin extended from one ear to the other as if she were enjoying her first ice cream cone.

I said, "Well, sweetheart, you made it. You are in the Rocky Mountains. You are officially a mountaineer!",

Later that evening, as we came back from our day's snowshoe, I noticed an especially-broad grin across Elaine's face. She was happier than I had ever seen her. She smiled back and said, "I think I'm going to wash my hair."

"You must be kidding," I exclaimed, but of course she was dead serious. She needed water, so I agreed to dig another tunnel down through the snow in the spot where I thought Wonder Creek might be hidden. When I finally reached the ice, I broke through and filled our cook pot with numbingly cold water. I handed the pot up through the tunnel to Elaine, who took it inside to the fire. While the water heated on the stove, I filled my water bottle from the creek and offered Elaine a drink. She drank deeply from the bottle, and after some discussion, we named this beverage "Magog's grog." When I took a sip from the bottle, my teeth began to ache, and soon I had an ice cream headache throbbing in my left temple.

Elaine laughed at me, then retreated down into the cabin to put on a short-sleeve blue shirt. She stepped out with shampoo, a towel, and her bucket of heated water. She used a cup to pour steaming water over her head, applied shampoo, and began to work her hands through her hair. She rinsed the shampoo away, and soon her hair began to freeze. She pulled it up into a cone seconds before it hardened into a vertical icicle. She looked like a unicorn. I knew right then that she was the brave and adventurous one. I took a photo of her hair and that massive grin just before she disappeared down the tunnel, back into the cabin to warm her head and towel off. From inside the cabin, I could hear her laughter.

3

EGEGIK, ALASKA

ALMOST EXACTLY SIX YEARS LATER, in the summer of 1979, Elaine was home in Oregon, five months pregnant with our first son, and I was in Alaska beginning my career as a wildlife filmmaker. That evening, I was standing on a barrier sand dune at the edge of the bitterly cold Bering Sea near a little fishing village named Egegik. The tide was out, exposing a ribbon of dark volcanic sand that stretched west five hundred yards to the point where it was being overtaken by a storm-tossed, violent gray sea.

The smell of death hung heavy in the air. The partially decomposed body of a harbor seal lay on the beach below. There were fish and half-eaten empty crab shells littering the sand. A raw, cold wind blasted in from the sea, churning up continuous lines of whitecaps, stripping the tops of the waves, and throwing foam across the sand. There was no way of getting out of the wind. Even the seagulls were on the ground, bracing themselves against the wind's relentless power. My hands were cold, my neck was cold—Alaskan cold.

I had come to this westernmost edge of Alaska, a newly minted assistant professor on the faculty of Oregon State University, to produce a television program about the decline of whale and other marine mammal populations worldwide. Film had become my passion. I had found a profession that suited my interests and skills, a vocation that would take me to wild places, put me in close proximity to wildlife, and satisfy my need for wilderness.

This film was to highlight the effectiveness of a new groundbreaking law, the Marine Mammal Protection Act. The new act, one of the first to take an ecosystem-wide approach to conservation, was important and had the potential to make a real difference to endangered whales and other marine mammals. The act was one of a number of similar laws, all passed at a time when our president and Congress understood the vital role government should play in guaranteeing a healthy environment and future for humankind.

My new friend Bruce Mate, a marine mammalogist at Oregon State University, was advising me on how to get footage of marine mammals. He had recommended I come to Alaska. That night, I was struggling to prove myself. This was the first film over which I had complete control and responsibility. I was not only the cameraman but also the film's director. It had been my idea to make it. I had found the funding and made the promises, but now I had to prove I could do the job. Other than youthful bravado, I had no good reason to believe I would be successful.

Typically, filmmakers follow the sun, paying close attention to the subtleties of light. If the sun is up, we are up. But in Alaska, for about a month in summer, the sun never sets. I had been up for more than twenty hours for each of the last three days. I was exhausted, both physically and mentally, and was profoundly unprepared for what was to come.

Standing on that beach, I also felt quite vulnerable. There were a lot of obstacles in the way, not least of which was the hostile environment surrounding me. Egegik sits in the Alaskan bush, in the middle of wild and untamed—perhaps untamable—country. There were thousands of square miles of storm-tossed black sea in front of me, nearly uninhabited Alaskan wilderness behind me, and somewhere off to the left, the Aleutians, a chain of mostly uninhabited mountains and islands, stretched from Kodiak to Dutch Harbor to Attu Island and from there straight on to Russia. I was a long way from any medical help and I knew it.

By the time I reached Egegik that July day, I had already been in Alaska for about two weeks, shooting film in several widely separated locations. For this job, I had hired an old college classmate as an assistant cameraman. Jim Hicks and I had begun this film on St. Paul Island in the Pribilofs, several hundred miles out in the Bering Sea. The Pribilof Islands were, quite literally, North America's frontier, a set of rocks located between Alaska and Russia. The island was also a large fur seal rookery, a breeding ground for nearly three-quarters of a million seals all packed in tight to one another on a thin strip of beach that ringed each of the small islands. The air was thick with the smell of seal excrement and the loud croaking noises of thousands of fur seals all competing for attention.

This island was now a refuge for the seals, but once fur seals had been severely over-harvested, mostly for their hides. On these islands, fur seals were easy to kill; they would let you walk right up to them. All you needed was a wooden club. Due to the Marine Mammal Protection Act, fur seals now enjoyed some measure of safety and, as a result, their numbers had climbed back to nearly one million. While the biologists on the island were pleased with the progress being made since the seals had come under federal protection, they were also worried the recovery might have stalled, and they were speculating that the cause might be linked to the seals' food supply.

After filming the rookeries on St. Paul Island, Jim and I had flown on to the village of King Salmon, where we were now concentrating on that part of the story—the seals' food supply. The theory was that human fishermen were directly competing with the seals for salmon and other pelagic fish. Biologists believed that northern fur seals depended upon sockeye salmon for food. As a result, the sockeye fishery was highly regulated.

The Alaska Department of Fish and Game strictly controls fishing pressure and allows only a portion of the sockeye population to be harvested on any given day. The season is also short, open for only a few hours at a time. When the fishery is open, Egegik resembles a madhouse. To be successful, a fisherman must work night and day, creating a frenzied atmosphere of boats rushing back and forth, airplanes zooming overhead, and fishermen wading out to empty their nets.

A few hundred men and fewer women scattered across thousands of square miles of land could not change the fact that this was still a wilderness. There were no roads into most of it. No way of getting in and no way of getting the fish out, except by air. People relied upon

airplanes to get them to the fish and to get the fish back to the processing plants in a timely fashion. There were airplanes of all makes and
models being used for this job. Some of them were quite old. With so
much money at stake, people had even pulled World War II–vintage
cargo planes out of storage, dusted them off, and pressed them into
service for this several-week-long season.

One especially popular airplane was the Fairchild C-119, the so-
called "Flying Boxcar." This cargo plane was designed for use during
WWII on unimproved dirt landing strips, with short takeoff rolls and
heavy cargos. It was used to carry armored vehicles—even light tanks—
into battle.

The C-119 was ideal for Alaska. It was nearly the size of a 727 passenger plane, was equipped with one-hundred-foot-long graceful wings,
each with a single massive Pratt & Whitney thirty-five hundred horsepower, twenty-eight-cylinder air-cooled radial engine mounted to its
leading edge. Perhaps because the C-119 was often used on marginal
runways and sometimes in combat, it had earned another nickname: the
"Flying Coffin." When the Fairchild crashed, not many survived. The
cockpit of the airplane was surrounded by Plexiglas, and the flight crew
sat on an elevated aluminum deck. This configuration made it easier for
the pilots to see what was around the nose of the airplane, but it made
a front-end collision almost certainly lethal.

From my perch on top of the sand dune, I slowly became aware of the
faint drone of a heavy, multiengine aircraft approaching. Searching the
sky, I tried to spot the plane but couldn't find it because the sound was
bouncing off everything. The mystery was solved when a huge airplane
screamed directly overhead and passed out to sea, scarcely thirty feet off
the water. Jim and I instinctively ducked.

As it headed out across the sea, the plane gained a little altitude,
wobbled its wings as if to signal someone on the ground, and banked
sharply to the left. As it turned, I was suddenly struck by the C-119's
beauty. From the side it had looked like an ugly flying boxcar, but now,
as it banked, it looked more like an elegant albatross, gliding from wave

to wave. Of course, an albatross glides almost effortlessly on wind currents, while the C-119 lumbers along with fuel lines the size of a man's thumb, with fifty-six pistons firing, screaming, and fighting for every foot of altitude.

The huge plane disappeared into the distant mist and silence slowly returned. The herring gulls again regained their footing on the sand, but the silence lasted just a minute or two when suddenly the Fairchild roared back into sight, coming in from my left, its wings level, its landing gear down. Without much effort, the giant plane settled, then glided to a stop on the beach right in front of us.

Such a huge airplane sitting on the edge of the sea in the middle of the wilderness looked out of place, but before the engines had fully shut down, it became abundantly clear that the plane was expected. Men appeared from out of a cut in the sand dunes to our right, a forklift materialized, and with a sense of urgency the men began loading big white tubs through gaping doors in the rear of the airplane. The plane was certainly odd-looking, a semitruck with overhead wings welded on, sitting on the beach in a wilderness with men and machines scurrying around in the semidarkness of an Alaskan setting sun. Odd or not, the plane was the center of action. It was time for Jim and me to move.

We gathered our gear and jogged down across the beach toward the airplane. The closer we got, the more fragile the Fairchild appeared. If ever an airplane was held together with baling wire and duct tape, this must have been it. The aluminum was dented, and there were a number of repair patches scattered across the fuselage. I imagined these patches might very well have been covering World War II bullet holes.

Jim and I dodged the forklift, skirted around the enormous slowly spinning propeller, and entered the Fairchild through a doorway just behind and beneath the cockpit. To our right was a huge open cargo bay, already half full of white plastic tubs overflowing with red salmon. The entire airplane smelled like a frozen fish warehouse. No one challenged us as we entered the airplane, so we squeezed past the tubs and headed for the cockpit. Turning to the left, we climbed two steps up to a small doorway onto the flight deck. It was immediately obvious that this plane had been designed for wartime; everything was painted OD—olive drab—and there were no comforts. Three well-worn seats were bolted to the cockpit floor, each with a metal back and what was left of a black plastic cushion to sit on. The entire cockpit smelled of a curious blend of dead fish and jet fuel. The control panels were ablaze in red and green lights.

When we arrived, both pilots were leaning back in their seats, taking a few minutes between flights to rest. The right seat was occupied by a young man about my age: tall, skinny, and handsome with delicate hands and fingers. He was wearing an old A-2 leather flight jacket, a symbol of the US Army Air Corps, with a white silk scarf tucked in at his collar. He made this job look insanely cool. The man in the left seat was older, had thinning gray hair, and was himself of World War II vintage. Deep lines spread out from the sides of his bloodshot eyes. He had an old, well-worn, dented metal coffee thermos in his left hand and a metal cup—the top of the thermos—in his right. As we entered the cockpit, he glanced up over the top of his steaming cup of coffee, showing neither surprise nor emotion.

The younger pilot had his feet resting on the airplane's instrument panel in front of the throttle assembly. A broad smile grew across his face the moment he noticed the large camera in my hands. I knew he would say yes even before I asked.

Our sudden presence in the cockpit didn't bother either of the pilots very much. No one spoke for a few seconds, so I eased into it. "This is a beauty," I said, looking around the cockpit. "Not built for comfort." There was no reply. "My name is Jim Larison. This is my colleague, Jim Hicks. With your permission, we would like to film what you're doing here." I explained we were making a television film, trying to portray the Alaskan frontier. "Do you mind if we shoot some film of you?"

The older man remained silent, but the younger pilot, the one who looked as if he were playing the role of Gregory Peck in *Twelve O'Clock High*, glanced at the Arriflex in my hands and the tape recorder Jim was carrying and said, "So, you're making a movie?"

"Yes, we are," I replied. "For PBS, we hope."

A half-second passed. I was afraid one of the pilots was going to say "no," so I kept talking. "Tell me about yourselves?"

The man I had pegged as Gregory Peck spoke first. He introduced himself and his father and told me he was a pilot for Hughes Air West out of Seattle. He was up in Alaska for a couple of weeks to help his dad. "We've been flying almost nonstop for the past two weeks, running fish into the processing plant in the interior."

"Looks like you are having a lot of fun," I said.

He swept his hand around the cockpit, and responded, "You don't get to do this sort of thing while flying businessmen around the lower forty-eight." He said we could have the run of the place. Anything we wanted to photograph was fair game. "We will be taking off in about ten minutes."

The older pilot lifted his blue eyes from his coffee, looked directly at me, and spoke for the first time. "Just be careful. Don't walk through one of those propellers."

I nodded agreement. Jim and I immediately got to work photographing the last of the loading process. I shot some film of one of the fishermen, working my way around the pilots, trying to catch a sense for the action. Jim followed along, recording sound to match the camera angle. We had to hurry because the plane appeared to be almost ready for takeoff.

This time, the young pilot came looking for me. "Would you like to fly along?"

Without so much as asking where the plane was headed or whether it would come back, I replied, "Absolutely. Wouldn't miss it."

Flying with these guys would not be routine. The pilot was younger than the airplane, which was a bad sign because that meant that the airplane was old and the pilot was inexperienced. But I could not do my job by retreating every time I felt a little anxiety.

I tried to put my thoughts aside by keeping my hands busy. There was plenty to do. I first took out one of my Leica M4 still cameras, hung it around my neck, and then took my lens cleaning fluid and worked my way around the Arriflex lens turret. I loaded a fresh roll of film, connected the battery, and then rotated the turret so that my wide-angle lens was ready. Jim was busy setting up the sound gear. Around his neck, he was carrying the Nagra III tape recorder, a monster of a machine filled with circuits, wires, and motors that weighed nearly twenty-five pounds. Attached to the Nagra, Jim had a Sennheiser 416 shotgun microphone blimped to prevent the sensitive sound gear from picking up wind noise. When things began to move fast, we would be ready.

The crew chief (he might have been another fisherman) offered his seat to me. Jim sat on a bench behind the copilot. My seat was behind the pilots in the middle of the flight deck. Whatever happened, this would be an ideal position from which to see and photograph the action. As everyone began settling in to his duties, the copilot turned to me. He pointed at the safety belt hanging unused from the bottom of my seat and made a motion with his two hands to indicate he wanted me to buckle up. What I had no way of knowing at the time was that this one simple act by the older pilot would save my life.

I strapped myself in, then glanced to my right to see that Jim also got the message. But he was sitting where there was no seat belt. He shrugged as if to say, "Nothing I can do about that." The fisherman who had given me his seat stood in the doorway. He too had no seat belt. A moment later, the younger pilot adjusted the throttles, flipped two switches, and one by one the engines sprang to life. As they began winding up, the cockpit began to shake violently, and the noise level rose until recording sound became impossible. Jim turned the recorder off and settled back into his seat.

Above the engine noise, the younger pilot attempted to make idle conversation—something about the cameras. No one could hear a thing above the roar, so I smiled back, nodded, and kept on shooting film. It was odd he had turned to talk about cameras while preparing to take off, but I was the one who started the conversation. Once again, I missed a key clue staring me in the face.

Father and son put on their headsets and started talking to each other electronically. The old man seemed to be telling his son to take the controls. Clearly the older man was proud of what his son had become. They were enjoying the moment. They talked as if they shared a very special bond, leaning in toward each other, smiling. The old man's smile was broad, infectious, and authentic. I couldn't help but like him. He reached over, put his hand on his son's shoulder, who pushed him away with an explosion of laughter. There was an uncommon tenderness in the old man's eyes. Perhaps more than his son, the older man showed the fatigue of a long day's flying. Pilots and airplanes were in short supply in King Salmon that summer. Everyone was pushing the envelope, working round the clock. The older man was especially tired.

Once again, the younger pilot turned to look at Jim and me. This time, I used my Leica to shoot a quick portrait of him as he reached above his head to make an adjustment to the control panel. Flight conditions were actually quite good that day. The wind was strong out of the northwest, coming straight off the water from left to right. So, the pilot reached down and eased the throttles forward. The airplane strained against the soft sand, broke free, and began to roll. Slowly, the young pilot turned the big plane around and began to taxi south along the beach testing the flaps, the brakes, and the engines as he rolled. I slipped the camera down to the level of the pilot's hand on the throttles, then slowly moved the camera up so that it could see the pilot, backlit by the windshield.

When the airplane reached the far end of what looked like the usable beach, our pilot gave the starboard engine a shot of fuel and at the same time stepped on the left brake pedal. The engine whined as the big plane spun around to face north. The wind was still steady from west to east, left to right. As soon as the airplane came around to face the wind, the pilot pulled the throttles back and waited while his father finished their checklist. The Fairchild throbbed with energy. I watched the pilots carefully, wanting to be ready, wanting to stay ahead of the action. Anticipating people's responses helped me to be sure the camera was pointed in the right direction and was rolling when action developed.

As I watched the pilot, something was off. This was one of the most critical moments of any flight. Pilots often say flying consists of thousands of hours of boredom, punctuated by a few brief moments of terror. Takeoffs and landings were supposed to be those moments of terror, yet this pilot did not appear nervous. Instead, he kept glancing back to see what I was doing.

Our presence was undoubtedly having an effect on the young man. He was all too aware that he was being photographed. People who are being photographed sometimes forget what they are doing. They put on the face in which they want to be remembered and lose sight of what is important. I was too busy doing my own job adjusting lenses, moving my camera across the scene.

It was now ten minutes before midnight. The sun was just off to our left, kissing the horizon. The sky was shifting from yellow to red and then to black as the light faded. Through a break in the black clouds, a ray of sunlight suddenly flashed across the beach, through the windshield, bathing us in a bright yellow glow. The young pilot put on his aviator sunglasses to shade his eyes, then pushed the twin throttles to the post, and the engines began to scream.

The forty-year-old bucket of bolts began its takeoff roll. Instinctively, I began cycling through my lenses, first the wide-angle lens because it took in the whole cockpit, next a portrait lens to capture expressions. When I look through my viewfinder, I see only the moving image, F-stops, focus, composition. I become invisible, as if I were not a part of the scene but an observer of it.

It never occurred to me that I should be afraid because everything that happened in front of my lens appeared to be happening to someone else. It is as if I were watching the pilots on a television screen rather than from the seat beside them. But of course, Jim and I were not watching the takeoff in the safety of our home. We were a part of this scene.

We had about two thousand feet of usable flat beach ahead of us before the shoreline curved abruptly to the right. We would have to reach takeoff speed by the time we reached that turn.

The throttles were now wide open; the engines gave as much as they could. The airspeed indicator began climbing through twenty . . . thirty . . . forty knots. The sand was wet, the tires soft, and the engines old. The plane had started out rolling north into a northwest wind, but it soon used up most of the straightaway beach. Still, the Fairchild had not reached takeoff speed.

A second passed, then two. As the mass of aluminum roared down the beach, everyone's attention was riveted on the ocean ahead. Five hundred yards, four hundred. Suddenly the pilot was forced to turn right toward the northeast, hugging the shoreline. But as he turned away from the powerful wind, the airspeed indicator began to fall. The great airplane, loaded with fish, was moving too fast to make the corner but too slow to take off—we were in trouble.

The pilots were rapidly running out of options. The Fairchild was beginning to feel light. As weight came off the tires, we lost traction with the ground. Centrifugal force began driving us left toward the sea. The propellers were pulling as hard as they could to the right, but momentum was forcing us relentlessly left toward the sea.

We had passed that do-or-die moment. It was too late to abort the takeoff. Faced with no other choice, both pilots, almost in unison, stepped hard on the left rudder pedal, turning the airplane sharply back toward the sea. They pulled on their yokes, and the nose of the great Fairchild rose reluctantly into the air, paying dearly for every foot of elevation gain. Its airspeed indicator dipped as speed bled off. Its engines screaming, the plane clawed for altitude as it sped out over the waves of the Bering Sea.

In the cockpit, despite the enormous roar of the engines, it suddenly seemed to be very quiet. The young pilot's face said it all. In his years of flying passengers from Portland to Seattle, he had probably never run out of runway. There was nothing he could do. He seemed to freeze up.

One second passed, then another. By this time, I had put my camera down, concentrating on the only thing that really mattered, the blur of water that flashed beneath the plane. Was it getting farther away, or was it coming up toward the landing gear? Was the plane climbing or stalling? We were a quarter mile out into the Bering Sea. The yokes were shaking violently in the pilots' hands; they were struggling to maintain some control over the airplane, but their efforts were sure to fail. They knew it, and because they could not hide their panic, I knew it also.

The older pilot turned to me—his face nearly white. Over the engines' roar he screamed, "We're going in!" He turned back toward the windshield, his chin sank into his shoulders, and he locked his jaw as if to brace himself against the inevitable.

My heart began pounding in my ears. I felt as if someone had hit me in the chest with a hammer. My heart ached. My arms tingled. Suddenly this scene became *very real*. I could no longer pretend this was happening only to the pilots in front of my camera. Whatever happened to them was going to be happening to us as well. Jim and I had stumbled into a nightmare.

A very long instant passed; then, at nearly one hundred miles an hour, the airplane shuttered as the nose wheel tore through the top of the first big wave. The airplane tripped as if it were an elephant running through mud. My camera slammed forward, hit the pilot's seat back, and was instantly torn from my now shattered, broken, and bleeding hand. The propellers knifed into the water. Cold water crashed into the hot engines. In a terrifying instant, Jim and I, the flight crew, perhaps twenty thousand pounds of fish, and a now-useless mass of twisted metal, abruptly dove beneath the surface and instantly struck the bottom of the Bering Sea.

The cockpit floor was shredded as the entire undercarriage of the plane was torn out from underneath us. The twin tails of the plane kept coming forward. Ten tons of fresh fish flew forward, slamming against the bulkhead behind our heads. The wall that separated the cargo hold from the cockpit ruptured under the crashing force of the heavy load. The fisherman behind me flew over top of me and slammed into the instrument panel.

Out of the corner of my eye, I saw Jim Hicks as he, too, disappeared into a tangle of metal. My chest slammed into the back of the pilot's seat, and my feet crashed down through what was left of the flight deck where the pilot's seat had been, through a jagged hole in the floor, trapping me in place. The cockpit was torn to pieces as it folded back under the massive fuselage. The crushing weight of the shifting cargo continued to drive forward, slamming me against the instrument panel but also, somehow, cushioning me from all the sharp edges and hard surfaces. The great weight of the cargo crushed me into a smaller and smaller space. There was nothing to breathe but a thick, smelly fish soup. I struggled to free myself but was shackled to the floor, entangled in shredded aluminum, unable to move.

We were all buried in dead fish, fighting for air, fighting for our lives. Just passing out would have been so easy, but adrenaline kept me mercilessly awake. Then, without warning, the cockpit walls tore open. The sides of the airplane opened to the sea. With a roar the cargo— perhaps five thousand fish—rushed out into the sea. Tons of salmon and a few people were ejected from the gaping wounds in the nose of the airplane. Blood and body parts flushed into the dark water. Then suddenly it was silent.

I had completely lost track of Jim Hicks. I didn't know where he was or whether he was alive or dead.

For those of us who had not been ejected but had been trapped under the wreckage of the fuselage, the worst was yet to come. As quickly as the salmon flooded out of the cockpit, the sea roared back in. One moment I was drowning in fish, the next I was drowning in arctic saltwater.

The airplane was now dead in the water. There was little hope my fate would be any better. I was thirty years old, and chances were that I would not be getting any older.

4

THE FLYING COFFIN

WHILE I WAS DROWNING at the bottom of the Bering Sea, Elaine was sixteen hundred miles away at home in Oregon, struggling through her first pregnancy. What would Elaine's life be like if I didn't make it out of that airplane? At perhaps the most important moment in any young married couple's lives—the birth of their first child—she was alone, and I was struggling just to make it home to her.

When I signed on to this filmmaking life, I had not fully appreciated the costs or sacrifices we both would be making. Every time I walked out the door on an extended filmmaking trip, Elaine would struggle to do the work of maintaining our home and family, alone in the woods of Oregon. When I returned from a trip, she would adjust to this itinerant visitor who was here one day, gone the next. She navigated around me, a single woman for weeks or months at a time, then married again when I returned to take up residence.

Somehow, Elaine was not angry with me for my choices. She simply accepted me for what I was, in her words, "driven." She would say, "You just don't know when to quit. You put your soul into everything you do."

Elaine always sees the good in every situation. "You should stop sometimes to smell the roses," she likes to say. At times I am so consumed by F-stops and camera angles and exposure latitudes of film, I don't know what country I am in, let alone what flowers might be growing under my feet. I see the world with tunnel vision, exactly as you might expect of a person whose eye is constantly pressed up against a camera's eyepiece. All that matters to a filmmaker is what comes through the lens. It's a strategy that may work for a photographer, but it can be disastrous when it comes to personal relationships. The fact that I still had such a strong relationship with my wife had more to do with her strengths than mine.

At that moment, my strategy of living life through the lens of my camera seemed like a foolish choice. The Bering Sea was inside the cockpit. I was struggling for each breath in the few remaining air pockets at the ceiling, trying to keep my head above water. As those pockets became fewer and smaller, my situation deteriorated. I began to feel as if there was no hope. I was drowning in freezing cold water. I wanted nothing more than to pass out, or even pass on, but was also frightened. Fear is relentless; it drags you back from the edge and demands you deal with the present. Adrenaline and an irrepressible will to live took over.

The water was excruciatingly cold, causing the muscles in the back of my neck to knot, producing fierce pain. The more they contracted, the more my head was pulled backward and the more difficult it became to keep my mouth closed. Water flooded down my airway, and it seemed that nothing could be done to stop it.

Blood circulated around in the seawater, but I couldn't tell whether it was my own or someone else's. My feet were still wedged into the floor beneath the pilot's seat. I could see no one else in the cockpit. Everything was crushed; the floor and ceiling met in places. Twisted metal and splintered control panels were everywhere. I hoped Jim was alive, but I had no idea where he was. I tried to stand, found one last air pocket, and took a deep breath, then curled over to try to free my legs. With my good hand, I fumbled, but they were securely lodged in the floor. When I straightened back up to take another breath, my head struck the instrument panel. It was too late. Ice-cold water had completely filled the cabin all the way to the ceiling.

Everything seemed hopeless. Perhaps for the first time in my young filmmaking life, I was forced to admit my choices had consequences. The camera had been recording the real world, not replacing it.

Just when I thought I was done, the younger pilot came back into the wreckage looking for me, risking his own life to save mine. He began prying what was left of his seat away from my legs, all the while holding his breath. We worked together on the seat—me pushing, he pulling—and finally it gave way.

Free at last, I began struggling to get out from underneath the fuselage through a gaping hole ripped into the side of the airplane. The two of us broke into the air. I vomited up a load of stinking fishy saltwater, coughed violently to clear my airway, and tried to thank the pilot for coming back for me. But just then, a large white-capped wave crashed into my face, driving me backward, slamming the back of my head against the fuselage. As the water retreated, I caught the last half of something the pilot was trying to say to me. "... *get away ... fire ...*" Together, we struggled around the nose of the wreckage, trying to put some distance between us and the airplane.

I swam, I stumbled, finally I crawled, desperately trying to reach the safety of shore. The Bering Sea was stunningly cold. A wave struck me in the back, sweeping me off my feet, but the tide was running toward shore that night, and I was being carried in its grip. Ahead, I could see two bodies on the beach. Jim Hicks was on his back. I could not tell if he was seriously injured, if he had been washed to shore, or if he had gotten there under his own power. Each new wave struck his body, moving it slightly. Farther down the beach, the crew chief who had been on board sat cradling his head. Blood poured from his jaw, a black empty space where his teeth should have been. He writhed in pain, moaning.

I crawled on my knees those last few yards, collapsed beside Jim's body, and put my hand on his chest. I could feel movement as he took a shallow breath. He was alive. Red, sticky liquid ran down my right hand, flowed to the tips of my fingers, and dripped into the sea, but I did not recognize my own blood.

My mind struggled to make sense of what I saw. I was in shock. What had just happened? How did I get here? Where is here? A few hundred yards out in front of me, a twisted, torn, and mangled mass sat like a javelin, driven into the seabed. Two identical, twin tails stood at precarious angles above the crashing waves—gray against the black sky.

White-hot steam rose from shattered, now silent engines. Jet fuel drained from the underside of one wing, spreading across the surface of the sea.

Something above caught my eye; I looked up to find a lone seagull floating by, seemingly oblivious to the wreckage beneath his wings. A wave swept up from the sea toward me, surrounded my legs, and ran through my boots. I had a camera around my neck and a lifetime of muscle memory. Without thinking about it, I lifted the Leica, pointed it in the direction of the wreckage and, without looking through the viewfinder, took one last photograph. The camera froze. I felt the film separate as I reflexively cranked the winding mechanism. As I let the camera fall back to the end of its neck strap, darkness came from inside my head and spread across the world. Slowly, I lay back on the warm sand, preferring darkness to reality.

5

RESCUE AND RECOVERY

IN THE HOURS THAT FOLLOWED, I remained in shock; my memory of those events is fragmentary. We survivors were apparently dragged from the sea's edge and taken by fishermen to their hut in the sand. Sometime later, I was able to cut through the fog and knew I was in an unfamiliar place.

It is difficult to describe how much pain I was in. From a distant room, I heard muffled, serious voices cutting through the dark. A soft flannel sleeping bag was on top of me, but I was still wet, wearing the same salt-encrusted clothes from the beach. I stank of jet fuel and fish. My boots hung down over the end of the bed, heavier than they should have been. I shivered, and then everything began to spin around and went black again.

During the next twenty-four hours, we survivors were evacuated from Egegik, first to an air force clinic in King Salmon where we were refused service by an obviously intoxicated doctor. He made some excuse about us not being active military, all the while we continued to bleed on his floor. Then we were flown on to a distant hospital near Anchorage, where our reception was much better. Much of what happened on those flights and in that hospital remains a blur to me today. I was just trying to climb out of a cloudy nightmare. My first clear memory was of a phone call to Oregon.

Elaine was alone in Oregon on her summer break from her teaching job, spending her time in our house in the woods. That day she was putting together a nursery for our soon-to-be-born son. Reporters were already hanging around the hospital trying to get the story for the morning papers. I was worried that Elaine might already have heard about the crash from some news outlet. But she was completely unaware.

Calls from Alaska in 1979 were routed through radios and landlines to the lower forty-eight states. On such distant connections, only one person could speak at a time. You never knew when the connection was good and when it was not. I didn't want to cause Elaine any unnecessary stress, so I tried to sound strong but calm.

"Hello darling. How are you?"

"Just great," she replied. And she went off on a description of the crib she was putting together.

Interrupting, I said, "Elaine, Jim and I were just in an accident." She went silent. "A plane crash."

And that was the end of the coherent two-way conversation. When Elaine heard me say *plane crash*, she began crying. As she sobbed into the phone, the transmission and the conversation became a one-way affair from Oregon to Alaska; the electronics of the phone connection locked in on the sound of Elaine's sobs, as if a radio operator had held the talk button down. The connection was horrible, but I heard her say, "I can't do this by myself."

I quickly jumped into the conversation, "We are OK. Neither Jim nor I is seriously injured. It was really no big deal," I lied.

Elaine could hear nothing from my end. She continued to sob, "What happened? Were you injured?"

I could hear her, but she could not hear me. Elaine couldn't understand why I was not answering her questions. Without an answer from me, her imagination ran wild. She assumed the worst and thought I was unable to answer. "Are you all right?" she kept asking.

"Yes, we're all right, really," I said, but she did not hear.

I continued, "The plane went down in the Bering Sea. Fishermen pulled us out—"

Abruptly, the line went dead. I didn't even get a chance to tell Elaine how to reach me by phone or which hospital I was in. Elaine was left with nothing. She was alone and didn't know if I was ever going to return home.

When the connection was lost, I sat in silence thinking Elaine had heard everything I said. I was hoping that she would not go into premature labor. Luckily our closest friends, upon learning of the crash, came pouring into our house all thinking the same thing, that Elaine would lose the child. One of Elaine's teacher friends brought over a rocking horse for the new baby, hoping that it would cheer her up. It just caused her to sob even harder. She was imagining that she might just have to raise this child on her own.

Bruce and his wife, Mary Lou Mate, came over immediately. He was also an assistant professor on the staff at Oregon State University. She was an intensive care nurse at the Newport hospital. The two of them came to help Elaine get through the day.

My next call was to my boss at the university, Bill Wick. I told him of the crash and our condition. Luckily this call went more smoothly. I gave him the telephone number where we could be reached, and he offered, without me asking, to do what he could to make sure Elaine was taken care of.

Bill hung up the phone and called Elaine. He told her that I was all right and gave her the hospital telephone number. Bill too was concerned for Elaine's well-being, trying to reduce her stress levels.

In comparison, I had it relatively easy. All I had to do was recover. I soon found that Jim's injuries were less severe than mine, and after a few days we were both healthy enough to return home. When we finally met that first time after the crash, we were relieved and happy to see each other.

"I imagined the worst," I said.

Jim was not making eye contact, so I avoided the subject of the crash. I watched him carefully. It was clear he was in a dark place. I worried that he would blame me for the mess, and I felt guilty that for the past few hours or days, I had been thinking only of myself and my problems, not worrying about Jim or what he may have been going through.

Aside from Elaine, Jim Hicks was undoubtedly my best friend. We had spent many years together, first in graduate school, then later as fledgling filmmakers at the University of Wisconsin. He had been a writer, and I was a photographer on the same university-based film-making team. In the evenings, when we were not working together, we competed on the handball court. In fact, Jim had taught me how to play. Neither of us liked to lose, but in handball someone always loses. Jim was strong and fit, despite having beaten back polio as a child. When he was tired, he would limp a little, but he never let that slow him down. He was every bit as tough a person as I had ever known. I could now see that his toughness was getting him through this traumatic moment. I hoped it would be enough.

Jim and I spent that last night in a hotel in Anchorage and booked commercial flights back to Portland and Madison. The idea of getting on another airplane was leaving me light-headed, but there was no other way of getting home and I needed to get to Elaine to make sure she was all right.

At six in the morning, the hotel phone rang. It was our wake-up call. Jim and I left for the airport without much more than a word or two between us. The sun was shining brightly as we climbed into a shuttle bus. When we arrived at the terminal, the cold Alaskan air was being sucked through the automatic doors to the main terminal. Jim and I avoided conversation until our flights were called, when he took a lighthearted swipe at me. "Hope we can do this again sometime."

For the first time since the crash, I allowed myself a small grin. "Don't ever say I never take you anyplace interesting, now will you?" He didn't laugh, so I continued, "That was probably funnier in my head than it was coming off my lips." Finally, he smiled. As he turned away and began walking toward his gate, I wondered if our friendship would survive this difficult moment.

Just then, the faint smell of jet fuel blew in from an open doorway down the concourse, triggering a cascade of unwelcome memories. My knees buckled and I abruptly sat on the floor. Sweat beaded up on my forehead. My shirt suddenly felt wet. The airport hallway began to spin around and over my head.

I struggled to regain focus. Somehow, I knew if I didn't control this thing, it would most certainly control me. I struggled to my feet, willing myself to just put one foot in front of the other. Ignore the headwind coming down the Jetway. My mind was screaming at me, *Don't do this. Don't go down that hallway.* But some part of me was also resisting. *You must keep walking.* I held my breath, gritted my teeth, and ordered my muscles to work one at a time. Left leg. Right leg.

Haltingly, I walked down the corridor and down the Jetway. Ahead was the doorway to another airplane. I hesitated before entering, then forced myself to step through the door. The flight attendant looked at me as if to ask, "What is wrong?" When the airplane began to move away from the terminal, I heard every rattle and felt the tires roll over every seam in the concrete taxiway. I heard the hydraulic fluids pushing through their hoses and the electric motors working to prepare the airplane for takeoff. The urge to get up out of my seat, to race toward the now-closed doorway, was overwhelming. My seat belt felt like a great weight, holding me down, preventing me from making a scene by trying to escape this place.

When the plane began its takeoff roll, I began hyperventilating. My hands shook, but the runway slowly fell away. With my good hand, I held the armrest as tightly as possible, the knuckles turning white under the strain. The back of my neck was again soaked with sweat. The woman next to me asked if I was all right and then reached for the call button on the ceiling above her head. I waved her off. Reluctantly, she let her arm sink back into her lap, all the while staring at me as if she thought I might explode at any moment.

On the way home, I looked out into the clouds and asked myself about Elaine. Would I find her curled up in a ball, unable to get out of bed? If she didn't want any part of this life or if she was afraid to let me out of her sight, what then? Would I agree to quit making films?

The Pacific Ocean kept slipping beneath the airplane as we hugged the Canadian coast; I was on my way home for what I knew was going to be a very tough conversation.

6

THE CONVERSATION

THE MOMENT THE SEAT BELT SIGN WENT DARK, I jumped up, eager to get off that plane. The aisle was an obstacle course, the Jetway too long. I snaked my way through the corridor. When I came around the last bend, I saw Elaine up ahead. She was crowding the doorway. When she caught sight of me, she side-stepped the agent and half ran, half shuffled, down the Jetway. No one was going to stop a pregnant woman in distress. Her protruding belly hit me first as she threw her arms around my neck. She was obviously emotional, but she was up, moving through life, and this was a good sign. In her embrace, I melted. All the strength I pretended to have vanished as she began to sob.

An audience of curious travelers fought to sidestep us on their way into the terminal. We stood close to each other, toe to toe, holding on. When the pilots came up behind me and the gate attendant respectfully asked us to move, we reluctantly let go. "Shall we go pick up your bags?" Elaine asked.

"There are no bags, just this carry-on."

She hesitated for just a second and said, "Of course . . . everything else was lost in the plane crash?"

"Pretty much."

And she turned her eyes away from me, wiping moisture from her cheek. "Tell me."

As we walked out to our car in the parking lot, I began the long story of the beach and the crash. I told her about Jim Hicks, about the hospital, and about the mess I left behind.

As we drove, she began to share her end of that phone call and how little she had heard. She shared her panic and about the friends who came to her aid. There were a lot of tears, and Elaine laid her head on my shoulder much of the way home. When we arrived at our house, we were talked out and thoroughly exhausted. We had shared all the critical details, but we knew a long, difficult conversation would occur sooner than later.

I suggested we put that conversation off until the morning.

"Tomorrow, then," she said and we went to bed, holding each other in a tight embrace for most of the night.

That next morning, even before the second cup of coffee, Elaine began. "What will our lives be like, from now on?"

I could think of no good answer.

Elaine began to cry. "I don't think I can take this. I can't lose you." She gasped for air and shook with a spasm as her voice caught.

I waited, not knowing how to ease her pain.

When she was ready, she continued. "Up to this point, I have been fine with you following your career even though you are gone a lot. We are a team, and that means I sometimes do one thing while you do another. But sometimes I feel like we're drifting apart." She looked down at her belly and wiped a tear away. "And it's not a good time to drift apart."

I remained silent. I knew she was full of anxiety and needed to have the opportunity to get it all said. When finally she regained her composure, she went on, "When you called me from Alaska to say you'd been in an airplane crash, I felt like I was being abandoned. Like this life you have chosen could end badly."

I looked at the floor and shuffled my feet. She was talking about more than the plane crash. She was talking about all the lonely nights, about the family growing inside of her, and what it would be like for our children to grow up with an absentee father or no father.

Breaking with emotion, she continued. "I don't see how this is going to work. You can't let our children grow up thinking they have been abandoned by their father." Elaine could see that I was struggling, so she tried to soften her message a bit. "I'm having trouble wrapping my head around what our lives are going to be like."

I apologized. "I'm sorry . . . I'm not sure I fully grasped what this life would be like either, but I can't just stop. This is what I want to do in life." Then I turned back to safer ground. "If I give in to my fears, what sort of man would I be?"

Elaine realized immediately that I was probably not going to stop my career before it had really even gotten started. She also knew I was not hearing everything that she was saying. She began again, softening her message yet again. "Last night, I came to understand that I was going to have to think differently about what our family would look like. I don't mean to say that any of this is a bad thing; it's just a different thing. I'm not asking you to give up your career. I respect you for what you are trying to do, but I have to come up with a way to deal with it all."

I tried to refocus our conversation on the immediate crisis, the plane crash. "Can you simply bury this?" I asked. "Can you put these past few days in a box and never go there or open that box again . . . just not let it overwhelm you?"

Elaine thought for a moment, then said, "Maybe, but you know what your brother [a clinical psychologist] would say, 'Deal with it, or it will deal with you.'"

After a moment of silence, I finally said something that was appropriate to the moment. "Tell me what I can do to make this easier for you."

She said she didn't know.

I wondered if either one of us would ever be the same again. We were going to have to build a life unlike any we had ever known before. After several minutes of silence, I assumed Elaine had said what she wanted to say, so I finished the dishes and started getting ready for work. The university lawyers were insisting I come up to the top floor of the administrative building to file a report and answer some difficult questions. I wasn't sure what sort of mess I was going to find when I got there.

———————

My secretary met me at the door. She was happy to see me walking upright. She ran her eyes over me, hesitating as they took in the bruises, sling, and bandaged arm. Then she turned to her phone and called the main office to let the director of the Sea Grant Program, Bill Wick, know that I was in. "He's here."

Bill came upstairs immediately. He closed the door behind himself. Once we were alone, we shared an hour of talk and back slaps. Bill was a truly good boss and was already becoming a good friend. He had hired me as an assistant professor; he was the one who had given me the opportunity to make films for Oregon State University. He wanted to hear all about Alaska but tiptoed around the plane crash. Mostly he asked about Elaine, how the film was coming along. Every once in a while, he'd slip in a question about the crash. "What happened to all that equipment?" More than anything he was just watching my body language, listening to how I responded to his questions. But I wasn't fooling anyone. Bill could see what everyone else could see; this plane crash had made an impact, and the impact was not just to my hand. My face said it all: I was shaken.

After Bill left, I went up to see the lawyers who seemed not to notice my bandages but were worried about the possible liability the university might have. Why was I on a cargo airplane? You weren't authorized to be there? Did my presence on the airplane in any way cause the crash? They kept pressuring me for details; I kept evading their questions because I didn't want to talk about the crash. Eventually, they took pity on me and let me go without the answers they sought.

A few days later, with my hand still wrapped in gauze and tape and after I had gathered together sufficient courage, I found myself in the darkroom down the hall from my office. I removed the film from the damaged Leica, the one I had been carrying around my neck during the crash. The camera had been destroyed by the saltwater and sand that had penetrated into its mechanisms, but the film inside was intact.

I washed the roll in fresh water to get the salt off and developed the film in a bath of D-76 developer. I needed to see what record might still exist of that night. When the film was dry, I pulled out a magnifying glass and glanced at the negatives. There was a photo of the pilot in the cockpit before the crash, reaching overhead to the instrument panel. A photo of his dad adjusting the airplane trim. And then there was a photo of the airplane sitting in the sea, broken, shattered, and steaming hot.

I printed that last photo, swirling it around in the developer and Hypo Clearing Agent, being careful not to get the chemicals on my bandages. As the image began to materialize, swimming in the chemicals, I began to tear up. Alone in the darkroom, I saw the airplane sitting in the sea, where a large wave was about to smash into it. The front end was crushed and split wide open. Its belly was torn off. The windshield had been smashed. The older pilot was captured in mid-stride, wading through rough water on his way to shore. The image was water stained and blurred from the saltwater damage, but otherwise it told a harsh story.

"You'll be OK," I reassured myself.

For a long time after the crash, I tried to make sense of that night. I wasn't even sure what had happened to the pilots or the fisherman after the crash. If I could just remember all the details of the crash, that would help. But you know what they say, "Be careful what you wish for." There came a time when remembering just didn't seem like such a good idea. For me, memories started to remind me of sharp knives, things you didn't want to play with. You could leave them in the drawer, benign, or you could pick them up and risk injury. To avoid the damage the "knives" might do, I decided to let them lie, to deny their existence. If I could successfully deny and forget, then maybe I wouldn't have to change anything I was doing. When no one was listening, I would whisper to myself, "Just move on. Bury the past." It didn't take long before I came to admit denial wasn't working all that well either. The smell of jet fuel, the sound of an airplane engine spinning up, even the simple sounds of seagulls could trigger another panic attack. Every sight, every sound, every smell from that day would come flooding back without warning, like the Bering Sea washing over top of me. Those memories made me feel as if I were drowning all over again.

I needed time, time to put this behind me, but you don't always get the time you need to put your affairs in order before the world places new hurdles in your path. Our lives were about to get a whole lot more complicated. I was about to be offered an opportunity that no one in their right mind could refuse. That big break, the one that all writers and photographers fantasize about, the thing I had been aiming for my entire young life, was going to be dropped in my lap. If I accepted what was offered, Elaine and I would be plunged right back into the eye of a growing personal and professional storm.

PART II

ON ASSIGNMENT

7

THAT BIG BREAK

ON A WARM SPRING DAY in early April that following year, everything changed. I was in Washington, DC, on a day just after the peak of the cherry blossoms. Robins were digging worms out of the grass on the National Mall. Spent flower petals drifted in the air, blanketed the sidewalks, and floated freely in the Lincoln Memorial Reflecting Pool.

As I walked around the park-like setting, I was struck by the sweet smells and warmth of spring. I had come to Washington for a university conference being held at the Hilton not far from the White House. That morning, I was feeling good because I had not suffered another panic attack on the flights from Portland to Washington. By that time, I had pretty much convinced myself that I was back—the worse of the trauma, I thought, may be behind me.

The conference was mostly made up of a bunch of boring meetings and lectures, but I was supposed to show *Mammals of the Sea* that afternoon to anyone interested and to those who hadn't seen it when it was broadcast nationwide on PBS earlier that year. In between meetings, I found myself in front of a buffet table piled high with donuts and Danish. As I hunted around for something to eat, a colleague approached from behind. Before I noticed her, Nada Yolan asked how I was doing. She had been talking to Bill Wick, who was not the sort of man to sugarcoat anything. He had told her about the plane crash in Alaska. Nada was obviously moved.

She hesitated before speaking, offering to pour me a cup of coffee. Nada was quite a bit shorter than I; when she turned to face me, she raised her eyebrows and fixed those large, black, dewy eyes on me. I was sure she could see right through the personal protective armor I had so carefully constructed. Nada and I had known each other for just a short time. We occasionally worked together, I as an assistant professor at Oregon State University; she as a midlevel manager at NOAA, the National Oceanic and Atmospheric Administration, the federal agency that funded my office. "So, Jim, how are you doing?" She was watching more than listening.

"Oh, I'm fine," I lied.

"Really?" she pressed. "Bill Wick tells me you are not so fine."

Glancing at the floor, I changed the subject, asking what was on her mind.

"I saw *Mammals of the Sea* when it was broadcast on PBS. Bill Wick made sure everyone in the national office saw it. We all thought it was great. I'm hoping you get a big crowd this afternoon when you show it."

"I must admit, it felt great to finally see one of my films on national TV."

"Bill tells me that it won the Silver Tusker at the International Wildlife Film Festival."

"It did. I was invited—all expenses paid—to receive the award in Las Vegas. The National Geographic Society won the Gold Tusker for their film, *Land of the Tiger*. A great film."

"It doesn't surprise me. The National Geographic is the best! There is something I wanted to discuss with you. I want you to meet someone. His name is Dennis Kane. He's the . . ."

"*Dennis Kane*?" I interrupted. "I know who Dennis Kane is—by reputation I mean. He's probably the single most important film executive producer in nature and wildlife filmmaking in the United States, possibly the world." Dennis was responsible for *Land of the Tiger* and just about everything the Geographic produced in those days.

Nada just smiled. "Have you ever met him?"

"No!" I said emphatically.

"Well, what if I could make that happen?" Nada went on telling me about her history with Dennis, but I could not hear much of what she was saying because my mind was now racing. She seemed convinced she could and should bring my film to his attention. I told her that I had been studying Kane's work, *Land of the Tiger* and also the *Living Treasures of Japan*. These were two of the very best television productions I had ever seen. In fact, I had studied and dissected these films endlessly.

The idea of one day working for the National Geographic Society had been a lifelong dream shared, I am certain, by just about everyone in the business of nature and wildlife photography. I had tried several times to get an audience with someone at the organization, but without an introduction, such a meeting was probably never going to happen. Now, Nada simply said, "Let's make a call."

The very next morning, I ducked out of my other meetings. Nada and I walked over to the National Geographic Society's executive suite; I was carrying my copy of *Mammals*. I don't remember the walk over or whether my feet actually touched the ground, but when we arrived, I paced back and forth in the lobby popping antacids to relieve the sour taste in my throat.

After what seemed like an eternity but was probably just a few minutes, Nada and I were led into Kane's office by his wonderfully attentive assistant Nola Shrewsbury. It was a big office—nearly a thousand square feet—but even so, it appeared to confine this man. The walls were covered with dramatic photographs of zebras and lions. There was a painting of Mount Kilimanjaro. On the adjacent wall hung a samurai sword. It looked like the real thing. On a shelf over his desk, there were four Emmy statuettes, each standing more than a foot tall, their golden glow flooding the room.

Dennis was on a landline but quickly begged off. He came out from around his desk, an imposing man. Like a lion, he dominated his domain. He swept his eyes over me. I wondered if he might not have been more at home traveling the world or camping on the Serengeti than he was confined between these white walls in an office building in Washington, DC.

There was a fist-sized hole in the wall above and behind his desk. When Nada noticed I was staring at it, she leaned in and whispered, "Dennis has a terrible temper." My stomach reacted by producing a new shot of acid.

But Dennis Kane was in a very good mood that day. Nada obviously knew Dennis, but I didn't know how. They looked odd together. Nada was maybe five feet tall while Dennis towered over her as they talked. Nada and Dennis seemed to have almost nothing in common as far as I could determine. She was a federal agency manager while he sat atop one of the most dynamic nonprofits in the world. Yet, it was clear Dennis was genuinely happy to see Nada. When he hugged her, he practically knelt down to get his arms around her petite frame.

As Nada's guest, I was extended a considerable amount of courtesy. Dennis greeted me warmly and turned back toward Nada. "So, this is the fellow you wanted me to meet."

"Yes," Nada took hold of my elbow, subtly pushing me forward. "May I introduce you to professor Jim Larison of Oregon State University."

Dennis extended his hand and firmly took mine. "A pleasure. Nada tells me I need to see your work."

My stuttered answer was almost unintelligible. Luckily for me, Dennis was not the sort of person to waste time with small talk. He immediately led us to a few chairs conveniently stationed around the business end of a well-worn seven-plate KEM editing machine. Dennis took my copy of *Mammals* and handed it to one of his assistants, who immediately began threading it across the top of the machine. I wiped the sweat from my palms and tried not to show how truly distressed I was.

Dennis leaned in and flipped the red lever in the center of the machine. My film began threading its way across the top of the flatbed editing machine. The sound of the electric motor and gears engaging and pulling the film forward by its sprocket holes filled the room. There was nothing for me to do but sit back and sweat.

Without moving my head, I kept glancing out of the corner of my eye, pretending not to be watching him, but I was desperately trying to interpret Dennis's expression. About two minutes into the film, I was afraid I had my answer. Dennis abruptly leaned forward and stopped the machine. Without a word, he sprang out of his chair and vanished down a hallway. Nada looked over at me and shrugged. Was he done watching, his patience exhausted, or was his attention span just that short? It never occurred to me that he might have liked what he was seeing.

A very long few moments passed as we sat in a stunned and awkward silence. I looked at the floor and shuffled my feet. When Dennis returned, he had a colleague in tow. A tide I could not control had swept into the room, and his name was Sid Platt.

This newcomer was far shorter than Dennis, but what he lacked in height, he more than made up for in bravado. His red hair and a slightly graying full beard brought color into the room. Unlike Dennis, Sid looked like he never got out of his office. He was slightly overweight and had very fair skin. He never looked directly at me. Sid was tightly wound and appeared annoyed at having been summoned to Dennis's office without any advance warning. What I didn't know at the time was that Sid was the director of the newly created office of Educational Films at the Society, a component, parallel department inside of the Television Division. Dennis wanted Sid to see my work because Sid was looking for talent.

I shook Sid's hand, and Nada offered him her seat so that he would have a good view of the screen. Dennis sat back down at the head of the editing machine and started rolling the film again. Everyone sat in silence for twenty-five minutes. Inside my head, I was fidgeting, wishing I had the chance to reedit the film. *That scene seems too long. Why did I cut that shot?* When the film ended, I was light-headed and sick to my stomach.

Dennis turned to me. "That was some very nice camera work." He looked back at Nada and thanked her for bringing me to his attention. He then turned toward Sid and with an almost imperceptible nod of his head, he signaled his wishes. "I think the two of you," he pointing first at Sid and then at me, "should have a talk."

Sid simply rose from his chair, looked at me, and without preamble motioned for me to follow him down the hall. I hesitated, looking at Nada and then at Dennis. Both tilted their heads in Sid's direction as if to say, "Go, man! This is your chance."

Once we reached his office at the other end of a long hallway, Sid simply turned around and spoke for the first time. "How do you know Dennis?"

"I don't. I only just met him."

Sid was skeptical. He seemed to think no one would have made it this far without a prior connection. "Well, Dennis certainly likes you, and around here, that is a very big deal." Sid simply spun around to the whiteboard behind his desk and began to describe the brave new world I was about to enter.

"We are putting together a new educational film office," he began, "and these are the first ten films we are planning to make this year. They will all fit together into a series on the physical and human geography of North America." He added, "I want our first series of films to look and feel much like the magazine itself, a sweeping visual portrayal of America, rich in imagery."

When I nodded my head to convey understanding, he continued, "At the moment, we are trying to find talented filmmakers to make each of the films on this board. The northeast region has already been spoken for, but if you want to work for the National Geographic and come in on the ground floor of this new film department, you can have your pick of the other regions."

My face instantly flushed purple. There was a loud buzzing in my ears and I gasped. Out of nowhere, my childhood insecurities flooded into my forebrain. I began to feel unworthy of such an invitation. How could I, a lowly university assistant professor, measure up to the National Geographic Society legacy? My mind began screaming, *You don't belong in such a group of elite photographers. Why is he making this offer? Say NO! You are going to fail!* I struggled to get control of myself.

Not even a half hour later, I was handed some paperwork. On top of the pile was an official National Geographic Society check with the Society's signature globe imprint, and somehow it already had my name printed on it. I had never before seen any organization move so quickly. I looked at the paperwork and gasped. This was more money than I had earned in the last year, working at the university.

When I looked up, Sid was speaking, " . . . can expect three more of these to come to you, one when you begin principal photography, one when you finish shooting the film, and one when you deliver the edited, finished composite internegative. We will, of course, cover all expenses incurred in the film's production. We want the film to be done by next fall."

He continued, but my head was spinning. I was trying hard to absorb everything. I drifted back to the paperwork in my hands and noticed a two-page contract under the check. Somewhere buried in the third paragraph of the contract was a guarantee of a million-dollar payment to my estate should I die in the Society's service. Given my recent history, that line caught my attention.

Sid saw I was hesitating, so he explained that no insurance company could be found to cover National Geographic photographers. "The work is just too dangerous and hard to explain to bean-counters. So, that's why the Society self-insures its people." I paused, not knowing exactly how to interpret this bit of information. But opportunity was standing at my door and I was certain it would knock but once. I would either take it and run, or I would never again get such a chance.

"So, if you agree, you should sign the contract."

Quickly, before Sid could change his mind, I scribbled my name where it said "signature" and Elaine's name where it asked for my beneficiary, but I was so nervous, my signature was completely unrecognizable. In a cold sweat, I sat back in the chair, stunned. My hands were shaking. To control them, I sat on my fingers.

When Sid finished describing what he wanted from me, he stood up and invited me to follow him around the office as he introduced me to staff: Nancy Rosenthal, Louise Millikan, Jean Berthold, and Suzy Poole. And then he introduced me to the postproduction supervisor, Carl Ziebe, a wonderful fellow with slightly graying hair and a light-hearted look. We startled him when we came into his office, and he spilled a bit of his coffee on his desk.

I said, "Oh God. Sorry."

He didn't miss a beat, cracked a tiny smile, and said, "Not God. Just Carl Ziebe."

I am not usually very good with names, but I realized instantly that I was not going to forget Carl.

As we entered the last office, Donald Cooper came out from around his desk. "Hello Professor Larison. I'm Donald Cooper." I liked this man immediately. Donald was also tall, over six feet. Compassion seemed to flow from his eyes and body language. He was dressed more formally than Sid, which surprised me, wearing a three-piece suit and silk tie. He started to say something, but Sid interrupted, "Donald is the assistant director of Educational Films. He will be your primary contact here at the Society. Want something, need something, call Donald."

Nada Yolan had been sitting on the far side of Donald's desk when we walked in.

"Nada has been telling me about your experiences, and I'm dying to hear about them . . ." He turned to Sid and asked, "Did you know this man has a rather colorful story to tell?" He then went on telling his fourth-hand understanding of the plane crash.

"OK, Donald, you can tell me all about it later. Nola is waiting in my office and needs to see Professor Larison." He turned toward the door, motioning for me to follow. We went back to Sid's office and I saw that Nola Shrewsbury was standing with a file in her hands. From the top of the file, she pulled an official letter on Society letterhead. At the bottom of the page, there was a gold-leaf seal with green, blue, and white ribbons pressed beneath the gold leaf. I quickly glanced at the letter, which began: "To Whom It May Concern: Mr. James R. Larison is directing on behalf of the National Geographic Society, the film tentatively entitled, 'The Mountain States' . . . " I glanced down at the base of the letter and it was signed, Dennis B. Kane, Director, Television and Educational Films.

"This is what we call *the dazzler*. It will be your letter of introduction," Sid explained. "You are to carry it everywhere you go and, if asked, show it as proof you are an official representative of the Society." He continued, "You wouldn't believe how many times we get calls from the switchboard and find that someone is impersonating one of our photographers. This letter will provide you with proof when you need someone's cooperation."

An hour later, when Nada and I emerged from the National Geographic Society headquarters, we were on an adrenaline high. The hot sun beat down on my face. I squinted, trying to get my eyes to adjust to this profoundly different world. What had just happened? What would this mean for my life? How would this affect Elaine? How would it affect my job at the university? Could I keep my job? What had I done?

The steady stream of questions flowing through my mind was eventually interrupted as Nada turned to me and with the biggest grin

National Geographic Society

WASHINGTON, D. C. 20036

DENNIS B. KANE
DIRECTOR
TELEVISION AND EDUCATIONAL FILMS

April 27, 1982

TO WHOM IT MAY CONCERN:

Mr. James R. Larison is directing on behalf of the National Geographic Society the film tentatively entitled "The Mountain States." He will be working as director and cameraman with his film crew throughout the Colorado, Idaho, Montana, Nevada, Utah, and Wyoming area.

The film is intended for the junior and senior high school audience, grades seven through twelve, and will be included in a series of films on the geography of the United States.

Any cooperation that you may extend to Mr. Larison will be greatly appreciated by the Society.

Sincerely,

Dennis B. Kane, Director
Television and Educational Films

DBK:jbr

written across her face, said, "My God. You did it." I was so excited I picked her up off the ground and gave her a bear hug.

"No, *we* did it." All of the tension that had been building up inside of me over the last three hours rushed out. "How will I ever thank you?"

But there was just no way I would ever be able to adequately repay Nada for what she had done for me. The only thing I could think to do was invite her to lunch. I picked the most expensive restaurant I could quickly find within a few blocks of the National Geographic office, and for the next two hours we relived the morning's success. In between toasts and pats on the back, it started to dawn on me. This was a moment of profound change. Nada asked me how I would tell Bill Wick and I said, "I have no earthly idea."

"That's going to be a tough one," she observed.

Of course, she was right, but at that moment, I was more interested in how Elaine might react. The last thing she knew I was going into a meeting with someone she had never heard of. But a lot had happened since then. She would be shocked to hear I had a contract in my hand. She would also be worried that this new contract would make our home life even harder to manage. When last we talked, there was a real sense that I might step back from my film career and concentrate more on my university duties. My university job would certainly pay our bills and would also be a lot less dangerous and stressful. But now, everything had changed.

I looked at my watch. At that moment, Elaine would be in school teaching math to her third-grade class. Our young son, John, would be at the sitter's. When should I place this call to her? Should I wait till she was out of school? Would she want me to wait? A half-hour later, Nada grabbed a cab. I headed back to my hotel room, put down my briefcase, and picked up the phone. Elaine would want to hear the news.

Elaine got a call over the intercom. "Elaine, you have a telephone call from your husband. He says it can't wait. We're sending someone down to take your class." As soon as Rod Harvey, her principal, came into her room, Elaine rushed up to the office and stepped into a private phone booth off the main office.

"Hi, Babe. You're not going to believe it," I began. "I was given a contract."

"What? What do you mean, *a contract*?" she asked.

I went on to explain the way the Geographic does business. They hire someone—a producer—to take charge of a film's production. They give complete authority to that person to get the film made, hire people, and arrange travel. "I have to submit a proposal to them by the end of next month. It has to include what they call a 'treatment,' which, in broad strokes, must describe what the film will say, what it will look like . . . what we will film and what it will cost."

"You already signed the contract?"

"I couldn't say no." And then, as if to soften the news, I added, "It came with a very big check."

There was a momentary pause. She was trying to wrap her head around this life-changing moment. I began fidgeting. Would this contract deliver a serious blow to our efforts to balance home life? Would it make Elaine feel abandoned?

Finally, Elaine broke the silence and surprised me. She seemed to have made a mental calculation. The decision could not be undone. She simply said, "I'm so happy for you. Tell me, what is the film going to be about?"

"The Rocky Mountains," I bubbled. "The film is supposed to look and feel like a *National Geographic* magazine article."

Elaine could tell I was excited, and I could tell she was holding back. In the end, she simply said she needed to get back to her class. "We'll talk when you get home."

That night at the Hilton in Washington, I sat alone in my room and tried to answer a few basic questions that had come to mind. Undoubtedly, the National Geographic contract would be a game changer. Would I have to resign my faculty appointment at the university?

My job with the university was permanent. The contract with the National Geographic Society was for one project. If I gave up my university post for a one-time gig—well, that just wasn't what any sane person would call a *bright idea*. But the National Geographic Society was a shimmering light, drawing me in. How could anyone say no to such an offer?

As I worked my way through the problems, I began to see a path forward. Faculty members have broad discretion to raise outside money, to adapt their efforts, and to determine how they spend their time. Just maybe I would be able to do both, the university's business and the National Geographic film. What would that look like? Would I need to buy some of my time back from the university or take a leave of absence?

For hours, sleep eluded me. I just stared at the ceiling, beginning to feel a lot like a pretzel. I was contorting myself, just to fit my life into what I already knew I was going to do. By two in the morning, I had begun to put together a possible plan.

———————

I flew back to Oregon thinking hard about our future. When I came downstairs that following morning, Elaine was feeding John. In between nervous laps around the kitchen, I fried two eggs. Between Elaine and me, there was this heavy air of uncertainty. No one knew how this was going to go. I was thinking hard about what I would say to Bill Wick. I burned the first eggs, then tried again. When two edible sunny-side up eggs were done, I sat in silence while John played with his food and Elaine tried to make sure that at least some of it ended up in his mouth.

Just seven days earlier, Elaine had been thinking I would be attending a somewhat routine university function, nothing life-changing, just a part of my normal university life. But she was thinking about the calls I'd made to her. She too was wondering if I would be able to keep my university job. If I left the university, what would that mean for our household income? How much more of my time would I be spending in the field? Would the contract deliver a serious blow to our efforts to balance our lives?

After breakfast, John began bouncing up and down on his rocking horse in our living room in front of our sliding glass doors, oblivious to everything except the thrill of the ride. When the springs beneath the horse drove John forward, his blond hair shot straight up three inches above his head. When the bronco jumped backward, his hair collapsed forward over his forehead into his eyes. He giggled with the fun of each repetition.

In some ways, I may have been riding a horse of my own that day and I, like John, may have been blinded by the thrill of the ride. These new filmmaking duties were going to have an enormous impact on our lives. As a mother, Elaine was being drawn in one direction while I was being drawn in another. Both of us felt the widening gap. I had promised Elaine on Lake Timagami I would always love her and never lose touch with her, but this new contract was threatening those bonds, straining our relationship. It was also no longer just about the two of us; Elaine was pregnant again and I now had an expanding family to think about. Somehow, we were going to have to build a family together that would look very different from any we had ever seen.

8

OUR FIRST ASSIGNMENT

JUST SIX WEEKS LATER, I drove up from Oregon to the airport terminal in Missoula with the back of the car filled with cameras, film, tents, and gear of all kinds. It was all a new experience for me, so I had just thrown everything I thought I might need in the car before leaving home.

I was deeply concerned. I had taken a two-month leave from my duties at the university. Otherwise, and perhaps more important, Elaine and I had resolved nothing. There had been no time to talk these things out. My contract with the Geographic was now setting the pace, driving our lives forward whether we were ready or not.

Jim Hicks came down the Jetway with his broad, square chin and a huge grin that stretched all the way from one ear to the other. He seemed not to have a care in the world. His body language radiated confidence, which helped me to feel better about everything. His hiking boots had a thick coat of snow seal, recently applied. He wore a red raincoat over top of a multicolored, not-so-flattering wool sweater he had knitted himself. He wasn't very good at knitting but seemed to enjoy the process. On his back, Jim carried a full daypack with a water bottle hanging from a D-ring. I knew immediately he was ready for what was to come. He seemed to have put the Alaskan plane crash behind him.

More than two years had now passed since I last worked with Jim, and in that time he had quit his filmmaking job at the University of Wisconsin and had moved to Illinois to join his new wife, Peggy Holmes.

Together they were taking over her dad's family farm. Jim had no experience running a farm, but he was committed and wanted to make this his new life's work. I never knew Jim to shy away from a challenge. I asked, "Aren't you missing the filmmaking life just a little?"

"Maybe a little."

Secretly, I think he was also happy to have a break from the farm. This film would give Jim the opportunity to keep his toe in the water as a filmmaker.

We talked briefly about each other's families and then I said, "I just can't picture you sitting on a tractor. How the hell have you gone from writing film scripts to digging in the dirt?"

"It's not as hard as you might think."

He kept talking about the farm as we walked over to the baggage claim area. He asked, "What's first on the agenda?"

"We're going to be busy. I've got us booked into a small motel on the west side of Glacier National Park. We start tomorrow by meeting the staff at park headquarters. You had better wear your thermals. It's going to be cold."

That night, we talked a little about the airplane crash. He told me about his reception back in Wisconsin. He never mentioned the word *trauma*. Jim is an intensely private person; it was difficult to get him to really open up. I've never been good at exposing weakness either. So, between the two of us, it was a short conversation—How you doing? Just fine, you? Not bad. So how about them Bears—it was just about that simple and unproductive. We shuffled off back to our respective motel rooms without knowing much of anything about how the other person felt. I still wondered if Jim held the crash against me in any way, but if he did, I was sure he wasn't going to say so out loud.

―――――――

The next morning, we met the Park Service road crew as they gathered around their trucks at the park headquarters building in West Glacier. The PR officer for the Park Service introduced us and handed us off to the crew chief, who was trying hard to pry his eyes open with a strong cup of coffee. He asked us to throw our gear in his truck, and we immediately headed for Logan Pass, Jim in the back seat and me beside the crew chief up front.

We spent a half hour or so skimming along the east edge of Lake McDonald and then turned up toward the mountains. At the lower elevations around the lake, spring leaves were just beginning to pop out of their buds. The early morning sunlight streamed through bright green shoots. But as we approached five thousand feet of elevation on the winding, one-lane road, we began to encounter winter. When we came around that last sharp corner, I could see a stack of heavy equipment parked nose-to-tail down the center of the road. A wall of snow blocked the road in front of the lead plow. This area, in summer, is known as the Garden Wall, partly because it is blanketed by spectacular flowers but also because it is so steep—practically a wall.

As we climbed out of the crew truck, the chief began explaining the process to the two of us. To get our attention, he stood right in front of me, less than three feet away.

With a no-nonsense expression, he said, "Now listen to me. Your lives may depend on it. We will be using four-hundred-horsepower D9 Caterpillars to 'pioneer' out on top of the snow. The operator will 'walk' the Cat out, cutting a path above the road surface. He will then back up and begin cutting thin slices off, one foot at a time, slowly working his way down until he reaches the asphalt."

I nodded and he continued.

"I want to warn you: this place is extremely dangerous. When the sun hits these slopes in two hours, the snow will become heavy and unstable. There will be dozens of avalanches coming down every one of these streambeds—this time of the year, we call them 'avalanche chutes.' Watch where you stop, where you stand, where you put your camera. Don't turn your back on an avalanche chute. Don't stand in an avalanche chute. When you have to move through one, just keep moving and keep your eyes up to make sure nothing is coming your way. My crew can't be spending all day watching out for you, so keep yourself safe."

"I understand," I assured the man. He also seemed genuinely concerned we might end up getting crushed under one of his machines on his watch.

"Just don't walk up behind a Cat without knowing that the operator sees you and acknowledges your presence."

The crew chief then turned us loose. Jim helped me by carrying the heavy tripod, accessory bag of lenses, and film magazines. I carried the Arriflex. We strapped on our snowshoes, then moved out in front of the lead Cat on the steep slopes of ice and snow, set up the camera, and filmed the process from a distance to gain some perspective.

The perspective was staggering. Giant snow-laden mountain peaks rose up a thousand feet above the roadway. The equipment, big as it was, was dwarfed by the size of these magnificent mountains. Beneath the Cat, a pile of snow at least twenty feet deep lay across the mountain slope.

I was searching for that one image, the one that would impress the Geographic staff. I wanted to capture a moment in time, and that moment would have to capture perfect light. I had spent years as a graduate student and then as an apprentice in film trying to learn to appreciate light and to capture in photographs what others often could not see. Photography, when done correctly, is art, and art does not come easily to a person such as myself. The key to a photographer's success comes down to his ability to see the different moods of light, then to capture that light in new and revealing ways. As a student, I became fascinated by the way light creates the illusion of a third dimension. Life is three-dimensional. Somehow photographers must use light, colors, shapes, and perspective to create the illusion of a third dimension in a two-dimensional medium.

Here, on that mountain, on my first National Geographic assignment, I was going to find out how well I had learned those lessons. The image, and perhaps I as well, would live or die depending upon the light I allowed to strike the film emulsion. Would I see it? Could I capture it? My future with the Geographic may very well depend on the answer to those two questions.

The work went on all morning. Every time the D9 reached the road surface, it would be surrounded by towering walls of snow. At that point, another crew member would move in with a giant snowblower to begin throwing the vast amounts of snow over the cliff.

At lunch that first day, the crew chief sat down and told us about an accident that happened a few years back when the D9 operator misjudged conditions. The snow beneath the Caterpillar had given way, and the Cat and driver had gone over the side of the mountain.

"I just had to watch the whole thing happen—like a slow-motion movie," the chief said. "I couldn't believe what I was seeing." The operator stayed in his seat. Miraculously, the machine stayed upright all the way down in a headlong plunge over the side of the cliff. "He fell nearly two thousand feet but lived to tell the story."

Jim and I got back to work after hearing the story, each of us paying just a little more attention to our surroundings. I had in mind the sort of shot I wanted and was determined to stay until I had it. The shot needed to be taken when the D9 was cutting a new section of snow, what the foreman had called "pioneering" out across the unbroken expanse of ice and snow. To make this shot, Jim and I had to put ourselves in harm's way. We had to be on the face of the steepest part of the wall, out in front of the Cat. We had to be close to the action. And I had to use a lens that would compress distance—essentially stacking the machine against the backdrop of the mountain cliff.

At the end of the first day, I knew we did not have what I wanted, so we kept coming back. Each day the D9 operator cut another half-mile of road, and each day, we were there to film the progress. Each day at dusk the men dismounted, left their machines on the plowed road, and walked back to their trucks. But as we walked the road they had just plowed, we encountered new avalanches that had come down during the day behind us along the road, and every morning the crew had to clear away those new avalanches before they could go on to cut another half-mile of roadway.

The work was hard, but it was also spectacular. On the morning of the third day, the sky was clear. The sun came over Logan Pass just as the Cat began cutting a new section of the road just below the steepest part of the pass. When the light poked over the pass, the Cat pioneered out across the cliff, belching smoke. In the background, the snowblower was cutting its way into an enormous pile of snow below an avalanche chute, throwing a curtain of snow over the cliff into the valley below. I knew right away this is what we had come for. I shot film until the camera ran dry.

When the road crew broke over Logan Pass at the continental divide, I was satisfied. Jim and I packed up and left Glacier National Park to begin working our way south along the Rocky Mountains.

———

Our next stop was the Blackfeet Reservation and an artist who worked in bronze. Bob Scriver lived in a teepee, not because he had to but because he wanted to, at the foot of the Rockies on the outskirts of Browning, Montana. When we drove over the last hill, I saw for the first time his summer home, a small encampment, three teepees sitting in a circle around a fire ring. These tents were set in a spectacular spot in the foothills of the Rockies. In the distance, the spine of the continental divide stood dark blue against the light blue sky. Quaking aspen stood in bright green bands between us and the mountains.

Scriver was perhaps seventy-five years old, bent like you might expect from a man who spent his entire life stooped over his artwork. I was surprised to see that he was not Native American. For a man to have spent so much of his life working on Native American art, you'd think he would be a Blackfoot himself. He was not.

Among the many things he had created was a bronze statue of an emaciated Native American hunter standing in defeat, seemingly carrying the weight of his people on his shoulders. Scriver called his bronze statuette *No More Buffalo*. It was a powerful piece of work that made a statement about the burden carried by all Native American peoples and about the loss of buffalo from the western plains. I wanted to shoot some film of this bronze statue and talk about what motivated him to do this work.

He was only too happy to welcome us into his teepee. In fact, Jim and I were stunned by our reception. As night began to fall across his foothill encampment, a bunch of local friends started showing up. Pickups pulled into the encampment. Pretty soon, there were forty people standing around the fire ring. A small family rode in from the south, over the hilltops on horseback, to join us around the fire.

Bob introduced us to everyone saying, "These are the National Geographic photographers I told you about." Bob was obviously a local celebrity, enjoying the moment. He pulled out dozens of thick rib eye steaks from a beat-up old cooler. Beer flowed freely. After several beverage shots of something I could not identify but could quickly feel in my kidneys, he began opening up.

"The National Geographic Society is the reason I am where I am today," he began. "I was a little-known starving artist with no prospects and no hope of ever breaking out of poverty. The big art studios wouldn't touch my work because I am a white man making Native American art. I made *No More Buffalo*, which sat on a shelf for a decade before one day a *National Geographic* photographer came along. I showed it to him. He shot a few hundred pictures of me and *No More Buffalo*. He then went away and I thought no more about it until May of that year, when a reporter from the *Missoulian* called to tell me I had been selected as the *premier Montana artist*. He told me *No More Buffalo* was featured in the May issue of the *National Geographic* magazine. My life has never been the same since."

"How so?" Jim asked.

"Recognition! I was invited to tour Europe, to display my work in Chicago, New York, London. My work went from being worth almost nothing and sitting in total obscurity to commanding as much as $10,000 in commissions for each small piece. When you called, I was only too happy to help. In fact, *anything* you want, name it, and it will be done."

Jim turned to me. Until that moment, I had never fully appreciated how much influence the Society's work has had on American culture. Here, in this man's simple statement was a lesson for me, one that would guide me in everything I did from that day on.

———————

After spending the rest of the evening eating and drinking around the campfire, Jim and I set out again, driving south. Our next stop was the Missoula Smokejumper Base at the west end of the Missoula International Airport. We spent the better part of two days flying with and filming their exercises. There were no active fires, so we had to be satisfied with training jumps.

From Missoula, we moved on, hitting every one of the states along the continental divide multiple times, filming a rodeo in Colorado Springs, miners at Kennecott Mine, a Native American powwow on the Crow Reservation, a day of branding cattle in Wyoming, Reba McEntire performing to a crowd in Colorado, mountain climbers in Jackson Hole, the Las Vegas strip, loggers in Bitterroot National Forest, roughneck oil men in Wyoming, buffalo and antelope on the range, and elk in Yellowstone.

Toward the end of July, we were back in Glacier National Park. This time, the snow had melted away and we had free access to the high-country trails. Jim and I packed all our camera gear into two sixty-pound backpacks, left our vehicle at the edge of Lake McDonald, and headed up a mountain trail toward Sperry Chalet and Gunsight Pass. Gunsight was known as one of the most spectacularly beautiful spots in the Rockies. Mountain goats frequented the pass. I wanted to capture on film the feeling of hiking in the mountains, and I could think of no better place to capture the beauty of mountains than Gunsight. But we were tired when we left the lake. We had already been running at full throttle for nearly two months, night and day. If we weren't shooting film, we were driving to the next location. We were growing a bit punchy.

As we hiked up the trail, we added physical exhaustion to our list of challenges. We had to climb nearly ten miles, all up, a gain of nearly four thousand feet through rugged terrain. When we reached the Sperry Chalet, we dropped our packs and made ourselves at home among the other hikers. The Chalet was staffed mostly by women. Jim struck up a conversation with the head cook. He asked her how she got her job at the Chalet. She told him that she had sent a box of her baked goods along with her application. "Kind of sealed the deal," she said. At dinner I told the other visitors to the cabin why we were there and made some lame joke about anyone not wanting to be photographed or seen with their present company at the Chalet to avoid our cameras.

When Jim and I were alone, I asked him, "Do you remember that time you, Elaine, and I shared a night together in that lean-to in the Porcupine Mountains?"

"Yes. Why?"

"Because that was the coldest night I've ever spent in the woods; nearly thirty below! Just before we went to sleep, you pulled out a flask of brandy. You said it was the good stuff and passed it around to warm us up. I don't suppose you have that flask hidden somewhere."

There was a moment of silence as we took a sip of his whiskey and each thought about that trip. We then went to bed, listened to the rain on the roof, and then Jim said, "I really miss my wife."

"Well, why don't you give her a call when we get down off this mountain? Invite her to join us for a few days. She can help with the filming and I'll get the Geographic to pay her expenses."

"Thanks, I think I will."

Luckily, the next morning dawned bright and blue. The mountain goats were all around us. I sat at the base of a big rock on the pass, and an old goat came right up to me. He sat down five feet from my lens and chewed his cud, unconcerned that I was there at all. Now I understood why there was so much matted white hair on that rock. This was *his spot*, and he wasn't going to let a human being stop him from enjoying the heat of a bright morning sun.

By the end of the morning, I had the one shot I needed—the goat overlooking the valley below with early morning, yellow light backlighting his thick white hair. We had captured a feeling of wilderness as it stands, full of life.

In late August, Jim and I headed south toward a small town on the western side of the Teton Range. On the drive down, I had told him we were going to have to confront our demons. We needed dramatic footage of the mountains. To get it, we were going to have to film from the air. I had made arrangements with a local pilot who made his living giving people glider rides over the massive stone walls of the Tetons. We arrived at the airport and were met by the company owner, who was also the principal pilot. He wore blue jeans, a western shirt, and a cream-colored Stetson in pristine condition.

"Afternoon. Are you the National Geographic photographers?" he asked.

"Indeed," I responded.

"My name is Norman—call me Norm. We are all set up for you. We've cleared our schedule of all other flights and distractions so we can give you two days of our undivided attention. All of our aircraft are at your disposal. Just tell me what you need."

This was more cooperation than I had expected. Jim and I looked at each other and I began telling Norm about our plans for this segment of the film. We wanted some unusual camera angles, I said, not just from the cockpit and not just from the ground. We wanted to mount a camera to the outside of his towplane airframe. Norman wanted to know where we would place the camera, so Jim started explaining his idea. He had welded together a mount for the camera to fit on the top side of the wing strut of a Cessna, in between the strut and the wing itself. He had tested the mount shortly after building it back at home and knew the mount would stand up to the force of the wind.

"I attached a camera mount on the strut of a Cessna 172; I can report it did not noticeably interfere with normal flight operations," he explained.

"OK, I'd like to see the apparatus," the pilot said. "Anything else?"

I explained our plan to strap a smaller camera to the top of the glider wing, on the leading edge if possible. The camera would then be able to film straight back along the wing so we would be able to see the moment the glider pilot disconnected the tow cable and peeled off, with the mountains in the background.

"I don't suppose you have tested that arrangement."

Jim spoke first, "No, neither of us has ever had access to a glider, so we will have to rely on your experience and judgment. If, in your opinion, the camera will disturb the airflow and lift over the wing, then obviously we shouldn't try it."

"Let me think about it."

That night, Jim and I talked over dinner. Neither of us had really flown much since our encounter in Alaska. I didn't know how we would respond to sitting in a cockpit again, especially in a glider.

"Are we biting off more than we can manage?" I asked.

"Maybe, but I don't see how we do our jobs if we don't do this. Somebody has got to go up in that glider and trigger the camera at the right times. That one powerful shot of the glider above the Teton Range can only be gotten this way."

"Shall we draw straws?"

"No. You're the photographer."

"Look," I said, "we need a camera on the ground filming everything from below. You handle that camera. I'll go up in the glider to trigger the remote camera."

Jim looked relieved, nodding agreement.

The next morning, we were at the glider hanger at 6:00 AM. Jim began mounting the camera to the leading edge of the left wing while I stretched the trigger cable along the underside of the wing, then taped it into place. Norman watched every step to make sure that we weren't doing anything to his airplane that would damage the wing or compromise its flight characteristics.

When we were done, he surprised us. "I had better take this flight by myself, just to make sure the camera doesn't cause the glider problems." And then he began strapping on a parachute. "I haven't worn one of these in a long while," he said. The pilot hesitated just a little as he buckled the chute around his waist and under his crotch but didn't let his anxiety get in his way.

"Do you really think you might need that?" I asked. "Will the camera affect the flight dynamics, in your opinion?"

"No, but I'd better be safe and I don't want either of you to get in a plane that is not flightworthy."

"I appreciate that," I said. But I was worried. What would I do if what we had asked caused this man's plane to stall or drop out of the sky? When his pilot took off, pulling the glider on a towrope, I bit my lip. Jim and I watched every second of the test flight, looking for any sign that the glider was having trouble, but from the ground, it looked stable. At no time did that wing dip lower. It looked like a textbook flight.

When Norman returned and climbed out of the glider cockpit, he said, "You were right. The camera made no difference at all to the flight dynamics." He stripped off his parachute, handed it to his assistant, and said, "We're ready to go."

I slowly climbed in the front seat of the glider to handle the on-off switch for the wing-mounted camera. Jim helped me strap in. "Are you sure you are going to be all right with this?" he asked.

"Just close the canopy before I change my mind, will you?"

Jim turned around and beat a path to the tripod and camera already positioned for the ground shot. I pulled my helmet on and moved the microphone up to my lips, "I'm ready."

Norman sat behind me at the controls. He waved his hand over his head to let the Cessna pilot know we were ready. Suddenly, the tow cable came up taut and we were jerked forward. One of Norman's men ran alongside the glider holding the wings level so neither would drag on the ground. As soon as we reached ten miles per hour, the airflow over the wings gave the pilot control and the man let the wing go. The glider lifted off first, and then the Cessna slid into the air. We were airborne. Butterflies began fluttering in my stomach. I felt a rush of adrenaline, and my face felt hot. I couldn't let this fear have its foothold. I was in a tiny little compartment—a closed-in space. The ground was speeding by under the fuselage. I was starting to panic. Silently, I screamed. *Control yourself, damn it.*

It took about twenty minutes for the Cessna to pull us to ten thousand feet. By the time the pilot asked me if I was ready to disconnect from the tow plane, I was. I had this thing under control; I was sure of it. "Cut loose," I said. With a wobble of our wings, Norman let his Cessna pilot know we were going to break contact.

There was a slight drop as the tow cable disconnected and we were on our own. The only sound now was the air rushing over the wings and around the cockpit Plexiglas. I asked Norman to take the glider up into a vertical stall, then drop over the left wing and regain level flight after falling a few hundred feet directly back toward the ground camera. He sensed that I was nervous and asked once again if I was ready, then pulled back on the stick. I rolled film in the outside camera as we climbed vertically into the puffy clouds around the Grand Tetons. As we climbed, we lost our forward momentum. The glider stalled and we began falling tail-first. Norman was a good pilot. He banked left and we dropped over the wing. I knew immediately we had the shot. The light was great, the face of the Tetons was in the shot. I'd done it, keeping my emotions in check while doing the job I was paid to do.

As soon as Norman had the glider on a flat trajectory, he turned toward the west face of the Grand Tetons. We spent about twenty minutes sliding in and out of a few cumulous clouds, losing altitude with each passing moment. For the first time in a long time, I was able to sit in an airplane and enjoy the ride. And the ride was spectacular! When we were just two thousand feet above the ground, Norman turned back toward the airport. We landed softly, rolled to a stop, and the right wing dropped to the ground.

I climbed out of the glider cockpit and said, "That was spectacular. We have it." Jim then turned to Norman and said, "If you don't mind, I'd like to try sitting in that thing just once."

"Of course."

Jim folded himself into the glider, preparing for his own ride. Because the camera was already mounted, I asked him to trigger the camera one more time just for good measure.

When all was done, I was quite proud of both of us. We seemed to be all right with the loops and rolls. My stomach was a bit queasy, but that was probably due to the loss of gravity and the G-forces, not anxiety.

The next morning Jim and I drove around the southern end of the Tetons and went straight to the Jackson Hole airport. Peggy was due to come in on the next flight, and from there we were going to go downtown to film the reenactment of an Old West gunfight.

Jim spent an hour or so teaching Peggy what she would need to know about the sound gear, and then we set up two camera positions for the shoot-out. Because we were working for the National Geographic, we had full access to the event. Jim took one of the cameras to the top of a nearby building where he could overlook the street, while I took the Arriflex S down to the street and moved in and out around the shooters. The announcer introduced us to the crowd as National Geographic photographers, so many of the tourists spent more time photographing us than they did the gunfight.

The three of us worked well together, despite having never worked as a team. Jim and I operated two cameras. Peggy worked the Nagra and shotgun microphone. Surprisingly, we had it in just one take. Neither of us felt the need to repeat the action or to come back on another day. Each of the gunfighters wore clothing befitting the Old West, sporting long beards and handlebar mustaches. They looked the part. The shot would end up leading our new film.

The next day we moved on to Salt Lake City, where we were to film a performance of the Mormon Tabernacle Choir. It was a formal affair. We were told we would have to do the job without disturbing the audience. Once again, Peggy handled the sound while Jim and I operated two cameras, one set up in the back of the room and another up front beside the choir.

That night, Peggy, Jim, and I sat down for our last meal together before heading home. Jim started, "I want to thank you for this opportunity. I got to see a lot of the West that I'd only read about before." As he gave me a smirk, he added, "And shooting film with you is always a treat." I sensed a bit of irony in his voice.

"None of this would have been possible without you."

Peggy jumped in. Looking directly at her husband, almost under her breath, she said, "Now for the hard part," and nudged Jim forward.

Jim continued, "I am not going to be able to do this again, Jim. The farm is just too demanding. The crops are on their own schedules; I probably won't be able to break free for long film trips again."

"You're going to give up all this and become a sodbuster?" I joked.

Peggy spoke first. "He'll do just fine down on his knees in the dirt."

I was sad but was expecting this.

Peggy continued. "I'm sorry, Jim. But my dad is getting on in years. He needs our help on the farm."

"I know. Really, it's OK. I hope we can stay in touch."

But we didn't. Our lives diverged from that day forward. I would quickly come to miss Jim a lot. He had been in my life for more than ten years as a friend—almost a brother. Jim went back to Illinois; I went back to Oregon. We would rarely see each other after that day in Utah. Our very different lives just got in the way.

I was completely exhausted. Jim and I had run nearly thirty thousand feet of film through the Arriflex cameras and had recorded a hundred rolls of sound tape. We needed a break. Jim and Peggy hopped the next flight out, and I began the long drive back to Oregon. When I arrived home, Elaine and John were outside on the porch. I had no idea how long they had been out there waiting for me to arrive. They were actually jumping up and down. Elaine was yelling, "Daddy's home! Daddy's home!" She was doing her best to make this a memorable moment in our young son's eyes. He was barely two years old, a little young to remember, but it was really sweet to see.

I spent an hour putting John to bed that night talking to him, asking about the things he had been doing. He showed me "his camera." It was the one I had around my neck when the plane crashed. It was now not much more than an inert, useless hunk of metal. Nothing worked, but he held the camera up to his face, pressed his eye up to the viewfinder in the back of the camera, and said, "My camera."

"I see. Can you take a picture of me?"

"Yes . . . click, click. See, Daddy, I took your picture."

Elaine came in the room suggesting I let John sleep. We backed out of the room and went downstairs, where Elaine had a candle on the dinner table ready for the two of us. We talked well into the night about the things that we'd missed in each other's lives. The big topic that night was how her second pregnancy had been going all summer. Elaine was only about four weeks away from her delivery date, so she was big. Just moving around was a challenge. I asked her a million questions. "I'll bet you're uncomfortable," I said.

"A bit. This one is a little rowdy." She offered to have me feel her belly, so I did, and for the first time I got a chance to feel what Elaine's life must have been like. This baby acted like he was trying to kick his way out of a jail cell. I should have known right then we were in for it with this boy. Elaine just grinned as the baby continued tumbling in her belly.

In late September 1982, Ted was born, seven pounds, six ounces, and a torrent of energy. With Elaine spending the night in the hospital, her mom was staying over to help with John and to be present for the newborn boy. When I brought Elaine home, the child care duties doubled or maybe tripled. It was clear: Elaine was going to have her hands full with this one. I stayed home to help raise our sons for as long as I dared, but by January I had to return to the field to finish shooting *The Mountain States*.

To replace Jim I hired a kid named David, who was a film student at the University of Montana. We went first to Snowbird, Utah, to film skiers, then on to film wildlife in Montana, and we finished up somewhere in Yellowstone National Park filming geysers and buffalo in winter.

At the end of that first year of filming, I was very glad indeed to return home. I practically had to reintroduce myself to my sons, who were living in the relative peace of our mountain home in the deep forests of the Northwest. I brought a couple of gifts home from Yellowstone for the boys, a stuffed buffalo for John and a wildlife T-shirt for our infant son, Ted. John slept with that buffalo until the stuffing came out and it completely fell apart. Ted wore his shirt as if it was a pair of pajamas until he outgrew it. Elaine hoped these tangible gifts would remind our sons of their father when I was away.

Our mountain home became my hideaway for the next few months as I buried myself in family and university duties, attempting to make up for all the time I had been away. At night, after the kids were in bed, I began the slow process of editing *The Mountain States* film, working practically nonstop every night and weekend, all through the winter. It was peaceful, it was quiet, and Elaine and I had time to grow back together.

At the end of that long winter, when it came time to deliver *The Mountain States* to the National Geographic, I began to worry there wouldn't be a next film—at least not one funded by the National Geographic Society. Many times, I had thumbed through *National Geographic* magazine, read the society's books, and watched its television specials. Rarely did an author or producer appear in the credits more than once. Somehow, I needed to convince Sid to fund another film. I hoped this time it would be one of my own ideas. Bill Wick hoped it would be something about the oceans and the Sea Grant mission. Much of my time that spring was spent thinking about how to keep everyone happy, the university, the Geographic, Bill Wick, Elaine, and of course, myself.

I called Sid's office. A new voice answered; Sid had apparently promoted Nancy Rosenthal and was breaking in a new assistant. The new secretary, Frances Ingram, knew instantly who I was. I told her the film was ready. She made reservations with United for me to fly back to Washington. She booked a room at the Jefferson hotel, one of the most exclusive and classic old five-star hotels in Washington. The motto at the Jefferson was "sophisticated serenity," and it was everything it advertised.

The hotel was only about two blocks from the White House and three blocks from the National Geographic headquarters. A car picked me up at the airport, then drove directly to the hotel. When I checked in, the manager said, "The National Geographic will be paying for your stay. It will be our pleasure to make you as comfortable as possible."

My room was filled with antique furniture, fine linen, and a bouquet of flowers. I had never before been surrounded by such elegance. I was not expecting any of this; it left me astonished but also very lonely. All I could think about was Elaine and how much she would have appreciated this. When I went down for dinner that night, the waitress knew who I was before she even seated me and, without being asked, brought me the most spectacular assortments of Stilton blue cheeses from Nottinghamshire, England, and a bottle of fancy champagne. My taste buds were experiencing a high completely unknown to them. Dinner, too, was nothing short of stunning. For a hick from Oregon, this place was otherworldly. I stuck out like a rough-around-the-edges country bumpkin. Everything about this place made me miss my wife.

The next day, Frances met me in the National Geographic Society's magnificent museum/lobby. A twelve-foot high world globe surrounded by a fountain set off the room. Sid had not yet arrived, so Frances showed me around, then took me to Donald Cooper's office.

Donald was really good at such meetings and I was not. He began by trying to put me at ease, asking me about my family, my life in Oregon. He asked about John and Ted, and I began to loosen up. He told me about his two daughters, Katie and Chloe. It was clear immediately that the two of us shared a common bond; our children meant everything, and neither of us could stop sharing the things we liked best about our kids. Eventually we got around to discussing the filming, how it had gone, what I had "in the can." It was a slow, easy, enjoyable exchange. He was trying to get to know me. I wanted him to like me.

Sid arrived shortly after nine. He blew through the room like static electricity, booming orders, leaving no doubt who was in charge. His red beard seemed to match his explosive personality. Sid didn't waste time on chitchat. He immediately called in Louise Millikan, the researcher assigned to this film, and suggested we all retire to the editing suite to see what I had to show for all the summer's effort.

Once again, I sat around a flatbed editing table at the Geographic, hoping for the best. When the film came to its end, Sid said nothing; rather he seemed to simmer. Something just beneath the surface was bothering him. It was impossible to read Sid if he didn't want to be analyzed, so I turned toward Donald, who was concerned I might be getting the wrong message from silent Sid. He said, "Just what we were hoping for."

Sid didn't contradict him, so I was left with no real sense of what was bothering him. But the pressure was off. Donald was happy. Louise seemed happy as well. Donald turned toward Sid and said, "We have to get this to the other producers to show them what we want this film series to look like." Sid nodded, and finally I felt relief.

I ended up spending the whole day with the three of them. Eventually, we all moved on to Sid's favorite restaurant in Georgetown. Both Sid and Donald liked what I had done with the Rocky Mountain film; that was clear, but I still worried there might not be a second film. I didn't know quite how to bring up the subject of another contract.

But then Sid did it for me. "Would you like another assignment?" Sid asked.

Surprised, I stumbled, "Well, I would. Of course I would."

Sid cracked the tiniest of smiles, something he rarely did, as he noticed my thinly veiled enthusiasm spilling out.

Over the next hour, Donald outlined what they had been thinking. "We want to do a small series, not unlike the geography series you helped us make last year, but this series will be about the ways we use the Earth's resources. There will be at least two films in this smaller series, one to be called *Riches from the Earth* and another to be called *Riches from the Sea*." Donald went on to say that he wanted the film to show both the need-driven motivation for resource extraction and also to deal with the costs. "What does resource extraction look like on the ground?"

Sid jumped in at this point and said, "With your background in ocean studies, we thought you'd be the perfect choice to produce the *Riches from the Sea* film." And then as an afterthought he added, "If you want it."

I tried not to act too happy, but I was about as opaque as a pane of glass. Without really having to ask, they were already thinking about how my next film would fit into my university duties and responsibilities and tap into my environmental background. Donald looked over his glass of wine. I could see immediately this was his doing. He seemed to know, without me ever having to say anything, that they would have to make an effort to tap into my university connections.

"Take some time. Write up a treatment with a budget," Sid went on. "Get back to us within, let's say, two weeks." The conversation then drifted off topic. I tried to stay engaged but slowly drifted away thinking about how I was going to make a film about the wealth of oceans when I had almost no experience filming underwater.

When I returned to the Jefferson, Elaine and I talked candidly by phone. She was relieved knowing the Geographic staff liked our first film and was happy they wanted to continue doing work with me.

In the middle of all the good news, I said, "You know, I don't know a thing about filming underwater. We don't even have an underwater camera, housing, or lights, any of the things we will really need for this job."

"Did you tell Sid that?" Elaine asked.

"I didn't want to blow it. But I don't even have the necessary experience with scuba. I haven't been in the water for two years and will have to find someone to give me a crash refresher course . . . possibly upgrade my PADI [Professional Association of Diving Instructors] dive certificate." The truth was, Elaine and I had each obtained our basic diving certificates more than ten years earlier with only one open-water dive, in Devils Lake, Wisconsin. Since then, we'd made a few freshwater dives, one of those in Lake Superior, where we nearly froze to death. We had never even been in the ocean. We were novices!

"Jim, maybe this is the wrong time to bring this up, but you just got a letter from somebody named John Mansfield at WGBH in Boston. I opened it. I hope you don't mind."

"Of course not. What did he say?"

"I'll read it. 'Dear Professor Larison. I like your proposal. I think the film you have proposed, *Farmers of the Sea*, might just fit into our Emmy award–winning *NOVA* science series. I need to meet with you soon to discuss the ideas you have for this film.' He goes on to explain their process."

I exclaimed, "Oh my God!"

Elaine continued, "He's asking you for a budget and a detailed description of content. He says he wants the film ready for the fall 1984 lineup. He asks, 'Is that schedule realistic?' He wants an answer from you by the end of next week so he can put together his broadcast schedule. He sounds just a little bit desperate and seems to be implying this is a done deal. Is it? Did you commit to him?"

"Well, it was a long shot. When I wasn't sure if I would be asked to continue working for the Geographic, I started sending out feelers. But they were just feelers. I didn't expect such a quick or positive response."

"Well your hook just came back with a whale. What are you going to do?"

"I don't know. I just don't." Fishing around in my pocket for a Rolaid, I hung up the phone and sat at the window, staring, playing with my pen. There was no sleep that night. In fact, there wouldn't be much sleep for the next two years.

The whole way back from DC to Oregon, I fidgeted in my airline seat, trying to wrap my head around the opportunities and challenges I would be facing starting the moment I landed in Portland. How was I ever going to be able to handle all this work? How could I have gotten myself so far overextended? And how would I handle all the travel—all the airplane flights? Was I ready for all this?

9

THE CAYMAN TRENCH

READY OR NOT, THE TEMPO OF OUR FILMMAKING lives was about to take off like a hydrogen-filled rocket. To be successful, I was not only going to have to learn to travel the world with a mountain of film gear, a challenge in and of itself, but I was also going to have to somehow learn to shoot film underwater. I had no idea how I was going to do either. I would need to purchase a long list of new equipment, a new camera, a flatbed editing table, a pile of new lenses, a meter, dive gear, an underwater housing, and lights. The list seemed endless as well as endlessly expensive.

To make matters worse, these projects were intimately and perilously intertwined. Both films required extensive international travel, but neither film alone had a sufficiently large travel budget to do all that I wanted to do. Only by combining the funds could we afford to travel as widely as was necessary for either of the films. Keeping everyone happy, especially the Oregon State University administrators, was going to be a delicate balancing act.

While I spent the next few months dealing with logistics, scheduling, staffing, and funding problems, Elaine had her own issues to deal with. She was being torn by loyalty to her husband and love of her children.

She realized, perhaps better than I, that this filmmaking career was tearing us apart.

"I think I'm losing you to your career," she had once said.

The only way to fix this problem was to do everything possible to hold on to each other. But she was a mom. Her maternal instincts were tugging at her. She loved being a mom and was the best of moms, but Elaine also wanted to continue being my partner in life. If I was going to be off in some other corner of the world, she wanted to be there, too.

Like many principal breadwinners, I was expected to make a living to support my family. Some people spend eight hours a day at work and come home to enjoy their family lives. Others do it by being away from home for short periods of time. They, too, had time for family. But my job required both, eight hours a day in my university office and extensive travel that would take me away for months at a time. In addition, when I was home, I would have to spend hundreds of hours at an editing bench cutting film. I couldn't hire someone else to do the work because everything depended on my own artistic talent and filmmaking skill.

There was no doubt: I was going to be working at least eighty hours a week for the foreseeable future. To avoid being an absentee father, I decided to bring the postproduction work home with me. That way, I would have to be away from Elaine and the boys for only eight hours a day, plus the long trips. The rest of the time, I could be at home if I built and equipped an editing suite in our house.

A Steenbeck editing table, not unlike the KEM in Dennis Kane's office, was delivered to our home a month later. The thing weighed close to five hundred pounds. We had to get it up a flight of stairs to the only available room in our home, an upstairs bedroom. I asked a couple of builder friends to wrestle the thing up the narrow staircase. They got it to the landing, then realized they'd have to take the doorjamb off to finish the job. Lucky I had asked a couple of carpenters to help.

After spending most of the spring planning, I realized I would be traveling almost nonstop for most of the next eighteen months. There would be one long trip through Hawaii, Singapore, the Philippines, Hong Kong, Indonesia, and Japan. I would also have to make a number of shorter trips, one each to Mississippi, Nova Scotia, Wisconsin, Maryland, Texas, the Gulf of Mexico, Panama, and Scotland. For most of this work, I could rely on colleagues at other universities scattered around the United States and world, but I also was going to have to hire help. I hired a couple writers and assistant cameramen, then began assembling the gear I would need.

Whenever I put together a film trip, Elaine knew she could join me, but most of the time she was just too busy raising our sons. She kept an eye on my travel schedule. One day, she decided she wanted to come along on a short trip to the Gulf of Mexico.

In August, Elaine's mom came out to Oregon to stay with the boys while Elaine and I flew to Miami, then on to the Cayman Islands for the first time as a filmmaking team. Just in time, really, we discovered our way forward. Elaine was going to learn to do the underwater lighting. I was going to do the camera work, all part of *Riches from the Sea*. To make this work, I packed everything into the shortest time frame possible, just to reduce the amount of stress Elaine would have to deal with being away from home, but even so, this was going to be difficult for her.

To prepare, we spent much of that spring acquiring additional scuba training. Elaine especially was still not comfortable underwater. She had spent a good deal of time learning to swim, practicing in the university pool, and taking scuba lessons with me in Madison. But we both had only basic scuba certifications; neither of us was adequately trained for the job at hand. On one of our previous training dives, Elaine had panicked, needing to surface and get her head out of the water. At the minimum, she needed some additional time at depth, and we would both need to qualify for an Advanced Open Water certification. It certainly wouldn't hurt to get a Deep Diver specialty card.

To meet this need, I found Steve Adams, a master dive instructor with PADI, based close to our hometown, who had the necessary skills. He was now teaching all the scuba classes in Oregon. He had tattoos running the length of his arms, weighed about 250 pounds, and was as strong and fit as you might expect from a navy man. He agreed to privately tutor us so that we would be ready for the Cayman dives. As payment for this special treatment, I agreed to hire him to be our dive master in the Caymans, a win-win because I would have someone with real skills watching over us.

Over the next months, we threw ourselves into an intensive training program. Steve worked to fit all the necessary dives in before we were to leave for our next film trip. He took care to make certain that Elaine gained confidence in her own abilities and spent a good deal of time ensuring that we would be able to respond appropriately to emergencies. He even took us to Puget Sound to make sure we could handle heavy currents, dry suits, and cold water.

Our second major problem was equipment. Aside from Jacques Cousteau and possibly Al Giddings of James Bond movie fame, there were very few people in the world at that time with the sort of gear needed to be successful filming underwater. No professional cameras were made for underwater work other than the ones invented by Cousteau and his team, but these were proprietary and unavailable to us. The only lights I could find were made by Al Giddings. Luckily, I was able to buy a set of these Giddings lights left over after a Bond filming. They looked dangerous because they were regular 110-volt halogens that required a waterproof housing of their own with a cable running to a generator above in a boat. Electricity running through water just didn't seem like a really smart thing, but we had no choice.

Elaine was the one who was going to be handling the lights, so I worried constantly about her safety. If water seeped into the light head housing, Elaine would likely receive a life-threatening electric shock.

The only underwater camera housing available on the market cost as much as my Arriflex camera itself and would dramatically restrict my access to the camera's working components. I couldn't afford such an expensive addition to our gear at that time, nor was I sure the housing would be flexible enough to permit me to do the job anyway.

My solution to the problem was to design my own housing. For help, I turned to an engineer at Oregon State University's school of oceanography. Rod Mesecar had extensive experience fabricating machines that would stand up to the saltwater environment and perform under great pressure at depth. His idea was to use machined heavy-duty, tubular PVC with O-ring-sealed end plates. The front of the housing was fitted with an optically perfect, nearly bulletproof, shatter-resistant glass window, big enough to accommodate an extreme wide-angle lens and sturdy enough to stand up to the enormous pressure underwater. The rear of the housing consisted of another O-ring-sealed cap. Once removed, I would be able to access the camera's film magazine and battery without disturbing the camera itself. A set of handles would be attached on either side of the housing and an O-ring-sealed ocular port was included so I would be able to look through the lens, focus, and frame each shot. The right-hand grip was to be fitted with a plunger that would electronically start and stop the camera's motor.

Neither Rod nor I recognized the one real weakness of this housing, the hole that ran from the outside of the housing through the wall to the on-off switch on the side of the camera. We thought this hole would be sealed away from water by the epoxy resin that would hold the handle in place.

———————

On February 3, 1983, Steve, Elaine, and I took our new housing and lights and flew through Miami heading for Grand Cayman. This was to be the first of many dives the three of us would have to make for *Riches from the Sea*. I had done everything I knew how to prepare for this trip but had no way of knowing if it was enough.

On a spectacular warm morning, while floating above a stunningly beautiful aquamarine reef, I stepped off our dive boat and entered a spectacular new world. The air temperature was eighty-four degrees, the water temperature was eighty-one degrees, and the seas were calm. Visibility was unlimited. I could see the bottom some 150 feet below me as clearly as I could see my own hand. A school of baitfish glided to my left. A large stingray flew through the water and came up to my face mask as if to ask, "What are you doing here?"

I turned back toward the boat and gave Elaine an enthusiastic thumbs-up. She pulled her long hair back away from her forehead, slid her mask down over her eyes, and reached back for her regulator. Steve asked Elaine if she was ready, then gave her a gentle nudge backward over the side of the boat. There was a small splash. I immediately came around in front of Elaine to see that she was comfortable and breathing normally.

I then signaled for Steve to put the lights in the water. I slowly moved my hands close to the lights without touching them. When I felt nothing, I gingerly took the handles of each of the lights in my gloved hands. I turned the lights over so that I could inspect them to make sure they were not leaking. Only then did I hand them to Elaine. I returned to the surface, put my hand up, and signaled for the camera. Steve picked the housed camera up and extended it out over the side of the boat for me to take. I checked the camera, touched the on-off switch to see that all was in working order, and then peered into the lens opening just to be sure there were no leaks.

Steve was a big man, constructed with generous amounts of muscle and bone—the sort of body you typically see playing tight end on a professional football team. He usually wore a short-sleeved T-shirt matched by wetsuit leggings that were worn thin at the knees and had been bleached almost colorless by hundreds of hours of exposure to the sun. Whenever he came into the water to join us, Steve would hold off at a respectful distance from the camera so he wouldn't interfere with one of our shots, all the time watching to make sure Elaine and I were safe. His hands were usually folded in front of his chest and he breathed slowly—a skilled diver if ever there was one.

We were diving about three hundred miles directly south of Havana, Cuba, along the edge of what divers called *the blue wall*. The water in this part of the Caribbean was unusually clear, largely due to the adjacent deep water and the upwelling of rich cold water that comes up from enormous depths of the Cayman Trench. I chose the Caymans as a shooting location for this film because the reefs were known to be healthy and because the island had not yet been discovered by the growing tourist industry. The island was occupied by very few residents and was known only to a few diehard dive enthusiasts. We had the place to ourselves.

I was especially happy on this trip because Elaine was becoming an integral part of the filmmaking process. By taking over the underwater lighting responsibilities, we were going to rediscover that team we had begun to build on Lake Timagami. With each dive, she would grow more at ease and better at lighting each individual scene. As we headed for the bottom that day, I was struck by how comfortable she already appeared in the water. Her long, brown hair trailed behind her as she moved. Sometimes it would sweep around and flow straight out in front of her mask as the currents switched directions. On that day, she looked ecstatic at being in the Caymans.

I was delighted with our choice of shooting locations; visibility was as good as it could have been. The water was so clear that it felt like we had stepped off the roof of a ten-story high-rise and were now drifting in midair, ever-so-slowly sinking toward the street below. It was a wonderful day and the perfect film location.

The purpose for this first dive was to test our underwater housing and lights. Throughout our descent, Elaine and I each ran tests of our equipment. When my depth gauge read ninety-two feet, Steve signaled it was time to begin leveling off. I could scarcely believe we had already sunk so deep. It was difficult to tell how far down we had gone. I shot a few images of the sand/coral bottom. A giant grouper came up to me and moved between my legs, brushing up against me as if it were a pet dog.

I glanced over at Steve, and he was studying his decompression table. This was why I needed Steve. When filming, my mind is on the camera. I needed someone to ensure that we did not stay too deep for too long. We had spent just fourteen minutes at depth, a total of forty-three minutes underwater. Steve signaled it was time to begin a slow ascent. When we reached ten feet, Steve signaled for us to hold while the clock ticked and we allowed the nitrogen in our bloodstream to escape. At one hundred feet, nitrogen can build up in a diver's bloodstream. If nitrogen remains in a diver's blood when he surfaces, it will form life-threatening bubbles. Steve made sure we made all of our decompression stops and watched the clock to make sure it was safe to surface.

The equipment was ready. When our heads came out of the water, Elaine spit out her mouthpiece and said, "That was amazing."

Later that day, we made two dives on South Beach shooting film of a moray eel and hundreds of jackfish. We established this as our preferred pattern—three dives each day, each time shooting a magazine of film. When the magazine came up empty, we returned to the surface. At the end of each dive, I would wash the housing with a mild soap, permit it to dry, then open the back to retrieve and replace the spent magazine and depleted battery. Steve spent the same amount of time cleaning our dive gear in preparation for the next dive.

At 10:00 PM on our third day in the Caymans, we slipped into the water beginning a night dive on the *Oro Verde* wreck. The old ship sat in fifty feet of water, half-buried in sand, and was full of marine life, much of which came out only after dark. As we entered the massive tomb-like ship in the dark, I felt a tingling sensation run up my spine. I was beginning to feel a little claustrophobic. But the film opportunities were too great to resist.

When we were not actively filming, our underwater lights were off. When we needed a little light to orient ourselves or to coordinate with one another, we used tiny red pen lights so as not to disturb the wildlife or destroy our night vision. In the semidarkness, you could see things that you would never imagine existed. When we looked up through the water column, we could see stars and the moon distorted by the seawater above us. A faint blue phosphorescent glow radiated from the gently rippling waves above.

Unlike in the daytime, we could not regulate our depth so easily because there were simply no points of reference. We simply moved with the shifting currents, while Steve monitored his depth gauges to make sure we did not sink too deep.

It was a little more difficult coordinating our actions in the dark, but Elaine and I quickly learned to deal with the new surroundings. We rarely got outside of arm's reach from one another because touch was the only way we had for communicating.

In the darkness, we busied ourselves shooting film of the coral inhabitants. A giant moray poked its head out of its concealed hiding place, seemingly to beg for food. Steve worked hard to keep the light cables free so that Elaine could move with the camera. But the farther we swam, the harder Steve's job became. As Elaine and I slipped deeper and deeper along the bottom, Steve fell farther behind. When we reached the massive coral bommie that, by prearrangement, was to be the farthest most point for this dive, I looked around and couldn't find Steve. Elaine swept her light around looking for him, and we saw a mass of cigar-shaped, white creatures all swimming in formation, overtaking us. The mass was a school of about a hundred thousand small anchovies all moving in synchrony. They quickly surrounded us, bumping into us. They were attracted by Elaine's lights.

I signaled Elaine to move a few feet away from me and to shine her lights back at the camera, because I wanted to backlight the anchovies against the white, bright light. It was a highly unusual thing to do but effective if what you wanted was a feeling of mystery.

When I finished with that shot, I again looked for Steve. At first I couldn't find him but then slowly realized he was above us on the surface, frantically swinging his light from side to side in an effort to gain my attention. He was attempting to warn me of something—but what?

Then the mass of slow-moving fish suddenly turned and darted directly at me, pelting me with their bodies. The anchovies were frightened. Something was out there. They dashed in unpredictable directions, panicking, trying to escape whatever it was in the water.

Suddenly, a six-foot Caribbean reef shark flashed through the cone of light cast by Elaine's lights. It passed less than three feet in front of the camera, its mouth wide open, its jaws extended as it attempted to snag a mouthful of fish. When the shark snapped its mouth closed, I could see the tails of two or three anchovies protruding from its jaws. Elaine and I were in the middle of a feeding frenzy of at least a dozen sharks.

I cranked the camera up to max speed so I could slow down the action as the sharks, one by one, flew through the frame. Somehow, the sharks avoided us, targeting just the anchovies. As a shark passed about two feet over my head, I saw the long, pointed, black-fringed pectoral fins; they looked almost like wings extending out from the shark's torpedo-like body. Another shark came closer; its dorsal fin brushed the front lens port of my camera housing.

We didn't seem to be in any real danger. These sharks were not known to be man-eaters. This was the same species that we had been filming all week. Of course, a shark could misjudge our position and slam into us by accident, but I was not terribly concerned about that possibility or about whether the sharks had malicious intent.

When I ran out of film, I signaled Elaine. As soon as Elaine turned off the lights, the anchovies moved away. I consulted my compass, and together we began working our way back toward the boat. We had less than seven hundred pounds of air left in our tanks, so we began a slow ascent to conserve what little remained. Steve caught on and began collecting the light cable, following us in.

Later in the week, we dove as deep as 120 feet to photograph gorgonian coral on the Cayman wall. As we had hoped, the reefs in the Cayman Island area were spectacularly rich. They had not been heavily affected by human activity and, as a result, the footage captured the enormous diversity and beauty of healthy reefs.

That very next day, we packed everything up and flew from Grand Cayman Island to Dallas, Texas, where I planned to film one of the most important threats to coral reefs—offshore drilling rigs. I sent Steve home with the dive gear while Elaine and I went to the nearest hotel for the night. I had made prior arrangements with a wildcat company of oil drillers to film one of their rigs out in the Gulf of Mexico. They had just punched a hole into a reservoir of oil and were eager to have their success captured on film. Their public relations officer told me they needed the publicity to attract financial backers.

The next morning arrived thick and humid. Elaine and I hopped on a helicopter provided by the company and headed out into the Gulf toward the oil rig some eighty miles offshore. I wanted to show how much oil exploration occurred in the nearshore water of the Gulf of Mexico, and I wanted that footage to capture the potential danger of such rigs so close to productive coral formations.

This was to be Elaine's first experience on a helicopter. I had flown many times in UH-1 Huey helicopters when I was in the army, but this would be the first time I would be flying in a helicopter since the Alaskan plane crash and I wasn't sure I'd be able to handle it.

I climbed into the rear right seat, busied my hands with my camera, and pushed any thought of flight operations and oceans, crashes, and drowning from my mind. When all the instruments registered in the green, the pilot turned to me and I gave him a thumbs-up. The helicopter lifted off from the big "H" painted on the concrete pad, banked sharply to the left, and began to climb. Elaine looked at me but didn't say anything. She was watching my reaction, gauging my state of mind.

The oil rig was out in the Gulf of Mexico, so it took about forty-five minutes to chopper out over the water. Elaine kept asking me if I was all right. I said that I was, and then she asked if the dot on the horizon was the rig. I nodded my head as the helicopter closed the distance.

Over the intercom, I asked the pilot to take us down to the deck and fly low. The moment of truth had arrived. "I'd like to have the water in a moving shot of the oil rig," I said. "If you can, please take us to twenty feet and sideslip the right side of the helicopter toward the rig." I knew that this would be the best single shot we could get of the rig. The water moving through the foreground would clearly establish the ocean environment, and the rig standing tall against the sky, breathing fire and smoke, would say everything I wanted to say about ocean drilling. It would be worth the risk of flying low to get this one, all-important shot.

With a good deal of anxiety, I stepped outside and took up a position on the helicopter skid. The rotor blast plastered my pant legs backward and tore at my shirtsleeves. But the good thing about a helicopter's rotor wash is that it tends to pin you against the side of the helicopter, rather than blowing you off the skid. As we slowly slid sideways toward the rig just above the rolling waves, I cranked the camera's motor up to maximum speed and ran through about five minutes of film in just over two minutes of clock time.

From my position outside the helicopter, I could smell jet fuel, but it did not elicit a reaction from me. I was being pounded by the wind, but otherwise I was fine. The shot was dynamic, and that is all I really could focus on at the moment. Maybe this was the key; keep my mind and hands busy and maybe I'd be able to handle the risk and fear. I stepped back into the helicopter and gave the pilot a hand signal to proceed.

When we landed on the rig helipad, we quickly learned that oil rigs were unusual places. Essentially, they are tiny islands cut off from the rest of the world, with their own rules and laws—or maybe I should say lack of laws. For the men—and they were all men as far as I could tell—who work on the rig, there is nothing but work, sleep, and food.

The work is hard, and the food is great. The rest is just plain boring. There were two or maybe three shifts of work. When not on duty, the idle workers have very little to occupy their minds and hands.

We were told that many of the workers stay on the rig for months or even years at a time, trying to avoid entanglements with federal and state authorities. As a result, they rarely get to see women.

These were pre-internet and pre–cell phone days, so communication with the mainland was also limited. The only contact between the rig and the mainland was done by short-wave radio, and the only radio was controlled by the company. We, and everyone else on the rig, were cut off from everything and everyone.

Two very large men met us on the helipad. The rig crew had been warned that one of the National Geographic filmmakers would be a woman, so special precautions were made. What I imagined was the largest, meanest-looking man on the rig was given the assignment of watching out for Elaine's safety. The man never introduced himself. Instead, he took the Nagra tape recorder from Elaine, saying only, "This had better not be your damn purse." Clearly, this man had not volunteered for the assignment, and I wondered just how safe Elaine would be in his company. For the rest of the day, I kept a close watch over her.

For twelve hours, we worked to capture the process of drilling at sea. I wanted to show the nature and difficulty of the work. For the men who worked on the rig, life was obviously very dangerous. There were massive steel pipes and chains moving with great speed and force. Our companions were truly worried that some piece of flying metal might strike one of their guests. I probably didn't help reduce their concern. Every time I wanted a shot of some workmen, I would move in very close to the action with a super-wide-angle lens. Pipes and chains rattled all around me and swung over my head with terrific force—and often without much warning. But the wide-angle lens was the only way to really get the feel of movement and action. Being close was essential if I wanted my footage to be powerful and have the feel of the place.

Elaine spent a lot of her day watching to make sure I didn't get hit. One time, when I moved in too close and Elaine moved right in behind me, her bodyguard grabbed her arm and pulled her back away from a fast-moving chain, just as a machine dragged it across the deck. Elaine looked at the man, and above the noise and clatter, she thanked him. After that, he paid more attention, trying to keep her from harm. I, on the other hand, was on my own.

The rig stood more than a hundred feet above the surface of the Gulf. If one of us slipped and fell, we would not survive the impact with the sea below. On one side of the rig, a giant boom protruded laterally. At the end of that boom, a terrific fireball of natural gas shot perhaps two hundred feet into the air. Our guide told me, "This is what we call the 'Christmas tree.' We struck oil last week and we are now burning off the excess natural gas that sits on top of the deposit. The gas is being vented through the drill shaft. Be careful because everything on that side of the rig is dangerously hot."

At around six in the afternoon, Elaine and I were invited to the mess for dinner. When we arrived, we found what I imagined was about half the rig's crew. The place buzzed with activity and conversation, but as Elaine walked into the room, the conversation abruptly stopped. The entire room went silent. Elaine had everyone's attention. She waved to the crowd, and everyone started whistling and making other inappropriate sounds. Her bodyguard scowled at his coworkers and barked, "CALM DOWN, GIRLS!" The tone of his voice put an immediate end to the catcalls, and I realized why this particular man had been chosen to watch over her.

We sat down and were immediately handed two bleeding, hot, twenty-four-ounce sirloins. "Yikes!" I said. "I haven't worked hard enough to deserve this."

The cook just growled. "They only come in one size," and then he disappeared back into the kitchen.

The man who was coordinating our visit to the rig left his seat at the head table and came over and sat down next to Elaine, facing me. He told me that as I had requested, the helicopter would be arriving in about a half hour. "When would you like to have it ready for your aerial filming session?" he asked.

"I'd like to be in the air just as the sun sets. That way the sea will be dark and the Christmas tree will show up very well against the dark sky and sea."

"No problem," he said. "The helicopter will be yours for the duration of the day, and when you are done, it will take you back to shore."

When Elaine and I finished dinner, we were ushered to the helipad. The pilot was there waiting. I introduced myself, and we began talking about the shot. I told him I would be needing the most dramatic shot of the Christmas tree possible. I wanted to get in close to the fireball, "as close as you can without risking our lives," I said. "Hold the helicopter just to the east of the fireball. I want to get the setting sun in the shot."

I continued. "That means we can't be shooting down. We need to shoot straight at the rig and the fireball from its own height. With that angle, there is a very good chance that the helicopter's blades will be in the shot, so you will need to wait for my signal, then roll the helicopter on its side and tip the blades back away from the rig and out of the shot.

"I will begin shooting just as soon as the blades clear the frame and before the helicopter falls off toward the sea. You will need to repeat the action a few times until I am confident in the film footage. Try to angle the helicopter to get the maximum amount of time possible before the helicopter begins its fall toward the sea." I then explained that I would be using a variable-speed motor to speed the camera up to its maximum. This would have the effect of smoothing out any bumps and would also mean that two seconds in the air would translate into about six seconds of screen time.

The pilot had learned to fly in Vietnam, so he was, I suspected, fully capable of the maneuver. He nodded his head to acknowledge what was expected of him. I knew from experience that these war-trained pilots could do just about anything with their machines. What he needed to do here was not nearly as demanding as avoiding incoming machine-gun fire on a battlefield.

Twenty minutes before sunset, we took off. To make the shot, I would have to step outside the helicopter on the skid again. When the time came, I slid the door open and we were immediately struck by the hurricane-force wind generated by the rotor downwash. I loosened my seat belt and climbed outside. Elaine held on to my jeans' belt; she thought her hand might provide me with just a little additional security. From our position in the sky beside the Christmas tree, we could feel the incredible heat of the burning natural gas. The rotor wash kept us bathed in fresh, cool air from above and reasonably comfortable, but the radiant heat cut through the downdraft and baked my face. My skin felt as if it might ignite at any moment.

As the sun set, the pilot and I worked together to get the shot. The helicopter engine made far too much noise for any verbal communication to be effective, so I put my left hand on the pilot's shoulder and held the camera on my right shoulder. When I was ready and the camera was rolling, I twisted the pilot's shoulder to indicate it was time and in which direction to roll the helicopter. He got the message immediately and rolled the helicopter onto its left side. A second later, as expected, we began to fall off toward the sea.

On our third try, everything came together and I knew we had what we had come for. The shot was everything I had dreamed about. I signaled the pilot to head for shore.

When we finally got back home and pulled down our driveway, the boys came running. Elaine dove into their arms and everyone began squealing. I lifted Ted up. He had a big bruise over his left eye. I looked at Peggy Colman, our neighbor and the kids' caregiver. She said, "Bee sting."

Elaine had left the Caribbean far behind and was back into mom mode. John and Ted had a pile of stories to share. As I listened, I came to believe it was time to make a change in our lives. These boys, now five and two, were old enough to begin sharing our world.

10

HART MOUNTAIN

AFTER FINISHING AND DELIVERING *RICHES FROM THE SEA* to the National Geographic Society, Elaine and I sat down to watch *Farmers of the Sea* as it was broadcast nationwide on the award-winning PBS science series *NOVA*. The date was November 13, 1984. The Nielsen ratings came out the next morning, putting the show's audience at four million, which, in those days, was a healthy audience share. Our phone rang continuously all through the evening with friends and colleagues calling to say how much they enjoyed the show.

The day after the broadcast, I realized how exhausted Elaine and I both were. I had spent almost two years on airplanes in far-flung parts of the world shooting these two films. With the exception of two short trips to the Caribbean, Elaine had spent that exact amount of time raising two active young boys all by herself in Oregon. We were spending too much time apart. I was really missing my sons. Elaine's life was filled with child care. Mine was full of strange hotels, metal film cases, and tight airplane seats.

One evening, I returned from work and told Elaine I had an idea. I told her that I had been talking to people at the university who wanted me to make a documentary for television about the Hart Mountain National Antelope Refuge. "What if we did this as a family?" I suggested. "This could be an opportunity to spend time together on a desert mountain in southeastern Oregon." We could forget about all the packing and unpacking, flying, and staying in hotels. We could plant our feet in the wilderness long enough to listen to the wind and birds. "This will be our chance to introduce our boys to the natural world," I said. "We can travel as a family and live in the mountains while I make this next film. Best of all, it will probably take about two years to make the film, and a lot of that time we will be on our own in the mountains."

"What does Sid think about this? Did you ask him?"

"Not really, but he wants us to begin production of a film about DNA, and I can do both at the same time. The DNA film will be a laboratory film, so I can pack it into the winter months when the mountains will be inaccessible anyway."

Elaine looked at me with those penetrating eyes. She saw the possibilities and quickly agreed. John and Ted were still too young to contribute or to come along on the day-to-day shooting, but they could explore and experience life on a mountain for themselves. The top of the mountain was a flat mesa. There was a dirt road that ran from Plush, Oregon, to the top, so I arranged for a camper-trailer to be pulled up onto the top of the mountain so that we would have a home base from which to live and work.

By the time we crawled into bed that night, Elaine was way ahead of me. She had a sense of what she wanted our family to look like. "This is how we can introduce our boys to the wider world," she told me. She thought the best way for us to blend all the competing demands on us would be to live as a family and involve the boys in our lives. If that meant taking the kids out of school for extended film trips, that was what she planned to do. "They will have experiences no other child has ever had," she said, "and they will be better for it." As a teacher, she could provide them with the things they might have missed in school.

It was decided. As soon as the winter snow retreated off the top of Hart Mountain, the US Fish and Wildlife Service hauled the trailer in from Lakeview. We set up our home away from home.

John took off exploring that first morning, found a big bone in the sagebrush, and dragged it back to the trailer. "Look Mom. I found a dinosaur bone." No one could convince him otherwise.

"You should show that to your father when he comes back. He'll be impressed."

Caring for the boys was still going to be a full-time job for Elaine. She would have no time to help me with the filming, so I hired a student at Oregon State University to carry camera gear up and down the mountain. Jeff was a strong kid, just beginning to find his way in the world, but excited to have the chance to develop his photography skills.

The Hart Mountain film fit nicely into my vision of how I should be using film as a tool. The film was to be about how this particular wildlife refuge was being managed for both wildlife and cattle. The US Fish and Wildlife Service, which had jurisdiction over the refuge, wanted to satisfy the needs of all user groups. It was a controversial idea because wildlife refuges are, by law, supposed to be managed for wildlife. Unlike Bureau of Land Management or Forest Service land, where managers are free to balance the needs of different user groups, refuges are supposed to be just that—refuges for wildlife. The large vocal environmentalist organizations in the state believed that cattle had no place on the Hart Mountain Antelope Refuge, while the ranchers, many of whom had grazed their cattle on this mountain before it was designated a refuge, were not about to relinquish their grazing permits without a fight. Ranchers, not just those in the Hart Mountain area but all over the West, wanted nearly free access to public lands to graze their livestock, while most everyone else wanted some of the vast western lands to remain wild, free, and natural.

I had agreed to keep an open mind and portray the management effort but made it clear to my sponsors that I would be making my own judgment about how well the strategy was working. I was happy to be making this film, because it would draw on my expertise as a wildlife ecologist and would speak to my primary concerns for the health of ecosystems. It was a chance to make a statement about wildlife and the management of public lands in the West, a subject that had been near and dear to my heart ever since I had been a young boy hiking western trails with my father.

Every day for most of the first fall, Jeff and I would pack up and leave before dawn to climb the mountain in the dark, spending the day inside blinds we had constructed in key locations. We would come back every night well after sunset, exhausted and ready for bed. We concentrated first on bighorn sheep, then switched over to mule deer, and finally to pronghorn. Along the way, we picked up footage of migrating birds and sage grouse.

Hart Mountain was a hostile environment in which to film. Most of the time, we were shivering with cold; the rest of the time, we suffered from the heat, water loss, and direct sun. Most mornings, we wore insulated underwear, heavy Carhartt pants, and camouflage coats. But the wind howled up the western escarpment of the mountain, spilled over the flattop high desert plateau, and cut its way through whatever we wore. Even the iconic sagebrush was no match for the relentless push of cold air scouring across the eight-thousand-foot top of the mountain. Most everything, including the sagebrush and the stunted trees, struggled to survive, growing best in the folds and irregularities in the ground where the wind was less severe.

Many of the animals we photographed spent the bulk of their time in the streambeds or on the lee sides of rock outcrops where food was more plentiful and energy demands lower. Jeff and I spent a lot of time hunkered down in these sheltered spots. Our camouflaged blinds were staked to the ground so they would not blow away and to prevent flapping in the wind, which would have been a dead giveaway to our presence. I often used a long Canon lens to focus on the animals as they browsed down in the streambeds, oblivious to our presence.

We spent almost one entire fall on the western face of Hart Mountain filming the bighorn sheep rut. Each evening, as the sun sank in the western sky, its rays began bouncing off the surface of Hart Lake two thousand feet below us, acting as a giant mirror. We were trying hard not to be seen, but all the while we were lit up like a deer in the headlights, bathed in that hot mirror's glow.

One afternoon, about one hundred feet above us, a half dozen large full-curl rams grazed the steep rock wall. They started chasing each other across the face of the mountain, pushing and striking each other with enormous force. The sound of their sturdy horns clashing together echoed across the face of the mountain. The sheep were too busy to notice us below them, so Jeff and I approached without worrying we would be discovered. I set the camera up in between two boulders; Jeff erected a camouflage net across in front of the camera position in an effort to blend in. Soon the largest full-curl ram pushed his smaller competitor over the side of a drop-off. The smaller animal fell to within ten feet of us, almost landing on top of our blind. Jeff jumped back to avoid being hit, but neither ram was hurt. Both just kept fighting each other as if we didn't exist.

Many times, the intense yellow light on Hart Mountain reminded me of just how I came to be a filmmaker in the first place. It seemed, now, to have been ancient history, but in 1970 when I was just beginning my graduate school work at the University of Wisconsin, I was intensively schooled in the importance of light to photography by an accomplished German photographer by the name of Fritz Albert. Fritz understood light. He had once worked as a filmmaker for the Luftwaffe and after the war had come to America on a Fulbright scholarship. At Wisconsin, he was a professor of journalism, and I had been his student. Fritz was widely regarded as a master filmmaker—perhaps the best university-based film-maker in the country. He was also a perfectionist.

Fritz often spoke with his gnarled, arthritic hands, saying, "You must remember a camera is just a tool; it has no talent. It is not the artist. You must learn to use it as a painter would use a brush." Photography, he would say, is an art performed in chemistry. Images are formed when silver halide crystals react to the energy of light. Exposure is determined by the amount of light we permit to strike those crystals. "You must understand, what you see on a page or on a screen is not actually the thing that was in front of the camera when the exposure was made. It is a bad copy." Photographers must learn to use the tools of chemistry to trick the viewer's mind into thinking they are viewing the world when they are really just looking at a fake.

Now, on Hart Mountain, I was putting all his training and all my acquired skill to good use, watching the light as it developed through the day, measuring it carefully not only for intensity but for its color. I wanted to convey just the right feeling about the mountain and its wildlife. The key would be to blend these colors with appropriate music to set the mood. As we moved through the seasons, I worked to get my camera in the right place at the right time to capture critical moments of color.

———————

That first spring, Jeff and I took a break from filming the landscape and the wildlife to tag along with Chuck and Sherry Messner, local ranchers, who managed cattle on the refuge. When we first met, I had Elaine and the boys in the truck with me. The Messners pulled up alongside us in their beat-up Ford pickup with its dents and scrapes, dragging a large branch of sagebrush under their front bumper. Talc-like dust covered their entire rig. I couldn't see much through their windshield either. The truck groaned to a halt. When Chuck turned the key off, the engine continued to sputter and the truck shook as a few cylinders just refused to quit. Chuck levered himself out of the driver's side, came around the door, and offered a huge calloused hand. He wore leather chaps, boots with spurs, and a black hat stained almost white with his own body's salt. Sherry came around the front end of the pickup wearing exactly the same thing. Both were covered in dust, and each had a wad of chewing tobacco bulging from beneath their lower lip—two identical, slightly bowlegged buckaroos.

Chuck took off his hat and slapped dust from his leg chaps. I could see a neat line dividing his forehead. Above the line, where his hat protected his skin, his forehead was nearly white, but below that line his face was sunburned, weathered, and cracked to pieces. No doubt, his hat was a fixture. He probably never took it off except to use it as a dust swatter.

Stiffly, we talked for a bit, making our introductions. At first, neither Chuck nor Sherry seemed to be the chatty sort. They were soft-spoken and honest as rain, but guarded. They didn't know me, and they were not going to trust me until I showed I was worth the effort.

John and Ted made all the difference. It was hard not to like our two outgoing boys. Ted, especially, kept interrupting the adults to ask about those spurs, leather chaps, and saddles in the back of the pickup. "Excuse me ma'am, but what's in your hair?"

Sherry knelt down to show Ted her braided pigtails, one on either side of her face, each woven around a piece of rawhide, hanging down to her chest. "How did you do that?" While Chuck and I talked about the mountain and the cattle, Sherry unwound one side of her hair to show the boys another way of being, how a western woman lives in the desert. Eventually, she stood back up and spit a dark liquid into the dust; Ted paid close attention.

It took a while for Chuck and Sherry to warm to us, but in the end, we became good friends. The Messners lived close to the land. Their wisdom sprang from their relationship with the land they worked. They understood the range and tried their best to be good stewards. They worked for one of the bigger ranch owners in the area but had full decision-making authority to manage the cattle on the refuge as they saw fit. They understood the need for some sort of balance between healthy ecosystems and ranching interests. Every day, they worked diligently to keep their cattle away from fragile streambeds, rotating their cattle through the various ranges frequently to reduce the overall impact of their animals on wild plants and animals. I asked Chuck about this practice. I walked away convinced he wasn't just doing it for the camera. Rather he seemed to want to do the right thing.

Chuck had big, black, horn-rimmed glasses, and Sherry had the darkest, deep brown eyes that lit up when she was excited. She was excited often. You could tell these two had grown up in the saddle; they sat effortlessly riding *with* rather than *on* their horses. Chuck rode a big gelding cutting horse that did most of the work without having to be told how. Chuck had ridden that horse for so long his body was partially shaped by it. Both Chuck and Sherry were skinny as fence posts but also tough as barbed wire.

I once saw Sherry sweetly talking to her mare, whispering in her big ears while caressing her long forehead. I quickly got the camera focused on her as she stroked her horse's mane. She stood close enough so the mare could feel her presence. She ran her hands down along her front left leg, took hold of the fetlock, and lifted the mare's hoof to check for any damage. She gently adjusted and tightened the belly strap, then seemed to ask her horse for permission to mount. She then slipped into the saddle with one fluid motion that screamed familiarity; this woman had done that many thousands of times before.

———————

That first spring, Chuck asked if we wanted to film the roundup and branding of cattle. Sherry specifically asked if John and Ted could come along for the festivities. "It's going to be a big party," she said, "with all the ranchers from around to help."

When we pulled up to their mountain camp, we were met right away by a small herd of the youngest family members who grabbed hold of our boys and led them off into the sagebrush. We wouldn't see our sons again till lunch. Ted was not quite four years old, but he especially took to the ranching lifestyle right away. Sherry liked Ted a lot and treated him with about the same level of affection she had shown her horse. She found a pair of chaps to protect his legs from the sagebrush and to make him feel more like a real cowboy. For a time, when lunch was being served, Sherry gave Ted her hat to wear while he strode around the camp practicing his roping technique. I noticed immediately that Ted had transformed himself into what he called a *cow-poke*. He had a Band-Aid covering his chin, the result of some rough-and-tumble play. His face was covered in grime after just a few hours roaming around in the dust. He also had a big wad of what I hoped was chewing gum in his mouth.

"What's that?" I asked.

"Tobackee," he said, as he spit on the ground just like he'd seen Sherry do. I laughed. Ted pulled out his borrowed lariat. As I walked across in front of the campfire, he threw the rope in front of my feet. My forward momentum carried me into his loop and dropped me to the ground. When I came up spitting dust, he was laughing. I dusted myself off, looked at Sherry, and found she was grinning broadly. I knew right away who had taught Ted that little trick.

That night, around a campfire, the kids pried a few stories out of Chuck and Sherry. The one that got the biggest rise from everyone was about Sherry's dislike for the alarm clock.

"One day last spring," she began, "Chuck and I were supposed to get an early start and ride up the south ridge to retrieve a couple of head that had wandered off." She had everyone's attention.

"At 5:30 the alarm went off! Darn near woke the dead."

The other kids had already heard this story a few dozen times but were wide-eyed anyway, just waiting for the rest. "When the clock was doing its thing," she said, emphasizing the word *thing* with disdain, "I pulled out my Colt and put a slug through the hour hand." Sherry spit on the ground as if to say, "And that was that!"

"Really?" Ted screamed.

"Yep! Knocked that thing clean across the bedroom," she said.

There was a half second of silence followed by a bunch of hoopla, and then Ted asked, "Right there in the house?"

Sherry just winked and nodded her head as if discharging a firearm inside a bedroom was common practice in her world.

Ted looked at Sherry and then at Chuck and was beaming from one ear to the other.

Chuck simply raised his eyebrows. "What could I do?"

For the rest of the evening the boys pretended that they were blasting their own alarm clocks and blowing the gun smoke from the ends of their hot, imaginary barrels.

It took nearly two years to make *Sagebrush Country* because we were on the timetable of the wildlife. I needed to film different parts of each species' life cycle and could concentrate on only one species at a time. In the fall, we filmed the ruts and mating; in the spring we filmed the birth of young. On a hot summer day, we filmed a rattlesnake up close, shaking its tail at us.

On a particularly cold morning in October, Jeff and I rose before light and headed toward the rimrock on Hart Mountain's west side. We were met by a very big man with a full black beard, a radio strapped to his chest. He was clad in head-to-toe desert camo. He saw our four-wheel-drive truck pulling up and ambled over to my side of the vehicle.

"You Jim Larison?"

"Yes. Are you Andy?"

"I am." Just then someone came on his radio asking for help with a decision. Andy held up one finger to me as if to say, "wait one." I listened in on the radio chatter but couldn't tell what the fellow on the other end wanted of his crew chief.

Andy was the crew boss for a bighorn sheep capture team based out of the Nevada Department of Wildlife. He, his team, and a few biologists from the Oregon Department of Fish and Wildlife were planning to use a helicopter to herd, capture, and transplant some of Hart Mountain's excess bighorn sheep to other locations throughout the West. The bighorn on this mountain were a big success story. The original dozen or so adults had been transplanted to Hart Mountain from the Rocky Mountains about a decade earlier and had immediately begun multiplying and rebuilding their population. The Hart Mountain Refuge was now a place where wildlife ecologists from around the West could come to find seed stock for transplants to other desert mountain ranges. They were all working together in an attempt to rebuild bighorn populations throughout the West to their former range.

Eventually Andy came back to me. "Let me give you the lay of the land. We have a helicopter up on the ridgeline." He pointed up to the west and I could faintly see the black dot moving from north to south across the top of Warner Peak. The helicopter was too far away to hear, but it was swooping back and forth not more than a few dozen feet off the ground. Periodically, I would see a flash of light as the sun bounced off the aluminum aircraft.

"The pilot tells me he's spotted bighorn and is trying to cut a suitable group of young males and females out of the bunch. We're sett'n up down here in this meadow," and he used his thumb to point over his shoulder to a snow-covered flat that, in summer, was a wet meadow.

He continued to explain they were making a corridor for the animals to run through. They planned to hide men in the sagebrush on both sides of that corridor. "When the helicopter herds the sheep down out of the high country, my men will rise up, begin shouting, waving their arms, and directing the sheep down the corridor into the meadow and the trap.

"We have strung netting along the throat of this meadow. If all goes according to plan, the sheep will run right into it," he continued. "The netting will collapse when the sheep hit it and will fold in on top of them, restraining them.

"We've found that the animals will calm down almost immediately when we put blindfolds on them. Anything we can do to reduce the stress on the animals."

"Where do you want us?" I asked.

"Probably down on the far side of the net. The sheep will run down the corridor, right into you. Once they are restrained in the net—*and not before*—you can move in for close-ups. Just be sure you're quiet. No shouting or yelling."

"OK, no problem. We'll be as inconspicuous as we can be."

Andy continued to explain that once the sheep are blindfolded and restrained, the helicopter will move back in and lift the sheep one at a time back to the horse trailer up on the hill. "We keep the trailer dark inside to help calm them. Once we have seven animals in the trailer, they will keep each other company."

A half hour later the first band of sheep was in sight. Overhead, the nimble helicopter kept moving left to right, back and forth, clearly herding the sheep down the hill into the jaws of the corridor. Almost precisely as Andy had predicted, he spoke a command into his short-wave radio and his men jumped from their hiding places, closing in on the fleeing sheep. The sheep ran at full speed down the valley right into the black netting. When the first ewe hit the net, the whole system collapsed down over the tops of the sheep, holding three young females in place.

Not two seconds behind the first sheep were the biologists. They came in fast, tackling any sheep that were not already on the ground. Jeff and I moved in quickly and began filming all the details in close-up. The first man on top of each of the sheep pulled out a blindfold and slipped it over the animal's head. The animal stopped fighting and quieted down.

Over the next six hours, the biologists pushed a total of fourteen sheep off the mountain, seven of which were caught in the nets and taken captive. The operation was judged a complete success as the horse trailer moved off to deposit their precious cargo to a new home some-where in southeast Oregon.

I worked long days and long nights that next winter in my editing suite putting together coherent sequences for the film. I decided to use the best single images from all the wildlife species in an opening montage. The rattlesnake, defiantly shaking his tail at the camera, was going to have an immediate impact, so I chose that shot as the opening image. Elaine lob-bied hard for another set of images of sheep running in silhouette against the vibrant orange western sunset. The trick for me, as the film's editor, was to cut together these images in a seamless timeline that flowed from early morning yellow light to full-on blue midday light. I looked hard for the best music to help set the right mood for the film. This music would make all the difference, so I looked for something that would be a little bit mysterious, a little mournful, and western. I wanted to prepare my audience for the film's message. When the rough cut of the film was complete, I began writing its narration. I felt heavily vested in this film, wanting the messaging to reflect my environmental sensibilities.

When all was done, I began shopping the film around to potential broadcasters. I ultimately decided to take the offer from the Discovery Channel and locked a broadcast date down.

Sagebrush Country was an intimate, beautiful portrayal of wildlife in a refuge, but it was also a clear demonstration of how two groups of people, in this case ranchers and environmentalists, could come together in a good-faith effort to balance competing needs for resources. Perhaps more than any other film I had produced, this film was designed to stimulate discussion, to help people to see the value of wildlife and wild places and to consider these things when making major decisions about land use and management.

Sagebrush Country specifically showed how the Messners were care-ful not to overgraze the high desert and how they kept their cattle out of highly sensitive parts of the ecosystem to minimize undesirable impacts. It was clear the Messners were doing a much better job on the refuge than some of their neighbors outside the refuge on BLM land. It also showed, in the case of the bighorn sheep, that wildlife could coexist on the same range as a few cattle, if those cattle were managed properly.

We scheduled a preview of the finished film for university staff, families, and a few state politicians. By this time, John Byrne had been promoted to be the new president of Oregon State University. He came to the premiere and gave an introduction to the assembled crowd of more than four hundred.

Afterward, Bill Wick came to me, "You know we are going to take some heat for this film."

I was surprised. "What do you mean? Why?"

"Well, you might have been just a little too honest about the history of overgrazing in the West."

Bill was right, of course. When the film was shown nationwide on the Discovery Channel, we started taking heat. I was wholly unprepared for the amount of pushback we began to receive the moment the film was seen. The ranch owners thought the film was not sympathetic enough to their point of view. The film did nothing to change the minds of the environmentalists either, who still thought cattle had no place on a wildlife refuge. Bill came up to my office just after the film aired to prepare me for the storm he knew was coming.

"How bad is it going to be?" I asked.

"About as bad as it can get. President Byrne has already received two calls from eastern Oregon legislators. I expect it's going to get rough . . . and soon."

I was still naive about such matters. Maybe I didn't fully grasp just how much raw power films had.

The big ranch owners in eastern Oregon provided the most heat. They did not think *Sagebrush Country* was flattering enough to their industry. They especially found problems with the section of the film that dealt with the history of ranching in the West. They could not accept the way we portrayed the Messners and their effort to minimize the impacts of cattle on the range because to do so would implicitly acknowledge that good practices were not being followed by all ranchers across the West. Ranchers tend to be an independent group that objects when anyone tries to tell them how to do their business. But the land in dispute was owned by the public, not by the ranchers. The ranchers rented this land from the federal government. People and groups other than ranchers had a right to voice their opinions about the fate of the publicly owned refuge.

Despite the clear effort on my part to show balance and the value of trying to work together, the leaders of a ranch group known as the Order of the Antelope tried to get the film pulled from circulation. When that didn't work, they applied pressure on the hierarchy of the university and tried to get me "pulled" from the faculty. Byrne was drawn into the matter when a representative of the ranch/political caucus lobbied for my removal. These people were heavy donors to the university's foundation. As a result, they had some influence over what happened at Oregon State University.

I genuinely believed they would win this fight because not a year earlier, another colleague in the Wildlife Department had been pressured out—essentially fired—for similar views. But when the university president took Bill Wick's advice, standing up to the pressure, the ranchers backed off and launched a campaign to discredit the film.

In the end, their efforts did not gain much traction; the film was rebroadcast multiple times by the Discovery Channel, as produced. The following year the environmental lobby succeeded in ousting the remaining ranchers from the refuge, and eventually, the US Fish and Wildlife Service refused to issue any more permits to the Order of the Antelope for its annual gathering on the mountain.

To this day, I wonder what would have happened had the ranchers simply embraced the film and its message. They could have used the film to show that they were trying hard to act responsibly on the mountain. The film clearly showed, at least in the case of the bighorn, that cattle were not having a major impact on wildlife survival. The film, having been produced by a wildlife professor at a reputable state university, would have helped them make such an argument. Instead, they fought the film, refused to engage in a constructive dialogue, and lost the argument. They were forced off Hart Mountain.

Through no fault of their own, Chuck and Sherry were caught up in the political fight. When the cattle grazing permits were denied that next year, they lost their jobs and moved away from the mountain. The Messners had not only been good stewards of the land, but they'd been good to us and to our children. They had done their best to balance the competing interests and didn't deserve what happened to them.

From a filmmaking point of view, *Sagebrush Country* was one of our biggest successes. It went on to win just about every national and international award for which it was considered, including awards from the Outdoor Writers Association, the Wildlife Society, CINE, and the National Academy of Cable Programming.

By any standard, our family experiment was also a success. Bringing John and Ted with us to the mountain as we made *Sagebrush Country* had worked. The boys didn't seem to suffer from the hardships of living on a mountain or from the loss of time at school. Their connections to us, to each other, and to the natural world all seemed to have benefitted from the time we spent isolated on Hart Mountain. When Elaine and I had a moment to talk about the two-year experiment, we agreed we'd do it again exactly the same way.

11

A LIVING OCEAN

Shortly after the Sagebrush Country furor died down, I signed a new contract, this one for the production of our fifth National Geographic film, *The Living Ocean*. This film was going to be our biggest, most involved foreign assignment to date. I was planning to shoot a major part of this film underwater on Australia's Great Barrier Reef.

Because this trip was to be a long one, and on the other side of the world, we agreed to do this one together as partners and that the boys were going with us. Elaine was sure we'd be able to find child care once we reached Australia, no different than being in the United States. I was convinced the trip would be good for our sons. They were young, seven and four, but I had been only eight when my father had taken me and my brothers on that extended western driving trip. It had ultimately been good for all of us.

While a light rain washed across the oversized, vertical windows in our Oregon home, Elaine and I busied ourselves assembling the equipment for this trip. To prepare, I spent a good deal of time working with Rod Mesecar again, trying to build a safer underwater lighting system. I didn't like the Giddings lights, constantly worrying about Elaine's safety handling them. I convinced Rod to build a watertight enclosure for a cannibalized set of CINE 60 battery pack lights. To my knowledge, no one had ever tried such a thing before. I didn't know how well an underwater housing would react to the intense heat of a five-hundred-watt bulb in a confined space. If it worked, this new system would allow us to use direct current, which was far less dangerous in water than alternating current, and we would no longer have to haul around a generator or drag cables through the water.

The logistics of such a trip were daunting. Just getting to the reef was going to be an overwhelming task. Elaine packed the essentials for the family—the clothes, toiletries, things the boys would need. I concentrated on the quarter ton of film and dive equipment. The pile stretched from the office, through the living room, around the stairway, into the kitchen. Two sophisticated Arriflex cameras, ten lenses, three light meters, two Nagra sound recorders, microphones, a neat row of film magazines, and a hundred accessories—total value easily twice that of our house—blanketed the kitchen table and countertops. As I assembled this gear, I tested, logged, and packed each piece. The motion picture cameras, five Leicas, and two Nikonos underwater cameras went in four Halliburton heat-resistant cases. There was a case for underwater battery pack lights. There were eight thousand feet of motion picture film and eighty rolls of Kodachrome and Ektachrome in two lead-shielded cases. A tripod case, an underwater housing case, a power convertor for Australia's 220 electrical system, and then of course, all the dive gear, masks, snorkels, wet suits, regulators, and buoyancy compensators. To save room, we packed our clothing around the gear. We'd be lucky if we could squeeze everything into a dozen cases each weighing near the airline maximum.

When we were just about ready to go, our neighbors, Jim and Peggy Colman, came over for dinner and told us we were doing the right thing. They were strong advocates for including children in their parents' travels. They had spent their lives working for USAID, taking their children with them everywhere, even to Afghanistan. They assured us the boys would be better for the trip—more worldly and better balanced, and our family would become better connected.

Jim Colman immediately offered to join us for part of the trip. "We could take care of the boys while you are out filming." The boys loved the Colmans, so the idea took on a life of its own. Soon, the Colmans had booked flights to Australia. In the middle of our preparations for the trip, another friend, Janet Dennis, asked if she could come along also. She, too, offered to take care of our kids in Australia.

I had picked the Great Barrier Reef for this film because it is vital to the stability of the ocean ecosystem throughout a broad section of the South Pacific. So much of life in the oceans depends upon these reef systems, but in 1986 they were showing the first signs of extreme distress. Ocean ecologists in Australia had estimated that 10 percent of the Great Barrier Reef was already beginning to bleach white. People were still debating the cause for this ominous decline, but it was clear we were losing a vital habitat. Without coral reefs, the oceans could not survive as a viable ecological system. If the oceans died, what would that mean for the Earth itself? What would happen to all the people who depended upon protein from the oceans? The collapse of such a vital ecosystem would likely have severe consequences for humankind.

It was important to me that my sons got to experience reefs while they still existed. This could be a once-in-a-lifetime opportunity.

At the end of that next week, the long, tiresome Qantas flights to Australia began—two hours to San Francisco, five more to Hawaii, an overnight layover in Honolulu, and an early morning wake-up for the flight to Australia. It was another ten or eleven hours locked up in the airplane to Cairns, Australia. We crossed the international date line somewhere in the middle of the night in the vicinity of the Marshall Islands. By the time we would be landing in Cairns, our bodies wouldn't know whether it was day or night. I knew the trip would be hard on all of us, especially the boys.

Elaine and I hoped our sons would sleep on the plane going over, but of course, the trip was just too exciting. The moment the seat belt sign was turned off, John and Ted were up in the isles "helping" the flight attendants pass out dinners, telling stories, and dazzling everyone who would listen with tales of life's adventures and expectations for this trip.

Elaine looked at me, rolled her eyes, and let them go. "They're your boys," she whispered. It didn't look like the flight crew minded, so I closed my eyes and tried to get some rest. When I woke, the lights were dimmed and John and Ted were in the airplane galley playing cards with one of the flight attendants. Ted was saying, "There are going to be sharks, barracuda, jellyfish. We're going diving every day."

The flight attendant was doing her part, "Wow! That sounds like fun."

I decided not to interrupt.

Elaine said, "Everything seems to be under control back there."

We arrived in Cairns on a warm morning. The air was thick and full of moisture. We wore too many layers of clothes and began to sweat immediately. A Toyota van stood at curbside waiting for us, so Elaine concentrated on keeping the boys out of trouble while I loaded up. Then we pulled out of the airport heading north on the "wrong side" of the road toward the little coastal town of Port Douglas.

We stayed that first month in a rented home overlooking the harbor and the South Pacific. The rental house stood in a grove of trees located above the town. The house came with two pools and was wide open, as is typical for homes in the tropics. Our neighbor, Sandy, came over right away to welcome us.

"We're your next-door neighbors. We kind of take care of the place when the Wilsons are gone. Can I show you around?"

We walked through the house remarking at how open everything was. The walls weren't really walls at all. Small, closable, louvered glass panes were all that stood between the house and the elements. Air flowed freely up from the ocean through the house. Not surprisingly, wildlife crawled around the house just as freely as the wind. Geckos hung from all the windows, walls, and ceiling. We found them in the most unexpected places. As we walked outside, Sandy never stopped talking.

"You're going to have to be careful walking back and forth between the house and the pool. Snakes are a problem. Especially, watch out for coastal taipans. They are really poisonous and aggressive. The kids especially need to be careful," she continued. "I'll have my husband, PK, cut the brush back away from the path. That should help."

I was struck by how Sandy seemed to accept the snakes as a part of life. People in the tropics just deal with a different world. Life in Australia differed from anything we were used to. We would have to learn to keep ourselves safe. Sandy was just helping us to understand how one lives beside the coastal taipan without having a confrontation.

It took almost a week to settle in to the time change. For the next month, every day, Elaine and I traveled to the outer reef onboard a fast, sleek catamaran named the *Quicksilver*. Sandy and PK both worked on the boat, so they gave us the behind-the-scenes tour. The owners of the *Quicksilver* had donated their boat to us in an effort to promote their business with American tourists. The entire tourist industry in this part of Australia was dependent upon the healthy reef system.

On one dive, we were filming a dive master who was entertaining guests by feeding a four-foot barracuda. The dive master was pulling a small fish apart, feeding the barracuda a handful at a time to keep the animal close to his paying guests. At one point, he tugged on the fish to tear off a new piece of meat when his hand slipped and came away empty. The barracuda, expecting a new piece of meat, saw only the diver's glove and struck the empty hand. In an instant, the barracuda's needle-like teeth lacerated the gloved hand. Later, as I looked at the film footage, I could clearly see the attack had taken less than one-sixth of a second and was captured on just four frames of film—literally the blink of an eye. But the damage to the dive master's hand was extensive.

To the great credit of the dive master, he maintained his composure, clamped his bleeding hand under his armpit, then turned to me. He signaled me to ask if I would take control of the group of tourists while he returned to the *Quicksilver* for medical help. I agreed and hooked the camera to my dive belt, freeing my hands to help the group. The dive master left immediately so that his blood would not attract sharks. Elaine and I spent the next half hour gathering up the recreational divers and getting them safely onboard the *Quicksilver*.

That month Elaine and I made a total of fifty-two dives from the *Quicksilver*, spending more than thirty-six hours underwater filming life on the reef. It was everything I could have hoped for, with its rich, accessible, clear water. We filmed in detail all the different kinds of corals, the crabs that lived in the coral, the fish that made the coral their homes, the pelagic fish that came in and fed on the reef fish, the sharks that came in to feed on the pelagic fish. It was a complex system. We needed footage of all its interrelated parts if we were to tell this story adequately. I was especially attracted to—and spent a lot of time photographing—the brightly colored clown fish as they peeked out from among the poisonous fingers of the sea anemone. This symbiotic relationship seemed to capture the unique complexity of a reef system better than anything else.

Elaine and I were becoming a terrific filmmaking team. By this time, we had been working side by side for four years. I knew what she thought and she knew what I would need, often before I asked for it. Verbal communication was often unnecessary. Being connected in this way was a huge advantage because the job required close coordination. We frequently did not have the luxury of language as a medium for communication.

This was especially true when we were underwater. When I operated the camera, I had to be able to communicate with Elaine with the slightest movement of a finger, because a finger was often the only thing I had that wasn't otherwise busy doing something else. She had to know how to place lights, how much light to give a scene so as not to overpower the ambient light, when to move the lights, and how to link her light coverage to the angle of the lens. In the underwater currents, she needed to know not only when to hang on but also when to give the camera room. Ours was a partnership that depended upon learned and shared skills, experiences, and goals.

Every night when we returned to the rental house in Port Douglas, Elaine would take over child care duties and listen to stories about the day's adventures while making dinner. While she and the boys ran around the living room, playing hide-and-seek, I disassembled the cameras, cleaning everything, charging the batteries, and changing film magazines. I replaced film and batteries, resealing the housing O-rings. I would clean all the dive gear, removing the day's salt. This maintenance work took about three hours each night. To calm the kids down before putting them to bed, Elaine would sit them down in front of the tiny TV and put on *Inspector Gadget*. The kids loved it and would go on to talk about the show for years afterward.

Every morning, Elaine and I would return to sea for another day's work. Every night, we'd return to find our sons having a blast in their new surroundings. One time we returned to our temporary home to find the kids in the pool.

Ted was so excited he couldn't control himself. "Dad, Dad, you have to see me swim."

Elaine and I had been spending a lot of our free time trying our best to drown-proof our sons. Ted was not yet a swimmer. Nevertheless, he had made a breakthrough. He wanted to show us his progress.

"OK. Show me your stuff."

So, without hesitation, Ted jumped in the deep end of the pool, feet first. He blew air out of his lungs and sank to the bottom, ten feet down. Slowly, his body sank until his feet touched the bottom. Elaine looked at me, "Go after him!"

Before I could make a move, Ted kicked off the bottom and shot up to the surface with eyes wide open. When his head broke into the air, he gulped in a big breath and sank back to the bottom. He repeated the process over and over, slowly "walking" his way from one side of the pool to the other.

"He can't swim, but isn't letting that inconvenient fact bother him," I observed.

Elaine said, "That looks like something you might do."

Toward the end of the month, we all began prepping for the next leg of our trip. We closed up the house, said our goodbyes to Sandy and PK, and left Port Douglas driving south along the coast, headed for Gladstone.

The camera equipment was matched by another three or four hundred pounds of food, fuel, and other supplies. Once we arrived dockside, we loaded all our gear into the bottom of an open barge—actually a military landing craft—and wrapped everything in heavy plastic. At six in the morning we motored out of Gladstone and met the sunrise at sea on our way to a tiny coral cay in the middle of the reef, a research station known as Heron Island. The seas were mostly flat, and the sun beat down on us.

The island was about fifty miles offshore, but it was all smooth sailing. With a tailwind, the barge might have been capable of five knots, but the wind was right on the ship's nose, so we were going a bit slower. No one was in a hurry. True to character, John talked the deckhand into getting out a fishing pole and showing him how to troll. The boat was going slow enough to permit the boys' spinners to work in the water. By ten o'clock there were three nice Spanish mackerel lying on the deck.

Elaine and I were happy to be together on our way to a new place. We stood on the upper deck, watching John and Ted fish. All the while a gentle ocean breeze soothed our faces. I wrapped my arm around Elaine's shoulder and let our hips rub up against each other. Now that it was too late to do anything about it, I feigned a gasp, turned to Elaine and said, "Did you remember the battery chargers?" Elaine just stuck her elbow in my ribs without bothering to reply or even look in my direction. I stepped around behind my wife, wrapped my arms over her shoulders, and lightly kissed the back of her neck. Together, we stared out across the cobalt blue water and the cerulean tinted sky. We were together a long way from home, working as a family.

———————

By noon, the barge slipped through a manmade channel cut through a barrier reef and into a protected cove. We found Heron Island to be little more than a pile of pulverized coral and sand surrounded by an ever-expanding ring of spectacular living coral, which formed the barrier reef.

A small grove of trees on the island hid thousands of nesting tropical terns, known as "noddies," and a few buildings, including a biological research station. When we arrived, high tide was lapping against the shore, so the barge captain drove his vessel headfirst onto the sand and dropped its front door. Everyone walked off into the hot sand. The barge was designed to front-load and deploy tracked vehicles, so off-loading our equipment was not a problem. Everyone pitched in. The research station manager gave us the use of one of the station's cabins. We had a neat, clean little place, equipped with four bunk beds, a small bathroom, and a kitchen. The cabin provided me with a workbench, a place to clean cameras. By nightfall, we had our base of operations set up. We were ready to get to work.

The kids were wiped—they fell asleep immediately. Elaine and I took advantage of the moment to step outside. For us, the air was filled with an exhilarating sense of expectation. It took no time at all to reach the beach, where, beneath a coconut tree, we watched as the fading twilight slowly released a thousand hidden stars. In the moonlight we could feel a slight breeze coming out of the southwest. I could hear only the pounding of waves against the distant barrier reef and the gentle lapping of much smaller ripples against the inner island sand. As soon as the light began to fade, the nesting noddies stopped screaming.

As the twilight faded in the west, we were left with starlight. The moon had not yet come up. The lapping waves generated their own bright trails as the starlight reflected off air bubbles caught in the white wave tops. As we stood absorbing the night, Elaine searched for the Southern Cross.

"There it is. No matter how many times I see it, I love that we are standing beneath a whole new set of stars." Elaine had been looking forward to this opportunity, talking about the Southern Cross for weeks. This was a very special moment for her. "Proof positive we are in the Southern Hemisphere."

We had never before been on such a tiny island, surrounded by such a peaceful sea. At that moment, I felt nothing could compare to the tranquility of this place. It was priceless to be able to share such moments with Elaine. For the first time in our filmmaking career, I felt Elaine was really at peace knowing our children were just a hundred yards over our shoulder, sleeping peacefully.

This was a very romantic place and time. Elaine and I spent most of the night out on the beach. Neither of us wanted that suspended moment to end.

I devoted those first few days on Heron Island to exploring the magnificent reef. Heron Island was surrounded by a quarter mile of mostly dead reef that was, itself, surrounded by that ring of spectacularly colorful, living coral. To get to the living reef, I either had to walk out over the tops of the dead coral and sand at low tide or use a boat to go out through the channel, then cut around the outer edge of the barrier reef. In this way we would have direct access from the open ocean. Walking would be fine if we were going to snorkel but impractical if we were carrying fifty pounds of dive gear and another hundred pounds of camera gear. We needed a boat.

The biological research station manager offered us a fourteen-foot skiff with a nine-horsepower Yamaha engine. It was small for the task at hand, but it was all we had. The engine was below the legal cutoff, which meant I would be free to operate the boat in Australian waters without a maritime license.

On the second day, I readied my snorkeling gear and began the short walk out to the barrier reef with nothing more than a mask and snorkel. I was surprised when I came upon several deep blue water-filled holes just inside the barrier reef. It was low tide, so the level of the ocean had fallen below the lip of the reef. The inner, dead reef was nearly dry, but these deep blue holes were full of crystal-clear water. They looked a lot like giant bathtubs, sitting in the middle of dry coral.

I decided to dive into the largest of these holes. As soon as I put my head under the water, I knew this would be a very good place to bring the cameras. The blue hole was about the size of a large house, but it was full of trapped fish. As the tide had fallen, thousands of them had retreated into the blue hole for protection. Now, with the water low, they were isolated from the open water. These holes would be like my own private aquarium; the only difference would be that I would be swimming inside it and the fish would not be able to swim away from my camera.

Probing around the outside edge of the blue hole, I found that the coral on the surface had grown at a slightly faster rate than the coral lower down in the water column, and that difference formed an overhanging lip. I pulled a flashlight from my pocket and swept its beam under the lip. Hiding in the shade under the overhang was a wobbegong shark.

The wobbegong is not like any other shark. It isn't aggressive, and its skin is not abrasive. Instead, the shark looks very much like it is covered with loosely flowing feathers. As the shark moves, its skin floats through the water in undulating waves. When I touched the shark, the skin was soft, hence the common name for this shark, the carpet shark. It is a gentle creature and poses little danger to anyone.

That night, back at the cabin, everyone was excited when I described the blue holes and the wobbegong shark. John immediately began lobbying to make this trip out to the reef. The problem was, a trip to the blue holes would have to be made at one of the really low tides that come only every thirty days when the reef would be above water. The opening to the blue holes would stand high and dry. The only way to get there would be to walk out across the dead coral reef during low tide, to dive into the hole, then walk back to the beach before the tide got too high again. I put John to bed, then studied the tide charts carefully, trying to decide if this would be possible to do with a seven-year-old. I wanted to nurture John's curiosity, but I also wanted to share in his excitement as he explored something new. The next sufficiently low tide would not arrive for almost another month.

A few days later, our friends from Oregon, Janet Dennis and the Colmans, arrived on the island. They immediately jumped in and began providing child care, which freed Elaine and me up for filming. We began using the boat to gain access to the outer reef.

When the next really low tide did arrive, the weather was unsettled. A storm was kicking up from the west, threatening to dump rain on the island. John was both excited and adamant. He didn't care how miserable the weather; he wasn't going to wait another month for the next low tide. Despite a few misgivings of my own, I agreed to start walking out across the reef. If things started to turn bad, we could simply return to shore.

At exactly noon, John and I stood on the shore, watching the tide run out. I was waiting for precisely the right moment. The weather was not stable, but I wasn't too concerned. A rain cloud was approaching from the far side of the island, but it probably wouldn't start raining until after we returned from the blue hole. If it did start raining while we were out on the reef, the island and its reef would protect us from the worst of the wind, waves, or any surge of water pushed in by the storm.

I calculated that it would take twenty minutes to walk out on the sand over top of dead coral to the blue hole. The tide would be running out, so the movement of water would help push us along. If we left at exactly 12:20 PM, we would get to the outer barrier reef at about ten minutes before low tide. We'd have twenty minutes in the blue hole, and then we'd have to turn around and beat-foot it back to the island ahead of the incoming tide. Once again, the incoming tide would help push us along.

It all seemed like a workable plan, but then John was only a seven-year-old. How fast could he move across that inner reef? And if the weather soured, how fast could he retreat to shore?

I put on my wet suit because the air was cold. John didn't have a wet suit of his own, so he put on his mother's suit. It looked ridiculous hanging from his tiny frame. No one was going to be able to talk John out of this trip. We had to give it a try. I assured Elaine, "If things start to look bad, I will just turn around and walk back to the island."

We adventurers set off right on schedule. The water was deeper than it had been on my previous trip. The tide was still going out. The two of us half-swam, half-walked, for about fifteen minutes. All the while, I was watching the weather build behind us. By the time we reached the vicinity of the blue holes, I was a bit nervous. The sky was getting pretty black. The storm set in much more quickly than I had imagined.

Then, without warning, a wave of rain swept over the island, marching across the ankle-deep water and over the top of the two of us. It was coming down so hard that neither John nor I could see more than a few feet. Water was running down our faces, washing our sunscreen into our eyes, and partially blinding us. The rain hit the water so hard we could just barely communicate with yells.

"Put your dive mask over your face," I screamed above the storm.

We slid our masks into place and were pleasantly surprised to find that the masks kept the rain and sunscreen out of our eyes, so we could once again see. Now there was another problem. The water was running around the surface of our masks, funneling directly into our mouths.

"Put your snorkel in your mouth upside down, like this." We may have looked a little ridiculous, but the snorkels worked. We could breathe again.

I did not think we should go on toward the reef, but when we turned around to begin the trip back, the island was no longer visible. The rain was coming down so hard that we couldn't see anything. If I moved my feet, I would soon lose my sense of direction; without that we would be in trouble.

Our troubles were mounting. The tide streamed past our legs. The two of us were standing shin-deep in a cascade of running water. It felt like we were in the middle of the ocean, and it was only a matter of time before the tide would turn and begin to rise again.

Suddenly, the rain turned to hail. Big chunks of ice began pummeling us, striking us repeatedly on the sides and top of our heads, striking the surface of the water like so many incoming artillery rounds. I grabbed John and drew him underneath my own body the way a mother bird would protect her young. The hail continued to pound my back and head. At least John was sheltered from the worst of it, but he was shaking from the cold rain that had been running down inside his wet suit. There wasn't much that could be done, however, until the hailstorm passed by. I hoped that the storm would pass before the tide began to rise.

The hail was hitting so hard that the sound inside my hooded wet suit was deafening. The roar was quite painful. I reached up and pulled my suit away from my right ear. That helped a little, but I didn't dare let go of John's arm with my other hand for fear he would be washed away.

To John this was just another adventure. With a broad grin across his face, he looked up, diving mask over his eyes, a ridiculously too-large wet suit hanging down below his knees, shaking violently from the cold, and yelled, "Hey, Dad, who picked this trail?"

In the middle of driving hail, I found myself laughing out loud. I was proud of my son for seeing the bright side of that moment, looking at the world with eagerness and bravery. I was also concerned for his safety.

Luckily, the storm subsided as quickly as it had come up. In a few moments the sun blasted through and began to warm everything up. A giant double rainbow formed over the island. We were safe.

John, of course, wanted nothing more than to continue to the blue hole. The wobbegong shark was exactly where it had been the month before. John got to touch it for himself. He used my Nikonos to take a picture or two underwater.

That night, the stories flew around the dinner table. John told about the blue hole, the wobbegong shark, and the thick concentrations of fish he had seen. Janet Dennis and the Colmans made a wonderful audience. They listened with mouths agape to the young boy's version of the day's adventures.

Sleep came easily to no one that night. John was likely once again swimming among the sharks. Elaine was reliving that moment when the storm had seemingly washed her husband and son away. I was just happy things hadn't turned out much worse for John and me in the storm. I continue to hang on to that priceless memory of my son laughing at the hail, wind, and rising water, smiling from ear to ear.

12

TIGER SHARK!

FOR THE NEXT MONTH, the days blended one into the next. The weather was constantly fabulous, the reef was full of life, and a routine developed. Each morning Elaine and I loaded the cameras and dive tanks into the small skiff and headed out to the reef. We worked there all day filming each of the component parts of the reef ecosystem. Then when we returned—often exhausted—we would spend two or three hours cleaning O-rings, emptying film magazines, and charging batteries. When the day's work was done and the family came together over the dinner table, John and Ted would coax us to share every experience, every story, every new incident. The children had insatiable appetites for these nightly stories. The more exciting and vivid the better.

To John and Ted, the Great Barrier Reef was like a private zoological garden. Everywhere they looked, there were new, previously unexplored animals, each more spectacular than the last. A few were even quite dangerous. One time, John returned with a story about having seen a very unusual octopus in a foot of water, near shore. I asked him for details and he described a blue-ringed octopus perfectly.

"The octopus was light cream colored. When I got close, it turned bright yellow. And then started flashing bright blue rings at me."

The blue-ringed octopus is probably the most poisonous animal on the planet. It was warning John not to come any closer.

Elaine looked at me with an expression of complete panic but hid her expression from John, not wanting to scare him. Later, that night in bed, she said, "I think the boys should not have quite so much freedom while we are out diving."

I wasn't sure how we were going to be able to keep them out of trouble. "Maybe if we just warn them to keep their distance from animals they don't recognize."

———————

The longer we were on the island, the more we came to depend upon the boys to help with the filming. It became their job to maintain the aquarium. The aquarium was in the university laboratory wet room where we kept sample corals, fish, and other organisms. Each went into one of the tanks where it would live until I had time to shoot close-up images. The trick was to make the aquarium look as much like the real reef as possible so that the film would match the footage that was coming from the reef itself.

One day, after we had been on the island for just over six weeks, the weather turned sour. I decided that it wouldn't do any good to try to shoot film that day because the light levels were not high enough. Elaine and I loaded the skiff with buckets of coral, crabs, and fish from the aquarium. We wanted to return the animals to their rightful home on the reef.

The water itself was choppy. A stiff wind blew out of the south. Conditions were marginal, but if we stayed close to shore, hugging the lee side of the reef, Elaine and I thought we would have no problems.

The first stop was in shallow water. I wanted to return a clump of coral to the exact spot from which I had removed it four days earlier. We'd put a little flag on the spot just to make sure we could find its home. The water was only six feet deep, so I wouldn't need my scuba gear. Elaine handed me the coral as I slipped beneath the surface. It was a lot like planting a flower. The trick was to orient the coral exactly as I had originally found it. Corals are sensitive to light and currents. If I returned each coral cluster to the exact spot from which it had been taken, the coral would have the best chance of survival.

The next stop was out at the mouth of the channel. The coral clusters I wanted to return would need to be placed at a depth of twenty-five feet. The wave action was tossing the boat about. Neither Elaine nor I imagined we could take very much of that without getting sick. I put on my buoyancy compensator, scuba tank, regulator, and weight belt. Elaine automatically shifted her weight to the starboard side of the skiff while I rolled backward over the port side. When I came back to the edge of the boat, Elaine had the first corals ready in a bucket.

Just two days before, we had been diving on this exact spot and had found the reef to be absolutely beautiful. Today, without the sun, with a mean gray sea, the coral looked dark, cold, and just a little bit frightening. There had been literally thousands of fish here two days earlier; now there were none.

It didn't make sense, but I had a job to do. I found the little flag marker, took out my dive knife, cleared away a little accumulated sand, and planted the first coral cluster right where I'd found it. I turned back toward the surface. I felt alone. The coral reef was normally loaded with life. Fish were always swimming around; some even come up to you to peck away at your exposed skin.

As I started back up, something gray, powerful, and very large struck me from behind. The first stage of my regulator—the part that attaches to the tank—smacked the back of my head as my air tank was yanked violently upward. My mask flooded with water, leaving me defenseless.

Quickly, I tried to regain my equilibrium. I repositioned my mask, blew air into it to clear the water, then spun around trying to catch a glimpse of my attacker. It was already gone, having disappeared into the distance as quickly as it had arrived. A sick feeling spread through my stomach. Wild animals do not *accidentally* run into human beings. If something hit me, it was because it intended to hit me.

Suddenly the answer became very clear, making my knees weak. Sharks can smell their prey through their skin. Some people say that before a shark attacks, they sometimes bump their prey to determine if it tastes good. It came to me like a tidal wave; *that's* why there were no fish on the reef.

The fact that this shark had come in from behind me and struck my tank, rather than my legs or chest, was probably just luck and probably saved my life. I quickly spun around in a circle trying desperately to find my attacker but found only gray sea.

Sharks often turn upside down before they strike a human. They try to come in underneath their prey, mouth open, then bite and shake their head to tear off large chunks of meat. If I stayed on the bottom, just maybe I could deny the shark an easy target. My dive mask blocked my peripheral vision, so I couldn't see anything left or right or behind me. I located a large coral bommie to my left and quickly swam to its side, turned my back to the solid wall of coral, trying to melt into its folds.

Frantically, I swept my eyes left and right, searching for my attacker. In the distance there was movement—a dark shape—something coming out from the distant gray. I saw the eyes first, like headlights coming out of the gloom, yellow rings around deep black, cold darkness. A torpedo-like body was coming for me without hesitation, without judgment, but with agonizingly slow, lethal precision. Power and grace—the perfect predator. Of all the creatures in the world, this one might be the most terrifying. Gliding, no visible means of propulsion, yet coming toward me nevertheless. I was locked in the cold, steady gaze of soulless eyes.

At first this gray body was almost indistinguishable from the gloom, but as it came closer, its markings became all too obvious. Gray/green top, yellow/white belly, perhaps eight hundred pounds, at least twelve feet long. Blunt nose. Interwoven dark and light stripes running from dorsal to pectoral fin—*a tiger shark!*

Tiger sharks are one of the world's most aggressive and deadly predators. The stripes were faded and worn. It was probably older, therefore experienced. It was huge, probably a female. Tiger sharks regularly eat people; I couldn't help but think my time had come. Escape unlikely. Maybe even impossible. Death coming relentlessly for me.

On that dark, silent sea bottom, my stomach turned over. How could I possibly prevail over such strength and speed? So many teeth spilling out of that lower jaw, all deadly. Suddenly, at the last possible moment, the tiger shark jerked to the left and began a wide circle around me and the bommie.

Elaine was in that tiny boat up above. I hoped that she wouldn't get into the water to come looking for me. The longer I waited, the more likely it was that she would.

Top: Moments after the crash, I lifted my Leica to eye level and pushed the shutter release, capturing one of the pilots as he struggled through the surf to reach shore.

Bottom: I returned to the crash site to find the aircraft wreckage had been winched back from the sea. The violence of that moment was plain to see. *Photo by James Hicks*

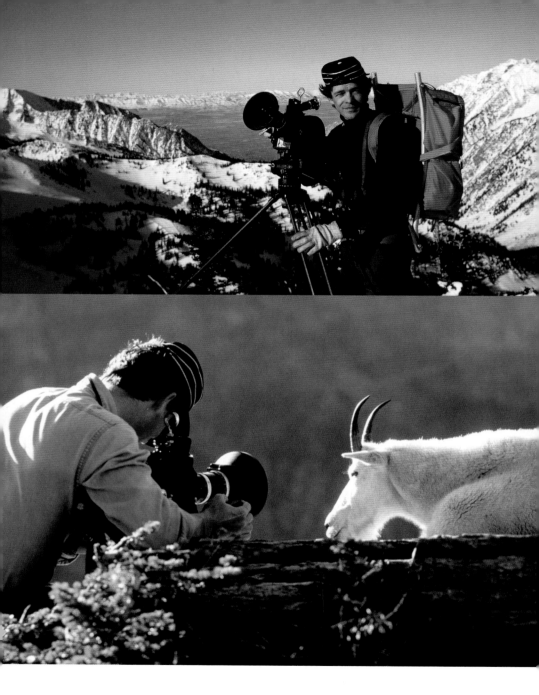

Top: On my first assignment for National Geographic, I spent most of one year high in the Rocky Mountains trying to capture on film the unique character of high elevation. *Photo by David Rassmussen*

Bottom: The key to obtaining good wildlife photographs is getting close to your subject. An especially cooperative mountain goat seems not to object to me or my camera. *Photo by James Hicks*

TOP: I folded myself into the tight glider cockpit, closed the canopy, and asked the pilot to fly directly above Wyoming's Teton mountains. *Photo by James Hicks*

BOTTOM LEFT: While filming *Sagebrush Country*, I crisscrossed Hart Mountain looking for pronghorn fawns.

BOTTOM RIGHT: Jim Hicks.

I have always been attracted to low-angle warm light such as that found on Diamond Head in the Hawaiian Islands.

Ted role-plays as a western buckaroo.

TOP: A curious four-foot barracuda inspects me and my camera.

BOTTOM: In the twilight just before nightfall, Elaine and I prepare to enter the Oro Verde shipwreck south of Grand Cayman Island.
Photo by Steve Adams

TOP: Steve Adams uses a banana to attract reef fish to the camera.

BOTTOM LEFT: John and Ted put on a show, wearing our dive gear.

BOTTOM RIGHT: John and I enjoy a moment together after our close up encounter with a wobbegong shark on the Great Barrier Reef.

After an especially deep dive, I decompress at ten feet, waiting for the nitrogen to leave my bloodstream.

Top: I rarely put down my camera when in the presence of wildlife, but this time, Elaine took the camera so that I might enjoy a moment with a playful stingray.

Bottom: With all the film exposed, I return to the dive boat after filming sharks on the Blue Wall in Palau.

TOP: In the morning light, I prepare to climb Mount Habel.

BOTTOM LEFT: I am preparing for a final push up to the continental divide on the Columbia Icefields.

BOTTOM RIGHT: After six hours of steady ice climbing, Elaine nears the top of the President in Yoho National Park, Canada.

TOP LEFT: Moments before breaking her leg, Elaine is caught in a whiteout and an electrical storm at ten thousand feet.

TOP RIGHT: On the evening after climbing Mount Habel, I take a moment to watch the remains of the electrical storm over the Wapta Icefield.

BOTTOM: Elaine takes a few days to ice her broken leg before beginning the long trek out of the backcountry.

Yoga at the Peyto Hut.

TOP: Members of the Corvallis Mountain Rescue Unit assist with filming on Mount Hood. *Photo by Ken Parton*

BOTTOM LEFT: I lead the way up a vertical ice wall on the Robson Glacier.

BOTTOM RIGHT: On the flanks of Mount Hood in Oregon, Doug McGuire (left) and Gene Griswold (right) help me reenact a climbing accident and rescue. *Photo by Ken Parton*

Elaine breaks a trail by moonlight at the base of Mount
Assiniboine in Canada.

TOP: Elaine records the haunting sounds of a howler monkey in the Amazon rain forest.

BOTTOM LEFT: Donald Cooper onboard a sailboat a few miles west of Tahiti.

BOTTOM RIGHT: Donald Cooper, Elaine, and I, filming the rain forests of Costa Rica.

Elaine and I enjoy a bird's-eye view of downtown Chicago in 1993.

The tiger came around, completing the first circle. I kept turning to face the moving shark. The second circle was smaller than the first. She was just being cautious. She had me. I knew it.

The tiger passed behind the bommie again. I spotted a long scrape down its side. This shark had been wounded before, possibly in a fight with another shark. When she came back around, she was closer still. Could I get to the boat without being killed?

On her next pass, the tiger shark didn't go all the way around the bommie. Instead, when she got almost out of view to the left, she abruptly spun around and came directly at me. This shark was done playing with her food. I looked right into that bottomless eye; it was revealing a lot more than I wanted to know.

With a flick of her tail she would, any second, go into attack mode and lunge at me. At thirty-six years old, I was as strong and fit as I would ever be, but was it enough? In this moment of personal peril, could I find the strength to survive? If only I could be brave enough to do what was needed: leave the safety of the bommie and swim to the boat.

I dropped the bucket and reached down to my leg holster. My knife hadn't been sharpened since we arrived on the island. I could not generate enough force from arm strength alone to penetrate that animal's tough, sandpaper-like skin, and I knew it. My only hope would be if I could strike the shark directly in its vulnerable eye. I didn't want to injure this wild animal, but I had to make a choice. It was a life-or-death situation—my life or my death.

As she passed less than a foot from my shaking body, I thrust the knife at her eye, but my aim was not good; in the murky water, I misjudged the distance. The knife struck the shark about two inches behind her eye, bouncing off. But the enormous shark had not expected to be hit. She flicked her tail once and disappeared into the gloom.

NOW! I pushed off the bottom hard, putting everything I had in me into the effort to get to the surface. I pumped my fins, blowing out air—or maybe screaming—as I went. The boat was forty feet away, twenty feet, ten. Once on the surface, I would be a sitting duck. The shark could hit me from below at any time. How would I get all that heavy dive gear off and climb aboard the boat in time?

I could feel the tiger behind me as I flew upward. I saw the boat above and aimed for the stern, where the ladder was affixed. I broke through the surface, ignored the ladder and grasped the transom. Without slowing down, I lifted myself—weight belt, tanks, and all—over the side of the boat. I spun around in mid-air and fell backward. My tank crashed against the metal floor with a frightening explosion of noise. Just then the shark's giant tail fin thrashed through the water inches behind my fins, smacking the shaft of the outboard, knocking our small skiff into the air and throwing a wave of water over both of us.

I spit out my regulator and gasped for air. "Holy shit! That was close."

"What? What was that?" Elaine screamed.

It took me several seconds to calm down enough to answer. "A shark. *A tiger shark!*" I lay on the bottom of the skiff gasping and shaking. It took me a few seconds to realize we were not yet out of danger. This tiny skiff offered little protection against an eight-hundred-pound hungry and determined shark.

I punched my quick-release harness, dropped my weight belt where it lay, and sprang to the engine. One pull and the nine-horse Yamaha caught, but it was facing to the side. When the blade engaged, it spun the boat in a tight little circle, nearly throwing both of us back into the water. Just in time, I straightened the skiff out and headed for shallow water with the throttle twisted to maximum.

My face mask was still hanging from my neck, and Elaine looked at me, stunned, "My God, you're white as snow."

On the way back to shore, once I had calmed down, Elaine and I decided not to share the details with the boys. But I was rattled.

For days later, I sat in a daze at the sea's edge behind the cabin. The waves washed in and flowed back out again. The tides rose and fell. The boys still played in the shallows. Elaine continued to make meals, periodically checking on me. Janet helped care for John and Ted. Not knowing what had happened, the Colmans asked if I was all right. But I sat and watched the sea. I neither filled my camera with new film nor charged the camera's batteries, nor even pulled on a wet suit. I just stayed on the beach, staring at the sea, imagining what almost happened.

Elaine asked me if we were done filming and I weakly replied, "We're about out of film."

She looked at me without judgment. "What do you say we call it a wrap?" she asked.

And we packed up and started the long trip home.

To be honest, I have had nightmares about dark gray shapes coming for my legs ever since we returned from Heron Island. In the middle of the night, even today, I kick out at imaginary shadows and sit up in bed in a cold sweat grasping to see that my legs are still attached.

PART III

LOVE OF WILDERNESS

13

THE UNFORGIVING WORLD OF ICE

It was just the nature of the job, really. You had to be flexible. One day, we were cleaning our dive gear after months of work on the Great Barrier Reef, and the next we were pulling our backpacks and climbing ropes out of the closet.

I had barely recovered from the tiger shark attack when Sid called to ask if we would make a film about ice and snow, all of which, he said, would need to be shot at high altitudes. Sid explained our sixth National Geographic Society film was to be about the physical geography of the western mountains and would have the title *The Rocky Mountains*.

"You are the ideal producer to make this film for us. You have the mountain experience and love of wilderness we need." He added, "But, you know this film will require you spend much of the next year on very dangerous ground." It was not really a question, more a statement of fact.

From the beginning, I knew this film would involve a lot of back-country living and technical climbing. Clearly, we would need support. Our camera gear weighed a lot; it was not designed to be used on the side of a mountain. We couldn't carry the camera gear together with a full complement of camping and climbing gear in our two backpacks. It would simply weigh too much. I also realized that all of our backcountry experience to date would not be enough. I would need to find someone to give us additional training.

To prepare, I signed us up with the Alpine Club of Canada. The club provided mountaineering training to its members, but it also owned a network of backcountry huts, scattered across the northern Rockies. If we used their huts, we wouldn't need to carry tents, stoves, or dishes. That would reduce the weight in our pack. Also, we needed to take advantage of their technical training camps.

Simultaneously, we forged friendships with members of the Corvallis Mountain Rescue Team in Oregon. Marti Keltner, one of the EMTs on the team, and her close friend Gene Griswold taught us what we needed to know to climb. Gene was the team's most experienced mountaineer. He once told me, "The important thing is to have enough training so that you clearly understand your limits." His implication was that we should not exceed those limits.

After many months of intense training, I thought I had it under control, but I would quickly learn, no one ever controls a mountain.

We began production of this new film at the base of the Wapta Icefields just north of Banff, Canada. One morning in early July we found ourselves standing side by side on a lateral moraine, a jumble of gravel, rock, and frozen water, gazing up at the base of the Wapta, where massive ice lays like a blanket across the continental divide between British Columbia and Alberta. The Peyto Glacier, one of the fingers of that ice field, flows in slow motion down from ten thousand feet, spilling over the vertical rock headwall to the valley floor below. The scene was stunning but at the same time harsh, nearly devoid of life. We were not above the tree line, but it was, nevertheless, too cold for much to grow.

Glaciers gather their strength up high in the mountains then flow as only ice can, down toward the valley, releasing some of their pent-up energy as they go, spilling into the flour-stained lake below. Understanding a glacier can be difficult for a human being because glaciers follow a rhythm measured in centuries. People take glaciers for granted and tend not to understand the importance of such ice fields to the world.

These massive repositories of ice are also vast reservoirs of fresh water, frozen and bound to the mountains.

In normal times, these glaciers release fresh water slowly, giving the valleys and lowlands a sustained supply. But in a world suffering from global warming, these glaciers are melting too fast. As the glaciers are threatened, so is the water supply for much of the West. To tell this story, I was willing to go to some length to get my camera to the top and even inside of this glacier. It was, after all, what Sid was paying us to do.

This trip up Peyto Glacier and across the Wapta Icefield would not be a particularly difficult climb. I had chosen it because the Peyto Glacier was easily within our skill set. It would give us a chance to ease into this film; we would practice our climbing technique before the more serious part of the filming later that year. On this first trip, we would concentrate on the massive area at the top of the glacier where it straddles the continental divide—the so-called "snow accumulation zone." This zone is vitally important because it is where a glacier receives and holds most all its mass. I wanted to show just how extensive those ice fields were. There was no way of doing that without making the climb.

Standing at the base of Peyto Glacier, I could feel a cold wind coming off the ice. We had already carried our camera and climbing gear down through the dense boreal forest, around the lakeshore, up through the rubble left behind by the retreating glacier. We were now putting on warm clothes, preparing ourselves for a steep climb up the face of the icefall.

That morning, I was trying to put all the things I'd learned from Marti and Gene to work. Marti had told me to study the ice "as if your life depends on it, because it does." I began looking for a safe passageway through all the crevasses so that we could access the top of the glacier where snow accumulates. I wondered if the snow bridges that cut across the face of the glacier would sustain our weight. I began plotting the least dangerous path.

To a climber, a glacier can look like a highway to the mountaintop—the easiest way to get to the summit. But Marti had told me that ice can be both a playground and a mortal enemy, all at the same time. Your survival, she said, can depend on things you cannot control. You can prepare; you can train. "In fact, you'd better do both." But if luck is not with you when you step onto the surface of a glacier, there is not much anyone can do about it.

"To some extent," she said, "all climbers, no matter their skill levels, are at the mercy of the mountain and the elements. Rule number one in mountain climbing is, bad things can happen! Rule number two is, no amount of preparation can change rule number one. Just be sure you do everything you can to prepare and be safe."

As we made our final preparations, the sun was just beginning to warm the high mountain air. I opened my pack and pulled out a sixty-meter dynamic climbing rope and my harness. Elaine dug around in her pack and pulled out her purple harness along with a rack of ice screws. I sat on a large boulder and began strapping on my crampons while Elaine stepped into her harness and pulled her hood up, then pulled on her helmet.

"Did you notice those deep crevasses on the left side?" I asked.

"Just above the *vertical* drop-off, you mean?"

I continued, "Those fissures in the ice are going to be a challenge. We'll have to skirt around them to the right, but I'm not sure how far out they protrude under the snow. I'll lead, make the ascent, put in protection, then bring you up on a tight line."

People sometimes say, "Love flows both ways on a mountain climber's rope." Indeed, an eleven-millimeter nylon rope, two harnesses, and a couple of figure-8 knots can bind two people together for better or worse. What happens to one climber almost always happens to the other.

Stepping in close to Elaine, I wrapped one end of the rope around her harness belt, quickly tying her off with a single bowline and a half hitch. I gave the rope a tug, pulled her to me, and gave her an unexpected kiss. I smiled at her, then measured out fifty feet of rope and tied myself in with a figure-8. I took the remaining rope, wrapping it around my chest in big loops so that it would be ready in case of trouble.

Elaine checked my gear then attached two premade Prusik cords to her climbing rope and stuffed the other ends into her jacket. She transferred all of her ice screws to my gear rack then checked to see that she had the necessary ascenders, carabiners, and a figure-8. While neither of us had ever experienced an emergency while climbing on ice, it paid to be extra careful.

Elaine and I had spent a lot of time prepping for this trip, outfitting ourselves with all the newest all-weather clothing. A lot had changed since those first days in Assiniboine. High-tech, ultralight gear was now commonplace. You could buy down clothing anywhere. Where once there were only a few European companies making hemp rope and rudimentary pitons, now there were dozens of companies in America and Europe making the most sophisticated gear for exposed climbing. All these expansion bolts, cams, ice screws, and figure 8s made mountains much more accessible.

Elaine and I spent much of our at-home time assembling safety gear, practicing its use, refreshing our memories about which knots to use and when, and assembling emergency medical gear. We took every precaution because climbers have to accept the risks and prepare for them. But we didn't let risks stop us.

Despite the ever-present dangers of climbing, I have always been drawn to film assignments that require high alpine work. Sid had obviously known that when he gave us this film assignment. Ever since that first trip into Assiniboine, I have known that mountains complete me. I have never felt so alive, so invigorated, so exhilarated, or so deeply happy as I am at altitude, where the air is thin, the ice is crisp, and the scenery is indescribably beautiful.

As a photographer, I have always been overwhelmed by alpine ice, by the way early morning yellow light streaks across the ice and backlights it, causing unexpected reflections and shadows to pop up. On this trip, I wanted to photograph the low-angle light as it passed through the ice, breaking down into a rainbow.

Few places are more challenging, exhausting, or emotionally draining as the top of a mountain, and few places are so rewarding. Elaine and I had spent a good deal of time trying to get into shape for this National Geographic assignment to make sure we could handle the physical strain, but exercising in a gym can never prepare you for a mountain. Mountain climbing is just so much more demanding. On a mountain, you can spend ten or even twenty continuous hours, expending maximal effort just to reach the top of some wall or to make it home or to reach safety. We were in the best shape of our lives when we began the Peyto climb.

But mountains require more than physical conditioning; they also require mental toughness. That morning, as we prepared to climb, I had no idea if we were ready for the coming challenges. But there was only one way to find out.

"Ready?" I asked.

"I'm just waiting on you."

I led off, stepped out onto the glacier, and paid out the rope. Elaine followed fifty feet behind. Shortly after we mounted the glacier and began our ascent, we fell into a rhythm, taking full-capacity breaths, once every other step, flushing the carbon dioxide and lactic acid out of our systems.

A half-hour later, when we reached the steepest part of the headwall, the rope behind me came up taught. Elaine had stopped. When I turned around, she was staring at the wall of ice in front of us. I asked her to move up the ice toward me so I could check her gear.

"OK?" I asked. "We've done more difficult climbs."

She nodded her head as if to say, *Go for it.*

I drove my ice axe into the steep ice and began to ascend. Elaine followed me up. Almost immediately, I began breathing hard. My heart began pounding. I looked back at Elaine and she seemed to be handling the work just fine.

I slowed to get over a particularly abrupt bulge of ice and Elaine asked, "Everything OK up there?"

I gave a wave. Elaine responded with a big grin. Clearly, she was proud of herself for coming up that steep ice. When she reached the top of the wall, she nearly screamed, "This is magnificent. That wasn't so hard." She swept her eyes across the vast ice field above us and gushed, "I love it!"

Mountaineering brought the best out of Elaine and me, strengths that can hide within a person until they are needed. Until you are forced to dig deep into yourself to find them, you will never be aware they exist. Now that we were on top of that steep ice wall, Elaine was having the time of her life.

I put my hand on her shoulder and said, "I think it's been a long time since I've seen that much joy written across your face." She pulled my balaclava down below my chin and kissed me. Elaine was happy, so I was happy.

I broke out the Arriflex and made a long panning shot of Petyo Lake and the toe of the glacier. The sun was now striking the ice, revealing all the crevasses in stark detail. I shot footage of the meltwater running down the face of the ice wall and showed how it cut a chasm into the glacier. I lowered the camera into the chasm and slowly pulled it back up along the face of the small waterfall of deep turquoise-colored meltwater.

Our plan was to spend three days traversing the Wapta Icefield. We were beginning at the north end of the glacier, planning to work our way west and south. That morning, after finishing the climb up the Peyto icefall and over the headwall—a vertical ascent of about a thousand feet—we began moving on up the belly of the glacier, slowly swinging around the hidden crevasses, coming to a southerly heading, gaining altitude with each step.

This part of the glacier was just a "walk," no real climbing involved, just miles of uninterrupted ice. There was a lot of time to set up the camera and capture the grandeur of the place. I filmed in detail the various types of algae growing on the ice and the parallel lines of rock and rubble strewn across the glacial surface.

As we came up off the toe of Peyto and mounted the central ice field, we began searching for the Peyto Hut. Elaine spotted it first, a tiny dot high above us on a massive mound of rocks. Elaine and I had permission to overnight in its relative comfort. At the end of our long day's climb, we cut left and ascended up the rock rubble to the hut for the night.

The place was empty, which did not surprise us because not many people make this long trek. The hut is located at eighty-two hundred feet, in about the most spectacularly beautiful place on Earth, about three hundred vertical feet above the vast expanse of the ice field, with a sweeping view of the glacier. The glacier actually wraps around the hut, flowing in from the continental divide on the left, coming all the way around to the valley floor behind to the right. There are large windows mounted in each of the front walls of the hut so that a person can sit at the dining table literally surrounded by the ice-covered mountain peaks. We unpacked and spent the evening photographing the rock, ice, and sunset. We sat at the table and played a round of cards by candle- and moonlight. The outhouse for this cabin sits on a nob about a hundred feet from the cabin almost four hundred feet directly above the ice. They say it's the very best seat in North America.

Elaine started dinner, filling the hut with the smell of spaghetti while I made our bed and dried our equipment. We were at peace together but also satisfyingly alone. After dinner, we went outside, where Elaine sat on the deck in full view of Mount Habel in a modified yoga lotus position. She sat there for a half hour, in her own world.

When the temperature began to fall, we put on our down coats and wool hats and watched and listened. The North Star, the Big Dipper, and a full moon reflected off the vast ice field below. Mount Baker and Peyto Peak blocked out the northwestern sky. The air was unusually calm. There was no one else within a dozen miles. Any remaining day-time warmth was rapidly being sucked up into the cloudless cold night sky. It was spectacular.

The view from the Peyto Hut is just plain magnificent, comparable to that early morning we spent on the snowfields of Assiniboine. I realized, as I sat there, that I would do almost anything to put myself in the presence of such beauty and serenity. Surrounded by such stunning scenery, the bond between Elaine and me strengthened. We sat in silence and soaked up the peace of wilderness. As I stroked Elaine's hair, I said, "Make me a promise, will you? When I die, spread my ashes in this place."

"If anyone is going to spread anyone's ashes," Elaine continued, "it's going to be you spreading mine."

I simply whispered, "You never know."

Elaine changed the subject and told me to take a deep breath. I did, and the cold air froze the moisture on the inside of my nose. It was a perfect moment.

The next morning, we woke early, before the sun came up. While Elaine stayed in our down sleeping bag enjoying its warmth, I went out into the crisp air to set up my camera on the deck. I put on a polarizing filter to make the sky shift from light to dark blue. The sunlight hit the mountaintops first, bathing them in yellow, and then slowly walked out across the face of the ice. I captured its progression in sped-up motion. When I had the shot, I retreated into the warmth of the cabin to eat an early breakfast.

We slowly packed up and climbed down to the glacier, strapped on our crampons, and crossed the glacier, making our way up the east side of the mountain. We were pushing our physical limits by climbing fast because we wanted to reach the summit in time to film the top of the glacier in early morning light. I also wanted to have enough daylight left after reaching the summit to move along the continental divide to the Bow Hut several miles south of us. We were breathing heavily and rhythmically. All was going according to plan.

The route up Habel was not terribly challenging but required a careful bit of route finding between thinly snow-covered, deep and dangerous crevasses on all sides of us. I continually scanned the surrounding snow, looking for telltale depressions that would signal the presence of a crevasse. We wore dark goggles to cut down on the brilliant sunlight and were roped together. We took a serpentine route avoiding the worst of the crevasses.

The climb took just a couple of hours from the surface of the Wapta Icefield to the top of the mountain's northeast ridge. Less than a hundred feet from the summit, the beautiful summer morning quickly turned black as a storm unexpectedly boiled up from the western valley below and flowed over top of us. Bracingly cold air blew across our sweating faces, and I shivered with the sudden temperature drop. One minute we could see the entire ice field a mile below us; the next we couldn't see each other.

I felt it first in my feet. The vibration was followed by a flash of light, and then thunder rolled in the black sky. "It's moving our way," I yelled above the rapidly growing roar of wind.

Elaine started to say something about the storm, but her words were lost as a bolt of lightning struck the slope less than a hundred feet over our heads, with an instantaneous, wake-the-dead deafening crash of thunder. My knees buckled as blue light flashed across the snow. I nearly came out of my skin.

I looked at Elaine and a few strands of her hair stood straight out from her head, pointed toward the sky. My ice axe immediately began vibrating and humming as static electricity buzzed and flowed through the metal blade and shaft. The axe was channeling the electricity, rapidly becoming the focus for the next lightning strike.

"Drop your axe!" I screamed.

Elaine's axe clanked against the ice. I pulled out a Prussik cord and ran it through the leash straps on our two axes. From that point on, we would have to drag our axes ten feet behind us for safety. For the time being, we were without the aid of our most important mountain climbing tool. We had to immediately retreat from that snowy and dangerous ridgeline.

On the way down that first pitch of the steep mountain, I heard Elaine scream and spun around to find her facedown on the ice, her pack driving her face into the snow. She was motionless. As quickly as possible, I worked my way back up the ice to her side, pulled her pack off her head, and turned her over.

Elaine spit snow from her mouth. "My ankle," she cried out. She clenched her jaw to stifle another scream, but she could not hide the pain. She was turning white and seemed to be losing consciousness. "I think I'm going to pass out."

"Hang on. Fight it! Stay with me." I removed her arms from her pack and spun her around so her feet were above her head, to increase the blood flow to her brain. I stripped off my own pack, then pulled her foot up in my lap. Gently I felt her ankle through her gaiters and tried to determine the severity of her injury.

We were still in harm's way, exposed to the full force and fury of the raging storm and at risk of being struck by lightning at any moment. As if we needed more evidence of the danger, the zipper on Elaine's coat seemed to be vibrating with static energy. Blinding flashes of lightning continued to cut their way from cloud to cloud just above our heads. I felt like my head would explode. "Stay low . . . keep your head down."

As I slowly manipulated the ankle, Elaine said through clenched teeth, "Ow. That hurts."

The right side of her ankle was already starting to swell. "Tell me, does this hurt?" I put pressure at the base of her fibula where it contacts the ankle and she screamed, pushing my hand away.

Before beginning my filmmaking career, I had spent eight years with the US Army Medical Services Corps as reserve officer; now my medical training was coming back to me. I suspected this was not a serious break. The fibula doesn't support much of a person's weight. "Elaine, I can't tell for sure if it's a bad sprain or a break. But if it's a break, it's not the tibia. Your pain seems to be localized to the base of the fibula."

Her eyes started to roll back into her head. "How bad?"

I didn't answer but said, "We're going to have to get out of this lighting strike zone before we can deal with this." I quickly tied a piece of webbing to Elaine's pack so that I would be able to drag it along behind us.

"I don't think I can walk."

"I'm sorry," I said, then abruptly lifted her up onto her good foot. She was on the edge of passing out from the pain, but we had no choice. "Let me take your weight." I slipped her arm over my shoulder and began slowly moving away from the storm.

Climbing down an ice field is always more difficult than ascending that same mountain face, even when the weather is good and when everyone is healthy. Doing so with a broken bone in a massive storm with zero visibility is very nearly impossible. Elaine let me take most of her weight and we started moving down the face of Habel, dragging our ice axes and Elaine's pack behind us.

From the moment the storm overtook us we were in a whiteout, surrounded by unbroken colorless snow. I was becoming profoundly disoriented, even losing my sense of up and down. Vertigo can overwhelm a climber caught in such a whiteout and can be lethal. Lightning again struck the mountain over our heads. I felt a concussive wave of air bounce off my helmet and backpack.

For a hundred yards I relied on our own tracks, the ones we had just laid down while climbing the mountain, to keep my sense of direction. But our bootprints were rapidly filling with fresh sleet. In their place, we could see only brilliant, unbroken white nothingness. No shadows, no definition. After about ten minutes, we lost that one remaining link to our escape path. With zero visibility and snow-covered crevasses on each side of us, we could ill afford to drift off track. Sleet was coming in from the west, driven by gale-force winds, pounding our heads, backs, and packs. I pulled out my compass for directional guidance.

Armed only with that compass and a rapidly disintegrating sense of direction, I led the way down what I hoped was the southeast face of Habel, struggling to keep all the weight off Elaine's leg. Slowly we moved out of the lightning strike zone, and within a half hour, we broke out beneath the storm cloud. I could finally see to avoid the belt of crevasses.

Once clear of the threat, we stopped so I could take a closer look at Elaine's ankle. The color was returning to her face, but her ankle was already purple. Her pain was localized to the point where the fibula attaches to the ankle. She had fairly good but painful control over her foot, so I fashioned a splint for Elaine's leg using our two ice axes—one on either side of her lower leg—and some one-inch tubular webbing and medical tape.

I stuffed the crampon from her broken ankle into the top of her pack and lifted her up again. Slowly we began moving directly south with ice still pummeling us, but our snow goggles protected us just enough to make progress possible. The sky was still spitting ice as we crossed the glacier, headed back toward the hut as if we were competing in a three-legged race. All the way across the glacier, I wondered about that rock and boulder field. How was Elaine going to manage that? But without complaint, Elaine hobbled for two hours, finally reaching the far side of the glacier. I left her pack at the glacier's edge and half-carried her up to the top of the moraine and across the threshold of the hut. By then, Elaine was shivering uncontrollably, half out of shock and half from the freezing wind.

The cabin was surprisingly warm, given the intense storm whistling through its windows. I wrapped Elaine in a down sleeping bag and struck a wooden match to light all four of the propane stovetop burners to begin warming the hut, then went back for her pack. The food in our packs would provide us with a margin of safety so Elaine could rest at the hut until the swelling in her leg began to subside.

I put on coffee to warm Elaine, poured soup and then food into her. I adjusted her down sleeping bag and returned to the stove to clean up.

For the next two days, I iced Elaine's leg and ankle with fragments of the glacier. Slowly the swelling began to subside while the bruising continued to work its way up her leg. She was unable to walk, unable to stand for long, even unable to make it to the outhouse without help, but the weather did break and was replaced by a warm western flow. Whenever she asked, I helped her hobble out onto the deck of the cabin where she would prop her leg above her head and soak up the mountain ambiance.

I began thinking about how best to get Elaine out of the backcountry. We debated whether I should go on ahead to organize a helicopter rescue, but Elaine shot that idea down immediately. "I don't need anyone to rescue me!"

This was a point of pride with her. We both felt climbers should own their own fates. We should not ask anyone to put themselves at risk to save one of us. If we made the decision to climb, we had to accept the consequences of our own risky decisions. I nodded agreement.

If I was right and Elaine had a hairline fracture of the fibula, she would be in a lot of pain walking out, but if I immobilized the leg against unexpected twists, Elaine could carefully walk on the leg without damaging it further. Neither of us, however, was under any illusion that this was going to be easy.

On the morning of the third day, we got out of bed early. Elaine took a maximum dose of ibuprofen. I made a hearty breakfast of pancakes, eggs, and ham, then immobilized her lower leg with tape. I told her she would probably not benefit much from a splint. We would need our ice axes for the long decent to the toe of the Peyto Glacier. I put Elaine on what is commonly referred to as a "short rope" to control her descent down the ice, to give her extra stability, and to help her keep her ankle joint straight while on a steep slope.

Slowly, without complaint, Elaine made the long climb down the length of the ice field and out across the terminal moraine, across Peyto Creek, around Peyto Lake, and up through the steep forest to our car, a distance of more than ten miles. When we finally reached the car, Elaine was stiff and sore but simply said, "I'm fine. I'm really not in that much pain."

While I doubted that she was telling the truth, I admired her strength and focus. I was lucky indeed to be married to such a capable, tough, and determined woman.

An X-ray of Elaine's ankle, done when we got home, confirmed the fractured fibula, and she was told she would need to wear a boot for eight weeks. Elaine immediately asked, "When will I be able to use the leg again?" She was thinking about our contract to finish *The Rocky Mountains* film, and the answer was three months. "But you'll have to ease into it and train."

Elaine and I agreed we would need an extension on our National Geographic contract. We had never before failed to deliver a film to the National Geographic Society on time, on budget, and as promised, but this was clearly going to be the exception. We wouldn't be able to finish shooting the film until Elaine's ankle healed. Sid would simply have to agree.

14

ROBSON GLACIER

Weeks passed. Winter came and went. By that next summer, Elaine's ankle had fully healed and she had resumed her running regimen to get back into shape. I was eager to continue shooting *The Rocky Mountains*. We drove up to our condo in Canmore, Canada, with Janet Dennis and her young daughter, Anna, in tow. Janet offered to care for John and Ted while Elaine got back to work.

This part of the film was going to be the most critical. We needed to get our camera near the top of one of North America's tallest peaks. Everything was different up there—ice, rock, and weather. You couldn't fake it. If we were going to make a film about the Rocky Mountains, we needed footage of this harshest of alpine environments. I had chosen Mount Robson because it is one of the most beautiful and massive mountains in the Rockies. Images from this mountain would be easily recognizable for what they were and where they had been shot. People who knew mountains would recognize and identify with the film footage.

The problem was, this was also a very difficult environment to work in. The weather was terrifically harsh and unsettled. The ice was extensive and expansive. If we worked on Robson, we would be pushing our skill levels. As a result, I had decided we were not going to make this climb by ourselves. I wanted to make sure we had all the support possible.

Asking the Alpine Club of Canada for backup support seemed like the logical choice. When I made my request, the club's leaders agreed immediately. We could dovetail our filmmaking with their General Mountaineering Camp, which was already scheduled for Mount Robson later that summer. The Alpine Club would heli-lift much of our gear in to the base of the mountain and then provide us with a support team once we were on the ice. I was confident we could do the job with their support.

Six climbers from the club met us at the junction of the Fraser and Robson Rivers. I could tell right away that all six were weathered mountaineers. Their boots were big and heavy, covered with scratches and gouges, and bore the markings of crampon straps. Each of these climbers—four men and two women—was experienced. In particular, their leader, Peter, was a tough old bird, a world-class mountain guide, a descendent of one of the original Swiss guides who came to the Canadian Rockies to help build a climbing community. Deep lines cut across his red face, the result of thousands of days of exposure at high altitude. He looked to be in his fifties but may not have been that old. He took his wool hat off and extended his right hand to me. I took it and felt like I had just taken hold of a leather boot.

Mount Robson was one of the greatest alpine challenges in North America. Many people attempt to reach its summit, but few succeed. It's not because the mountain itself is so impossible, though its infamous Kain Face is arguably one of the most difficult sustained ice climbs in the Rocky Mountains. The weather is what turns most climbers back before they reach the summit.

On this particular assignment my plan was not to summit Robson but rather to capture on film the climbing experience, using the mountain as a backdrop. We planned to film the ACC members as they worked their way across the Robson Glacier, ascending the ice field just below the Helmet and the Dome.

The first day was comparatively easy. We hiked up the Robson River in the rain, through a spectacular old-growth forest, around Kinney Lake, and then up a beautiful gully named the Valley of a Thousand Waterfalls. A cold blast of alpine air hit us in the face just as we broke over the top of Emperor Falls, which seemed to explode like a fire hose out of the high plateau and cascade over the valley. The trees above the falls were noticeably shorter, more weathered; all their branches came out from the downwind side of the tree trunks. The cold blast of fog-laden air cut through everything we wore.

The trail finally leveled off as we crossed a rocky, nearly treeless area surrounding Berg Lake. By then we were at fifty-four hundred feet. The map said that we were at the foot of Mount Robson, but it was completely shrouded in clouds.

Peter explained, "Robson has been known to go an entire summer without anyone ever seeing its summit."

A large, region-wide, high-pressure area was moving in, so I was hoping the weather would clear sometime while we were on the mountain. If it didn't, our film footage would probably lack the punch it needed and ultimately end up on the cutting-room floor.

As we hiked around the west side of the lake, we caught a momentary glimpse of the base of Berg Glacier. It looked like a huge waterfall, frozen in time, plummeting out of the cloudy sky. As we watched, a large piece of ice broke free and, in slow motion, crashed into the lake, joining a number of other icebergs already floating there. It took a few seconds for the sound to cross the lake, but we could distinctly hear the crashing sound of ice hitting water.

Peter was hiking in front of me. He turned and said, "These glaciers are retreating fast. When I was a kid, they came all the way down to the lake. Now most of the glaciers in the park have retreated, some of them a half mile, some more than that." This was the first time I had heard an experienced mountain climber talk about the damaging effects of global warming.

Once we cleared the end of the lake, we jumped the headwaters of the Robson River, cut across a large boulder-strewn terminal moraine, and began the gentle climb up to the toe of the glacier. At one time, when the climate was cooler and the glacier was expanding in size, it had pushed its way down this valley, carving and grinding these rock walls. But now the ice was retreating, exposing more of the underlying rock.

The temperature dropped another ten degrees once we reached the glacier, a localized effect of the ice that we would have to live with for the next several days. Everyone was tired when we reached the ACC base camp at the toe of the glacier. Elaine and I were given the use of a wall tent, already set up close to the base of the ice.

We woke at 4:00 AM. I flipped on the tiny battery-powered REI candlelight that hung down from the tent's aluminum frame. The walls of the tent immediately began to glow yellow.

"Must you get up so early?" Elaine complained.

I said. "What kind of photographer would miss the first light of day?"

"You don't need me for this," she groaned and rolled over to bury her head before the cold morning air could sweep inside as I opened the tent flap.

When I stuck my head out into the still-dark and cold morning, I was greeted by a vibrant, glittering star field overhead. The sky was completely cloudless. The sun was still far below the horizon, but the faintest of red light was just beginning to glow at the ridgeline. Everyone else was still in a sleeping bag.

I quickly slipped into my down coat, pulled on a stocking hat, and jammed my feet into climbing boots. Struggling to my feet, I became aware of an enormous black shadow blocking out the entire southwestern sky. Even at the early hour, in the absence of any real light, the mountain was impressive. We seemed to be in luck; the rain had stopped sometime early in the night. Our tents were almost dry.

Surrounded by nothing but cold stillness, I quietly broke out our backpacker's stove to make some coffee for Elaine. I struck a match and the stove took off. Ten steps behind our tent, I dipped into a rivulet of pure ice water pouring off the glacier and filled a small metal pot. Members of the ACC team were just getting around. While the water was heating up, I pulled out the Sachtler tripod and unzipped my backpack so I could pull the Arriflex out of its foam fitting and set it up to get a first-light shot of Robson. I waited for the light level to rise sufficiently for the shot. When I had it, I returned to the coffee and poured Elaine a cup.

I already had a full magazine of film footage before the sun broke over the eastern ridgeline. Most of that footage would show the building light on Extinguisher Mountain and the Kain Face of Robson. Elaine and the ACC team were up, speaking in hushed tones, trying not to wake the others. I removed the spent magazine from the camera, climbed back into our tent, and pulled the black change bag from the pocket of my pack. I placed the film magazine and a fresh roll of film inside the change bag, then slipped my arms inside through the sleeve ports. By feel, I replaced the spent roll of film with a new one.

We all ate a good breakfast then began breaking camp and shoving everything back into our packs. In a straight line, we all headed for the toe of the glacier. Elaine and I brought up the rear. In about ten minutes we reached the glacier and began pulling our ropes and climbing gear out of our packs. The sun was just then reaching the foot of the glacier, and when it struck my back, I was only too happy for the warmth. The base and edges of the glacier were streaked with large, easily avoided crevasses. Most everyone sat down to fit their ten-point crampons to their boots. We broke into three rope teams, and Peter gave everyone last-minute instructions.

As we headed out, the only sounds to break the mountain silence were our crampons loudly crunching into the ice, the tips of our axes biting into the glacier, and three climbing ropes dragging along the surface of the ice. I was reminded just why I like crampons so much. When you walk out onto slick ice, the crampons are the only things that keep you grounded; they provide solid footing on even the steepest of sections of the glacier and make the wearer feel like Spider-Man. They are designed to fit on boots that are equipped with steel shanks in the soles. These rigid soles provide a base against which the crampons fix themselves. Two of the points face forward so that a climber can jam his toes into the face of an ice wall to obtain footing where none would otherwise exist. With crampons, a climber can ascend vertical ice. But vertical ice can still be pretty tough on a climber.

That morning, the glacial ice was rough and jagged, with granular knife-like edges protruding. Rock fragments, dust, and algae gave the ice surface a dark appearance. When sunlight strikes it, the algae can make the ice look pink.

I was full of expectation and thrilled with the intense yellow light that was, by then, flooding in over Robson Pass. The surface of the ice was covered with a spiderweb of surface streams of water. Every few hundred yards we would find a place where the water had cut a sinkhole down through the glacier. The intensely turquoise meltwater disappeared into these holes, eventually flowing out from the glacier's toe.

I asked Peter if all this water was normal, and he said "the new normal." This new, warmer normal obviously troubled him.

Midmorning, we came upon a very steep ice wall cutting all the way across the face of the glacier. We couldn't avoid it. "I think we should take this ice wall head-on," Peter said. The vertical climb would be in the neighborhood of three hundred feet.

Elaine and I shot footage of the climbers preparing their gear for the assault on the ice face. To my surprise, each of the two ACC rope teams spread out to the full extent of their ropes, preparing to take the wall on the run without bothering with ice-screw protection. Elaine said she would be more comfortable with the ice climb if I was more conservative and put in protective ice screws as I led our way up the wall.

Several times as we climbed we moved on out in front, planted the camera in the ice, and then asked the ACC climbers to move on through the scene. Each time they would have to wait for us to set up a new camera position before they began climbing again. At the top of the ice wall, at about seventy-five hundred feet of elevation, we all stopped and came together to share a cup of hot cider. Peter began asking us about our filmmaking careers, so Elaine told him about the time we were diving, surrounded by sharks. She went into some detail about what filming predators was like.

"There were dozens of sharks all streaming by just three feet away," she said.

Peter looked at Elaine in disbelief. "My God! That would have scared the *BEJESUS* out of me."

Elaine and I threw each other a surprised glance, then, almost at the same time, burst out laughing. This man, who regularly climbs sheer mountain ice walls with little more than a few steel crampon spikes to hold him to the mountain, a man who had climbed the Kain Face of Robson many times, was telling us that he would be afraid to stick his head in the same ocean with a bunch of reef sharks? Everyone on the ACC team began to laugh along with us.

Within a few moments, silence took the place of the chatter, and we leaned back on our packs. The splendor of this place was overwhelming.

"Can you imagine a more beautiful picnic spot?" Elaine asked. Visibility was unbelievably good. I could see the entire mountain. To the right of the peak was the Dome and the Helmet, two "foothill peaks" on the way to Robson. To the left was the magnificent, ice-covered Resplendent Mountain, with its long, low-angle ice ridge connecting it to the Kain Face. In between was a long tongue of ice that wound its way up through the middle of all the peaks like a highway, reaching toward the Kain Face itself. Moments like these make climbing worth every bit of sweat it takes to get there. For the next hour, I worked to capture the scene on film.

For most of the rest of the morning, we filmed the climbers as they moved on ropes up the glacier. It was spectacular filming because of the direct sunlight and the breathtaking scenery. Centuries of wind-blown dust and accumulations of rock coated the ice and gave it an almost black appearance. About six in the evening, we began looking for a place to put our tents, ultimately settling on a spot at about nine thousand feet.

The place we selected was out of reach of any falling ice in a partially protected spot away from most of the wind. Finally, at about 9:00 PM, I decided to try to sleep. I turned the candle off and moved in close to Elaine in our tent. Feeling my cold skin, she wrapped her body around me to share her body heat.

"What have you been doing? You're so cold!"

"Admiring the view," I replied. "I hope the wind lets up by morning. It's the only way we are going to get a shot at this mountain."

Our tent flapped in the wind most of the night, making an all-too familiar racket that would have kept most people awake, but we were so tired, I doubted the flapping would bother us much. Elaine buried her nose in my neck and kissed me. I wrapped her head in my arms, the way I always did. She snuggled, trying to get as far beneath me as she could.

It was impossible to tell how long we slept, a few minutes or perhaps an hour. The next thing I knew, something that sounded like a rifle shot awakened me, but that was ridiculous; no one carried guns up here. It was dark outside our tent. I lay quiet for a moment, pulled the down sleeping bag away from my ears, and listened.

The wind had stopped so it should have been quiet, but it wasn't. In the distance, a low rumbling got louder with each passing moment. A second passed, then two. Finally, I realized what was making the noise. It was an avalanche of ice and snow coming off the side of Robson. The "gunshot" had been the sound of the ice breaking free.

"It's a big one," Elaine whispered.

We listened for a few seconds, and as abruptly as the sound had begun, it stopped.

"It's airborne," I guessed, but before Elaine could respond, the snow and ice crashed into the side of the mountain again and continued its rush toward the valley floor.

Elaine turned to me, "Will it reach us?" she asked.

"Not a chance."

A very long half-minute passed, and then, finally, the sound slowly died away.

By the morning, conditions had improved. There was a moment of silence. The mountain was gathering its strength. Clouds had begun forming on the lee side of Robson. They looked like smoke streaming out from the western flank of the mountain. In between the clouds, the summit occasionally became visible. A front was moving in. This was what everyone called the lull before the storm, but it looked like there might be a small window of opportunity for us to get our filming done.

Peter came over to where Elaine and I were preparing. "I suggest we leave the tents and bags here. If all goes well, we will be back by nightfall. If, for whatever reason, the filming takes longer than you say, we can bivvy overnight wherever we can find shelter from the wind and come down in the morning."

Breakfast was ready. We all ate well. I sought Peter's advice, ultimately deciding that Elaine and I would lead off. We were planning to set up a camera on a pronounced ice ledge visible from where we stood and film the ACC folks breaking camp, then coming up after us through all the ice. This entire section of the glacier was steep, so right from the start I tied Elaine in to one end of the rope and threw a rack of ice screws over my shoulder. When needed, we would be ready to affix two opposite-facing carabiners held together by one-inch webbing to each screw and then snap the rope through the gate of the outside carabiner. The system was commonly referred to as a "quick draw" and was designed to anchor climbers securely to the face of a mountain.

About a quarter mile out away from the tents, we came to the steepest section of ice. I could see the bergschrund, the topmost edge of the Robson Glacier, some distance above us. We needed to traverse across the face of the glacier before we would be clear to turn up the mountain's wall. The climb was about to become treacherous. As we moved laterally across the mountain, we became more and more exposed to steep ice and the precipitous drop-off below us.

We began to sweep up the ice face, headed for the flat spot where I planned to put the camera, when I noticed that the ice surface was a bit rotten, probably due to the previous day's sun and warmer-than-usual air. I used my ice axe adze to cut down to good ice before cranking an eight-inch ice screw into place. As I cranked the screw into the blue ice, I was reassured by what looked like good-quality ice coming out of the hollow center of the screw. I affixed a quick draw to the ice screw, snapped my rope into the outside carabiner, and continued on.

This was a very steep slope, so I began paying close attention to where I put each foot. I traveled about fifty more feet up a sixty-degree incline of ice before pulling out a second screw, but before I could use it, I heard a muffled crack.

Suddenly the rotten ice beneath me—everything within twenty or thirty meters—fractured and began to collapse. My left elbow slammed into the ice as my feet were swept out from underneath me. A ton of ice beneath and above me was sliding off the mountain, carrying me with it.

I kicked my crampons into the ice to gain some traction, but the speed of my fall was already too great. My right crampon caught in some firm ice as I sped past. The force of my fall tore at least some of the tendons that held my ankle together. My boot temporarily stopped, but my body kept sliding. As my head passed by my foot, my own boot hit me in the jaw. The force caused me to tumble over backward, bouncing down the mountain on my back, headfirst.

Reflexively, I tried to use my ice axe in a self-arrest, but when I slammed the point of my axe into the ice, my forearm came into contact with the knifelike ice surface. My coat and insulation layer were ripped away. The skin on my forearm was instantly torn off, and I dropped my axe. It flew away to the end of its tether and began clanking against the ice as I accelerated. In an instant, I sped past Elaine and continued my plunge off the mountainside.

There was nothing left for me to do to stop my fall. Our last line of defense was the nine-millimeter single nylon rope, but ropes do a climber absolutely no good if they are not securely fastened to the mountain. There was only one ice screw between Elaine and me anchoring us to the mountain, and there was a good chance the force of my fall would yank that screw from the ice. If that happened, our safety line would jerk Elaine over the side of the mountain with me.

Luckily, Elaine saw the collapsing wall and knew exactly the right thing to do. She was the only one who could save our lives, and her long hours of training paid off. She wrapped the rope tightly around her waist, clamped her right hand—the breaking hand—down on the rope, and braced herself against the violence she knew was coming. The terrific force of my fall jerked Elaine off her feet, pulled her out of her strong belaying position, and dragged her across the face of the ice toward the anchor screw. But Elaine refused to let go of the rope. She was determined.

Suddenly, I came to a violent halt as tons of ice continued roaring by my head, slamming into my helmet and shoulders and backpack as it rushed past me over the side of the mountain. Elaine too was being pounded by ice as broken fragments slid off the mountainside. She lay facedown on the ice with the rope running around her back, pulling her into the screw. She didn't dare look up for fear of being hit in the face by the collapsing wall of ice. A very long three or four seconds passed as we each tried to regain our wits, and then the ice crashed into the rocks below.

Hanging from our rope on the side of Mount Robson, suspended by my harness, two opposing carabiners, a terrific ice screw, and a priceless wife, I realized how much I had to be thankful for. Just as quickly, I was reminded of the pain I was in and how far we were from the nearest road.

We were also a quarter mile from the other climbers. We were on our own for the time being and still at some risk. The rope between us was taut. One ice screw was taking all the strain. We couldn't count on that screw holding forever, so I fished around behind me on my harness, pulling out another. I cranked it into the wall and clipped a second quick draw into place and snapped my rope through the carabiner. Only then did I dare look up at Elaine. She was still facedown in the ice, holding on and supporting my weight, struggling under the strain.

"Are you all right?" I managed to ask through a clenched jaw.

"Are you?"

"Thanks to you," I replied. "Do you have another ice screw on your belt?"

"No."

"OK. I'm going to take the weight off the rope. When I do, regain your footing and brace yourself. *Maintain belay*."

I tried to assess the damage. My pack was still on my back. The waist belt was cutting into me, taking the weight but making breathing difficult. The camera was still intact and hadn't gone over the side of the mountain. I tried to put weight on my leg, but the damage to my ankle made that difficult. I used my one good leg to lift myself up a foot or so, drove my ice axe into the wall to hold myself in place, taking the pressure off the rope so that Elaine could move and regain her footing.

Slowly I worked my way back up to Elaine, and she took in the slack rope as I struggled up the ice. When finally I reached her, we sat in stunned silence for a long time. We were still on an adrenaline high that dulled the pain but also gave me a sick stomach. I was proud of Elaine's quick reaction to the fall, stunned that this 120-pound woman had absorbed what must have been a terrific amount of force at the end of that hundred-foot fall. I put my hand on her knee and squeezed just to let her know how much I appreciated her at that moment.

The climbers below us looked like little ants moving across the ice. They seemed unaware of our condition. Finally, I told Elaine about my ankle. "I'm sure it's a soft-tissue injury. It hurts a lot, but I don't think anything is broken."

She noticed the blood caked around my forearm and asked about that. "Let me see." She pulled my coat sleeve up and could see most of the skin on the underside of my arm, from my wrist to my elbow, was gone. She moved down around me and probed the injuries to my ankle. I was still wearing my crampons, boots, and gaiters, so she couldn't really get a good sense for the injury. "Can you walk?"

I gritted my teeth and tried to assess our situation. "The only way I'm going to get off this steep ice is if I can keep my ankle straight, reduce the strain on the tendons."

"We can't do much to immobilize that ankle up here," Elaine said.

I thought for a long moment and said, "We're going to have to exchange roles. You're going to have to belay me down. If you keep the rope taut, it will take much of my weight. I should be able to manage."

I looked around and handed Elaine an ice screw. She used it to rig up a double anchor, running the rope through the carabiner. She repositioned herself to take the load, and I lifted myself up into a standing position using my good leg.

"Slowly," I said. "When the midpoint in the rope comes up to you, tell me to stop."

As I descended the ice, Elaine slowly paid out half our sixty-meter rope, taking most of my weight as I went. In a few minutes, Elaine yelled, "Stop."

I stopped descending and put in another screw, clipped in, and then pulled the excess rope down to me. When Elaine was ready, I put her on belay so that she could climb down to me.

"What are we going to do with that screw up there," she asked.

"Leave it. We have no choice. I'm not going to let you descend without top-rope cover, and I am in no condition to do that either. I've got seven of these cheaper Russian-made screws, which should be strong enough to use as top support. That should be enough to get off this high-angle ice."

Thirty meters at a time, we slowly worked our way down the ice until we reached the relative safety of the main glacier. By the time we came off the steep ice, the ACC team had caught up with us, and from there on down we had all the help we needed.

We were done filming. With the injuries I had sustained, it would be difficult making the descent down the glacier to the trail and then the long slog around Robson's base to the trailhead. When Richard had a moment to think about it, he suggested we try to get off the ice before nightfall. To keep the swelling down in my ankle, Elaine put a compression bandage on it. I didn't dare take my swollen foot out of my boot for fear I wouldn't be able to get it back in. Elaine wrapped tape around the outside of my boot and upper leg to provide additional stability.

That night, I was freezing cold and physically spent, but we dragged ourselves back to the base camp. The ACC folks made dinner for us while Elaine broke out our med kit, disinfected and bandaged my arm, and gave me a dose of some extra-strength ibuprofen.

About twenty minutes after I laid my head down on my rolled-up down coat, Peter came over to our tent. He had in his hands two little cups filled to the brim with a dark liquid. "Want some Jack Daniels?" he asked.

Elaine responded first, "Oh look, Jim. Your own personal rescue Saint Bernard." For the first time in days, I saw the faintest hint of a smile spread across Peter's face.

The drink helped, but not much. It was a long, fitful night. I woke to find Elaine quietly packing everything up for the long trip out. She had apparently been up for some time, talking with the other climbers. They were busy helping Elaine by stuffing much of our gear and camera equipment into their own packs.

"What are you doing?" I asked.

"You're not carrying anything. We've got this." She didn't seem to be in a mood to negotiate.

On the long trip out, I had time to think about what just happened. I was humbled by the fall. This mountain had provided me a lesson about ego and gravity, about the true nature of wilderness, and about my own limitations.

It had also given me the opportunity to see my wife in a new light. Elaine and I had begun our lives together with me leading the way. I was always the one who pushed us into new places and experiences. Elaine always rose to the challenge of each new experience, but she followed most of the time. Now she was most definitely leading, taking the responsibility to mend my wounds and to get me out of the backcountry, coordinating my extraction from the mountain.

Peter came over to me, nodding his forehead toward Elaine in a conspiratorial way. In a soft voice so as not to be overheard, he said, "She's tougher than she looks."

PART IV

ADVOCACY

15

THE LIVING EARTH

WHEN ELAINE AND I ARRIVED IN SID'S OFFICE, he was already sitting behind his desk waiting for us. Donald was on Sid's couch, as was Jean Redmond, the researcher who had been assigned to our next film project. The moment Elaine entered the room, both Sid and Donald jumped up, enthusiastically reaching out for her. Sid got there first and threw his arms around Elaine, which was something I never saw him do with anyone else. Most often, Sid wore an expressionless mask, the one that was so hard to read and contained no trace of a smile. But this morning he seemed almost ecstatic to see Elaine.

I had come to know Sid as a curmudgeon who projected a tough external demeanor, but Elaine had helped me to appreciate that he was not so crusty as he wanted people to believe. Elaine saw more deeply into people than I did. She was aware of Sid's softer side.

When Sid finally stepped back away from Elaine he asked, "How's that leg healing?"

And it hit me; I finally knew why he and Donald were so eager to see Elaine. While she and I had mostly forgotten about the climbing accidents, the National Geographic Society staff had not. This was the first time they had seen Elaine since sending us off into the Rocky Mountains to make that film, and they were concerned she had gotten hurt while on their watch.

Elaine turned slightly red in the face. "Good as new," she replied.

As soon as Sid was satisfied, it was Donald's turn, and he swept in, hugging Elaine even more enthusiastically than Sid had. I ambled over to where Jean was standing. The two of us just stared at each other in shock. She whispered, "What are you, chopped liver?"

With a broad grin, I said, "What do you think? Are they going to award her the Purple Heart?"

Donald heard the joke, then turned to face us. "Oh Elaine, did you bring Jim with you?"

Jean and I thought Donald was funny, but Sid was becoming restless, returning to the curmudgeon we all knew him to be. Almost as an afterthought, he said. "You know, I really liked *The Rocky Mountains*. You did a good job with that. I appreciate the lengths you went to for the high-altitude images."

"Thanks, Sid. It was *unforgettable*," I said.

Sid looked at me closely. Satisfied, he continued, "So, what's on your mind? What did you want to talk about?"

We had come to Washington that day to make a bigger-than-usual request, a request for three years of continuous funding for a film series. It was a big leap forward for us, but I was thinking we were coming from a good bargaining position, having produced so many successful films for Sid.

Without hesitation, I launched into it. "Elaine and I would like to propose a series of films about the biological health of planet Earth. Scientists the world over are becoming deeply concerned about the direct assault on the environmental movement in the United States," I said, "and I think we have an obligation to do what we can about it."

Up to this point, the environmental movement had enjoyed broad support dating back at least two decades. Rachel Carson's *Silent Spring*, published in 1962, had played a lead role in launching environmentalism in America. As her book's title suggested, Ms. Carson believed, if something was not done to curb the widespread abuse of toxic chemicals, we would one day wake up to a world without the sound of birds—a silent spring. I reminded Sid how Carson and her book had changed the world. A long period of bipartisan agreement, which we needed to preserve and conserve nature and stop using it as our own private cesspool, followed the publication of *Silent Spring*.

I then ticked off on my fingers the progress we, as a society, had made since Carson's book. The Clean Water Act was passed in 1960, the Clean Air Act followed in 1963, and the Wilderness Act cleared Congress in 1964. Gaylord Nelson organized the first Earth Day in 1970. That same year, Richard Nixon signed into law the National Environmental Policy Act and created the Environmental Protection Agency. In 1972, the Marine Mammal Protection Act was signed, and the Endangered Species Act followed one year later.

"All this work produced tangible benefits to society," I said, "producing cleaner air and water for everyone." By 1997, the EPA reported the cleanest air across the nation ever measured. The emissions of the six principal environmental pollutants were all down by one-third. The release of toxic materials generally were down by nearly 50 percent. The new agency reported that more than three-quarters of all lakes, rivers, and streams were now safer than they had been since the EPA started monitoring environmental quality. People could see the difference. The air was noticeably cleaner. The number of days of air quality alerts in our major cities had dropped precipitously. We no longer had to worry about entire rivers bursting into flames as happened in Cleveland in 1969.

"The disturbing part came after," I continued. Perhaps, not surprisingly, the more effective the environmental laws became, the greater the opposition from the industries being regulated. By the early 1980s the environmental movement was under direct assault; industry money was flooding Congress. Ronald Reagan was elected as a pro-development president and immediately installed James Watt as head of the Department of the Interior and Anne Gorsuch Burford as administrator of the EPA.

Burford's mission was to strip the Environmental Protection Agency of its power. Watt was installed to realign the Department of the Interior to favor development. These two administrators were wildly unpopular, and Burford was soon removed from office after Congress stepped in but only after she had significantly damaged the agency. Almost a third of the EPA's funding and a quarter of its professional staff were gone.

Elaine and I felt we needed to do more to argue for research-based decision-making. I knew this was going to be a stretch for Sid. While I was the one producer in Sid's office with a strong environmental background, I was also the one who was most likely to get him into trouble. It was my opinion that the National Geographic Society tended to avoid controversy. It generally did not say things in the magazine or books or films that might bring criticism. When it had dealt with controversial subjects, it had always been careful to present both sides of any issue and had shown a clear preference to avoid getting too far out in front of the science.

The films I was pitching would push some of these boundaries and might bring heat down on Sid's head. I was acutely aware of the dangers but thought we should push ahead regardless.

"The first film in the series will be titled *The Living Earth*," I said, "and will be about the nature of life on Earth." For this film, we would photograph the Amazonian rainforest, the Sahara Desert, and coral reefs, to show how life evolved and what role it plays in maintaining the Earth as we know it. I went on to explain that the second film would be called *Ancient Forests* and would be the most controversial of the three. It would be about the importance of northwestern forests as an ecosystem. "The third will be the most important film of the series," I said. "It will be titled something along the lines of *Earth's Biodiversity*." I hadn't yet decided on a title, but it would be about the interdependence of life on Earth and about complexity in nature. This final film would be the key to the whole series. "Together, these films will make a powerful environmental statement about wise management and use of natural resources."

Donald was the key. If he understood what we were trying to do, he could convince Sid. I was sure of it. Over the next few hours, I aimed most of my pitch toward him. The conversation went on well into the afternoon as we made our way to one of Sid's favorite Georgetown restaurants.

It was obvious Donald was in our corner already. He jumped in with unqualified support. "I think this just might be your most important contribution to our efforts here at the National Geographic to date." He then turned to Sid and waited for Sid to make the call.

Sid took his time. He looked at Donald, at Elaine, and then turned ever so slowly toward me. He seemed to be measuring his words. "Jim,

I'm going to give you a little room to run here. I'll sign off on this series for now. But we'll revisit this after each film in the series is done. I think you're fully capable of doing what you say. And I love what you have done for us thus far. Just don't get me into some kind of big environmental food fight."

As quietly as possible, I let out a long, slow exhale, paused, and then said, "I'll do my best."

Less than three months later, Elaine arranged for Bruce and Mary Lou Mate, who by this time had become two of our best friends, to host John and Ted at their home in Newport while we flew to Hawaii.

We landed in Hilo on a rainy day in mid-May to begin production of *The Living Earth*. This was our third trip to the Big Island of Hawaii for the National Geographic; the first two trips were to photograph Kilauea's eruptions. Now we were driving up the island's sister mountain, Mauna Loa, to the NOAA Earth System Research Laboratory.

As soon as we broke out on top of the layer of thick rain clouds, we could see the research station sitting on the top of the volcano, looking as if it were a lone sentinel watching over the Earth. In fact, that is exactly its purpose.

This first film in our new series was supposed to ask some very important questions. What makes Earth capable of sustaining life? What role does life play in making Earth habitable for humans? We hoped to demonstrate the ways all ecosystems on Earth are connected and interdependent and how human beings are utterly dependent upon these biological systems.

To make these points, we first needed to show how human beings were changing the gaseous makeup of the atmosphere. On Mauna Loa, we met with the laboratory's manager, Dr. Chin, and trained our cameras on the world's longest continuous record of atmospheric composition data. NOAA scientists on Mauna Loa have been measuring the carbon dioxide levels in the atmosphere nonstop since 1958. When the first measurements were taken, the carbon dioxide levels in Earth's atmosphere were just over three hundred parts per million.

Elaine worked directly with the lab manager, outlining his role in our film and making him comfortable with the camera while I lit the room and set up the camera gear. She hung a microphone around his neck while I adjusted the light and ran the cords. When Elaine thought he was ready, I rolled the camera and began asking him about the carbon dioxide readings.

His response was startling: "We have been monitoring the carbon dioxide levels in the atmosphere longer than anyone. Our data show that these levels are on an unsustainable trajectory. If something is not done, and soon, we will live in a very uncomfortable world in the near future, a world where crops will fail, weather will become more extreme, and people will be displaced." He went on to point out the effect of forests on carbon dioxide levels in the atmosphere. "An interesting thing about our data is that it not only shows the steady rise in carbon dioxide levels year to year, but it also clearly shows the importance of plant life on Earth."

When summer comes to the Northern Hemisphere, where the Mauna Loa station sits, carbon dioxide levels dip. This is because trees consume enormous amounts of carbon dioxide as they grow leaves. In winter, when many trees in the Northern Hemisphere drop their leaves, carbon dioxide levels rise. The data clearly showed this annual cycling is an indicator of the importance of forests to the oxygen/carbon dioxide balance in Earth's atmosphere.

When the cameras were off, our host advised us to head to SUNY in Buffalo, New York, where scientists were measuring carbon dioxide in ancient ice cores. By measuring the trapped gases found in older ice, these research teams had shown that preindustrial levels of atmospheric carbon dioxide hovered around 200 parts per million (ppm). Today those levels have more than doubled, climbing to 420 ppm.

Our work in Hawaii complete, Elaine and I began planning for the next part of the film, which was to be shot in the rainforests of South America.

We needed help with this part, because Brazil is a difficult country to move around in with a big movie camera. I turned to a native Brazilian scientist who was deeply involved in a study of the role of the Amazon in stabilizing Earth's water cycle. At the time, Elen Cutrim was a post-doctoral candidate at the University of Wisconsin; that's where I found her. But she was simultaneously a professor at the Federal University of Pará, in Brazil.

When I met her at the Atmospheric and Oceanic Sciences Building on the Madison campus, I found her to be gregarious and gracious, quick to help anyone who came looking for that help and uncommonly outgoing. She was articulate, though she spoke with a heavy Brazilian accent and I occasionally had difficulty understanding her. When Elaine and I arrived in Madison, a team of university computer specialists were analyzing Elen's data. An extensive array of satellite dishes covered the top of the twenty-story building where Elen did her work. The team sat around an equally impressive array of computers and screens.

Elen used her data to show us that the rainforest does not just benefit from all the rain that falls upon it—about eighty inches each year—but it recycles that water endlessly by generating much of the water vapor that rises up as mist and becomes rain.

I decided on the spot to highlight her research work in our film. Luckily our schedules were a match. Elen was planning a return trip to her home town of Belém for a family visit and to attend to her research sites.

A short two months later, Elen; her husband, Bill Sauck; Elaine; and I flew together to Belém. Elen was excited to be home, but Elaine and I were not looking forward to the inevitable customs hassle of trying to get a lot of film equipment through a country with tight restrictions on foreign journalists. When we stepped up to the customs counter, the agent typed in our passport number and then signaled to someone behind him. Usually when a customs officer does this it is a sign that things are going to become more difficult. A few minutes passed as we waited, and then an army officer appeared from a back office and began walking directly toward us. I looked at Elaine and said, "Oh brother!"

Before the officer had time to examine our paperwork, Elen came out from the line behind us and swept her arms around the man. She exchanged enthusiastic greetings, then turned to us and introduced the commanding general for all of Amazonia as her uncle.

Elen explained, "My uncle is in command of almost everything in northeastern Brazil. We are going to need his help with your filming."

The general asked us to follow him as he whisked us down a back hallway through customs, skipping all the formalities. He turned to me and asked for our paperwork, then handed it to a staff officer and barked orders. Just like that, we were in Brazil.

Two days later, Elen's uncle loaded us on one of his private airplanes and sent us to a small mining town on the northern end of the Amazon, near Carajás. From there, we took boats up the Amazon into the jungle. At one point, Elaine and I were completely surrounded by multiple canopy layers of trees with some leaves the size of small cars. There were millions upon millions of trees, all competing for space. Localized wind gusts sent shivers through the forest in waves.

Less than ten minutes after we arrived there was a flash of light just over the horizon. The wind picked up, and soon the sky began to fall in sheets. Vast amounts of water marched across the canopy, pummeling the trees and the pavilion roof over our heads. The word *rain* somehow fails to adequately describe what we were experiencing. It was more like standing beneath a waterfall with millions of gallons of water crashing down on your head. The roar of the rain made communication impossible.

The air was also extraordinarily thick. The sounds and smells were new to us. Billions of insects and thousands of birds were all fighting for their voices to be heard above the cacophony of competing calls. My senses staggered under the weight of it all. Elaine turned to me and said, "This is cool."

"Not the word I would have chosen." I was dripping with sweat.

Elaine was truly enjoying the sensory overload.

I was not. "This environment is going to consume our camera gear."

Just as the rain began to subside a little, a haunting, metallic-sounding voice echoed from somewhere below us.

"I think that's a howler monkey," I observed.

"It sounds like a machine starting up."

That next morning, we went looking for the source of that sound and eventually found a family of eight or ten howlers. The dominant male was covered in rich black hair except for his face, which was completely hairless, dark blue or black depending on the color of the sky. His eyes were intensely brown. He had a beard-like accumulation of hair beneath his chin. A female jumped from the adjacent tree to a limb above the male's head by using her long, prehensile tail as a fifth hand. The end of her tail was hairless on the underside.

We filmed as the lead male stood guard over his tribe and the family moved through the trees eating leaves, fruits, and some flowers. As I was changing lenses, I looked to my left just in time to see a bright yellow and black poison dart frog sitting on a leaf, observing me. The trees were full of hundreds of birds, seemingly all screaming at once. Elaine had her hands full trying to capture and separate the cacophony of sounds on her Nagra.

I could clearly see why the rainforest is considered so important to the Earth's ecosystems: there is just so much life there. One in every three known species on Earth lives in the Amazon. The Amazon is home to the largest collection of plant and animal life in the world. Despite its biological wealth, or perhaps because of it, the soil beneath the forest is known to be poor. Most of the nutrients in the Amazon are held in the forest canopy itself. When loggers or would-be ranchers or farmers come in, they strip the entire area of its nutrients. When forests are cut for farming, the farms always fail, because the nutrients have been burned or carried away with the logs. Once these farms have failed, the land remains impoverished and will not recover for many thousands of years.

Maintaining these forests as intact, viable ecosystems is essential if we are ever going to stabilize Earth's climate, preserve the Earth's biodiversity, or maintain functioning hydrologic cycles on Earth. I now clearly understood why scientists argue that our civilization may not be able to survive the loss of the Amazonian forests.

Not long after we filmed in the Amazon, we headed for the Sahara to film the expansion of deserts and the resulting impact on people who live around the edges of the desert. We dove deep into the center of the Sahara and spent a week at a tiny oasis named El Kharga to show how the desert sands were reclaiming the city, then moved on to the desert fringe to film the nomadic people who had been displaced by the growing desert.

Almost a year later, we were wrapping up the shooting of the film in Indonesia after having visited three continents and eight countries.

Elaine took up child care duties the moment we got back to Oregon. I buried myself in my editing room and began assembling the film's component parts. To open the film, I wanted to ask several key questions. I cut together a montage of images, one scene from the Egyptian desert, one from the Amazon, one from the boreal forests of Canada, and one from the steaming jungles of Indonesia. Over top of these images, I would set the scene by asking questions. "How does life in one ecosystem affect life in another?" "How does life in the sea affect life on land?" And finally, "If we damage life in one ecosystem, will that affect life in other ecosystems?"

From there, we would slowly march through the various major ecosystems on Earth, first the deserts of Africa, then the jungles of South America, then the boreal forests of the north, and finally the mountains and glaciers of North America. After making all the arguments, I would transition to the science. What do scientists already know about these subjects, and what work is being done to answer remaining questions?

To write this film, I hired an accomplished author with whom I had worked before. Joe Cone was the principal writer in my office at Oregon State University. He was deeply involved in environmental issues. He would bring a much-needed skill set to the film. It was Joe's suggestion that we use the footage we had of Mount Kilauea in Hawaii erupting. This dynamic footage, which we had taken both from a helicopter and from the rim of the volcano, would give him the opportunity to introduce the concept of global warming and the role of carbon dioxide and the so-called "greenhouse gases."

Luckily the footage Elaine and I had shot for a previous film of the volcano erupting was dynamic and contained ample evidence of volcanic gases, including carbon dioxide and sulfur dioxide being released into the air.

Sitting beside me at the editing machine in our house, Joe began helping to shape the film. "Once we establish the existence of carbon dioxide in the early atmosphere, we can transition to the role plant life has played in consuming and sequestering it." Joe wanted to show how algae captured carbon dioxide and sequestered it in the form of carbonate mounds known as stromatolites.

We then agreed to show coral reefs so that Joe could say, "Life still actively withdraws carbon dioxide from the atmosphere." Coral reefs are essentially made of carbonate. We would then go on to show that the forests of the world also withdraw carbon dioxide from the atmosphere and convert it to sugar, all the while expelling oxygen, which of course, all animals depend upon.

The film began to take shape as Elaine, Joe, and I started pulling together the essential elements that fall. The oceans play a key—but as yet not fully understood—role on Earth acting as if they were a flywheel, moderating the climate. Joe lobbied for showing state-of-the-art research being done at the University of Washington, where scientists were concentrating on ocean plankton and its role in rain cloud formation.

We all knew that by the end of this film, we would need to turn the narration around and ask about the role humans are playing, and should be playing, in preserving the health of global ecosystems. Joe wanted to make a specific endorsement of university-based research. We need, he would argue, to continue expanding our understanding of life on Earth through this research. Our survival would depend upon how well we understand the Earth's ecosystems.

16

OLD GROWTH

Living in the Northwest, Elaine and I became acutely aware of the intensive logging operations occurring all around us; you really couldn't miss it. Every time we drove anywhere in the western half of Oregon, Washington, or northern California, we were met by massive clear-cut scars and forty-ton log trucks flying down the roads headed to sawmills.

The forests were falling so fast we could no longer ignore the obvious; the problem of deforestation was not confined to the Amazon. On one of our many trips back to the National Geographic Society during the postproduction process for *The Living Earth*, I looked out of the window of the United flight as we flew over the Cascades in Washington state and could see nothing but clear-cuts below us stretching in all directions.

The second film in this new NGS environmental series was going to highlight forest management practices and the loss of the so-called ancient forests of the Pacific Northwest. Elaine and I wanted to let our audience experience an intact forest system: the eagles, bears, elk, fish, and clean water. We wanted the audience to come away with a bold yet intimate view of an intact ancient forest.

North America's temperate rainforests stretch from the redwoods of Northern California to the Douglas fir forests of Oregon and Washington, to the Sitka spruce and hemlock forests of British Columbia and Alaska. Pretty much across their range, the federal government was doing a bad job of managing those forests.

Over the centuries of western expansion, 90 percent of the original forests had already been cut. This loss was bad for everyone. Even current logging operations were only marginally profitable in the lower forty-eight states precisely because all the old growth had already been cut. Not surprising, the second-growth forests were smaller, hence less profitable. Most of the sawmills had closed, at last count about fifty of them in our area alone. Most of the loggers were either out of work or had moved on to other ways of making a living.

Increasingly, the big logging companies were shifting their operations to the temperate rainforests of Alaska, where there were still virgin, old-growth forests to be cut. I wanted this second film in the series to speak about these logging pressures, and I wanted to motivate people to stand up for such forests. I was planning to film in several locations from Northern California to Alaska, with the majority of the film being shot in the area around Juneau and Ketchikan.

Once again I hired Joe Cone, and the two of us spent nearly a year in the university library reading everything we could find on the history of logging. We found that the US Forest Service, as it was reshaped by Reagan and Watt, seemed happy to provide the logging companies with what they asked for. Politicians provided the money to subsidize the harvest with a massive network of publicly paid-for roads. The new Forest Service was influenced by recent graduates of the state universities of Oregon and Washington, where they were teaching foresters how to manage forests by using clear-cuts and intensive replanting efforts. These practices had the effect of replacing complex, intact ecosystems with sterile, replanted monocultures. They would call these stands "working forests," but they were little more than an agricultural crop masquerading as forests. The Forest Service's broader mission, to maintain and ensure the integrity and sustainability of the national forests, was almost completely replaced with policies that undermined the forest ecosystem itself.

As part of our research for this film, I flew to Ketchikan to meet Jack Gustafson, a habitat biologist with the Alaska Department of Fish and Game. As I was coming in on final approach to the town's small airport, I noticed busy oceangoing tugs pulling giant floating log booms toward town. I also couldn't miss the enormous piles of logs surrounding lumberyards and Ketchikan's massive pulp mills or the pickup trucks with rough-looking men and high-powered rifles zooming around town.

The town was so small that I walked from the airport to Main Street. When I found the building I had been looking for, I scanned the directory on the wall inside the front door, then headed for the second floor. Jack's office was inconspicuous, piled high with reports, journals, and books. My first impression was that he had too many responsibilities and too little time. He came across as a gentle, self-assured fellow, wearing a red flannel shirt, hiking boots, and jeans. He had a quiet, easy way about him that said, "I've known and liked you all of my life."

I wondered how Jack managed to live in this town. It didn't look like a good fit. Ketchikan was built around one short road carved out of dense Sitka spruce forest and squeezed into a strip no more than a couple of blocks wide and a mile long. Most everyone who lived in Ketchikan lived off Alaska's natural resources. Fishermen netted the North Pacific and tied up at processing plants in Ketchikan. Loggers cut their way along the fingers of the Inside Passage and floated their logs back to the Ketchikan mills. Sportsmen who flocked from the lower forty-eight states to the rich Alaskan wilderness to capture salmon and to shoot bear, moose, and Sitka black-tailed deer used Ketchikan as a jumping-off point. Jack worked to address fish and wildlife habitat concerns for Alaska's southeast region.

"Tell me what you need," he said. I described our goals for the ancient forest film. Jack took me to his workroom, and right from the beginning I could see why it had that name. Maps were spread out on every flat surface. The walls were covered with more of the same. There were a few small close-up photos of bear and deer on the walls sandwiched in between satellite imagery.

"The Tongass is the largest track of public land in the United States," he began. "It is blanketed in a mixture of Sitka spruce and hemlock. This forest has never been cut, but that is about to change. The logging industry has shifted its focus to southeast Alaska, on both Forest Service and Native-owned lands."

Jack continued. "Cutting these forests is going to have an enormous impact on the wildlife that live here. As a result, all the hunters and fishermen, all the tourists, and all the businesses that depend on them are going to be severely impacted. I'm not sure you will be able to recognize this part of Alaska fifty years from now," he added.

"That is exactly why I'm here," I interjected. "I really have two things to do. First, we need to find the most pristine old-growth wilderness area to portray the natural side and the diversity that exists there. Then we need to shift gears and film what logging looks like to include clearcuts, the pulp mills—that sort of thing."

"Well, then you really need to meet my wife. She's unique," Jack said. That was an understatement. On the way up the hill behind his office, Jack explained. "Jackie works for the US Forest Service."

My guard went up immediately, because while the US Forest Service may have been created in 1905 by Gifford Pinchot to protect public forest land, it had been severely compromised over the years.

When I walked into the Gustafson home, I was wondering how a woman who worked for the Forest Service was going to help me with a film about the benefits of old-growth forests. But Jackie was not your ordinary US Forest Service harvest facilitator. Instead, she was a leader in the Forest Service Employees for Environmental Ethics (FSEEE), a group of people within the agency who believed in ecological, sustainable management and environmental ethics.

Jackie was delightful, a little over five feet tall, one hundred pounds, and full of fight. She swept into the room, extended her hand, and said, "You're welcome in our home any time." She didn't sit down but offered me a seat and then sprang around the room, doing two or three things at once. She continued our conversation as if that was the only thing on her mind.

"We're not all that popular in Ketchikan," Jackie admitted. "But I believe our views are consistent with national interests in America. To the people in Ketchikan, we may appear to be environmentalists, but we're not. We are not against all logging. But harvest rates need to be directly tied to the growth rates of trees. If you harvest trees faster than they will grow back, you will lose the forest ecosystems that we all depend on."

Jack pulled out a map of the lower Tongass forest and, with a weathered hand, pointed at a large island not far from where we were standing. "This is Prince of Wales Island," he began. "Right here is a little-known virgin track of old-growth forest called Honker Divide."

Jackie jumped in, "Honker is an untracked wilderness sitting in the middle of the most pristine expanse of Sitka spruce and hemlock in the lower panhandle. It would be an ideal place for you to go if you want to film virgin, undisturbed rainforest."

Jackie continued, "The Tongass is one of the most beautiful, but it is also one of the most threatened in Alaska, so you will have to hurry. The logging companies may even reach the Honker before your filming is done. I think you should go into an old trapper's cabin on the Honker. It is old, but it could provide you with a base of operations . . . a way of staying dry while you film." She turned to Jack and asked, "What do you think, Jack?"

Jack turned the map around so I could see it, then pointed at a spot midway between Hatchery Creek and the Thorne Bay. "The cabin is located right here, at the base of a small open pool, just before you hit a small waterfall. This spot is ideal for several reasons. First, it hasn't been cut; second, salmon concentrate under the falls; and third, the concentrations of salmon attract bears. You could get footage of the forest, the river, the salmon, and the black bears all in one spot."

Jackie disappeared into the kitchen, coming back a minute later with a piping-hot pizza. Later, she returned with five containers of Ben & Jerry's ice cream. She had three spoons and as many bowls. We each ate more than we should have, then Jackie took the empties back to the kitchen. She returned a moment later with a toothbrush in her mouth. She was walking, talking, and brushing all at the same time. "I hope you get what you want from Honker. Anything we can do to help, just call."

Both Jack and Jackie, as it turned out, were up to their eyeballs in a political fight to spare Honker from the chainsaw. They were leading a political battle, the kind that few of us have the energy to fight and almost never win. The problem for environmentalists is that you can win the fight for years, as Jack and Jackie had with the Honker Divide, but lose it once and you've lost it permanently.

We had a film location and, more important, a role to play in the broader environmental struggle to save the Tongass. I saw it as my job to nationally publicize the unique environmental qualities of the Tongass and to demonstrate why it should be preserved.

All the way home that night, I thought about our sons, now twelve and nine years old. They were worldly beyond their years. They were good swimmers, loved camping and fishing. In some ways, Alaska would be a great place for them to grow, and this would be the best time to introduce them to an ancient forest. As my plane skimmed over Puget Sound, headed to Sea-Tac Airport, I became increasingly excited about what this trip might mean to us as a family.

Elaine met me at the Portland airport. On the drive home, I told her about my meeting with Jack and Jackie. And then I asked her if this wasn't the time to take the next important step in our development as a family. "This could be a great experience. John and Ted are ready for their first big wilderness trip."

"I can't tell you how happy that would make me!" Her excitement showed. "They'll love all the fishing opportunities." I watched as she began to wrap her head around the idea of taking our sons with us on such a long wilderness trip. A broad grin spread across her face. Elaine began listing the benefits.

Eventually, I interrupted her by saying. "We're going to have to find someone to come with us to watch over them while we are out filming. Whomever we chose, that person will have to be comfortable with bears being all around and be proficient with a gun for self-protection. They'll have to be a positive force in our kids' lives because they will be with them for days on end."

"Well, we're going to have to think about that," Elaine said.

"Just don't take too long. We need to leave inside of six weeks, and that person will need some time to prepare."

Eventually we settled on a friend with children of his own, a US Marine and a teacher whom Elaine and I had known for more than a decade. Rob Schulze was a good choice because he was familiar with outdoor living, had weapons training, and loved to fish and hunt elk. He was on summer break from his teaching job and was extremely excited about the offer.

When I asked him if he would be interested, he said, "Are you kidding me? Alaska? Oorah!"

With Rob on board, I began assembling a small mountain of cameras and wilderness survival gear. Elaine and I drove up to the Seattle REI outlet and bought two identical Old Town canoes, exactly the same model we had used so many years before on Timagami. By June, we were ready and caught the Alaskan ferry up the Inside Passage to Ketchikan. The canoes were strapped side by side on top of the four-wheel-drive Suburban. From there, we transferred to a smaller ferry to take us out to Prince of Wales Island.

We were in the field again and it felt good. The boys were so excited they just couldn't stop talking about all the things they were going to see and do in Alaska.

––––––––––

From the moment we drove off the ferry ramp and onto Prince of Wales Island, I could see why Jackie had suggested we hurry. Most of the southern end of the island had already been clear-cut and looked like a nuclear bomb had just detonated over the island. Log trucks the size of small houses rumbled this way and that down the dirt roads, throwing up blinding dust as they roared by. There was a sense of urgency in the air, driven by the profits to be made. Elaine and I had never seen such mass environmental destruction in our lives. We were heartsick.

Early on the second morning, and without much warning, we drove around a corner in the road and found ourselves in the middle of a huge log yard piled thirty feet high with freshly cut trees. The smell of tree sap and wood chips was overwhelming. A machine with a claw the size of an eighteen-wheeler rumbled by, scooped up an entire truckload of logs and, just as rapidly, roared in the opposite direction toward a pile of logs. There must have been twenty thousand dead trees lying on the ground that day.

We were spiritually depressed by the wholesale destruction of one of the last bastions of natural forest in North America. The only thing that would heal the emotional damage done to us was a heavy dose of wilderness. "It's time we head to the Honker Divide," Elaine said. I turned north.

It was a long trip. We bounced over unimproved dirt roads for most of a day, our diesel-powered gray Suburban packed to the ceiling, the four-wheel-drive option locked on, the two canoes lashed above, cutting through the marine air. Elaine kept her eyes on the map while I steered between bottomless holes in the roadbed. Ted and John bounced around in the back seat, all the while chatting about all the fishing possibilities. Rob stared out the window, awestruck.

"The Thorne River crossing should be just around the next corner," Elaine announced. As I came out of a gentle turn, there was an older bridge covered in road dust spanning Goose Creek. Below, tannin-stained water flowed toward the Thorne River. There wasn't much water running under the bridge, just enough to float our canoes. I angled off the road and ground to a halt on the flattest part of the shoulder I could find.

Before I could turn the engine off, the boys sprang to life. "Is this the river? Can I get out my fishing pole? What fly should I use, dry or wet? What kind of trout will I catch? Are there salmon in this river? Where are my boots?"

I rolled my eyes and turned to Elaine for help. "Actually, boys," Elaine said, "That would be a great idea. Why don't you see if you can catch dinner while we get these canoes in the water? Stay within our sight."

"That was a good choice," Rob grinned.

"As if we had a choice," Elaine shot back.

Elaine, Rob, and I began the tedious job of transferring four hundred pounds of gear from the back of the Suburban to the two canoes. For the next four or five weeks, we would have to live with what we were carrying with us. There would be no electricity to charge camera batteries, no medical help, and no radio contact. Careful planning was essential. If I didn't specifically plan for every contingency, I would come to regret the oversight. The canoes would have to hold enough freeze-dried food, film, and fuel to last at least a month. We could catch fish to stretch our supplies to last six weeks. Next, we loaded the tents, sleeping bags, dishes, stoves, water pumps, and clothes. Then the extra paddles, life jackets, rope, cameras, lenses, tape recorders, microphones, and fifty rolls of movie film. It would be a tight fit, but everything had to go into waterproof bags in the two seventeen-foot Old Towns.

I had prepared for the worst. I expected that we would arrive on location to find the ground wet. It would be raining when we set up tents, raining when we cooked food, and raining when we shot film. Everything had to be planned to account for vertical curtains of water. Most important, tents had to stay dry—the cameras could never get wet. There had to be some way of drying our clothing. How do you keep dry when you are in the middle of weeks of nonstop rain?

Most of our backcountry gear was designed for climbing mountains and was made of breathable fabrics, but as anyone who has tried living in such rain gear can attest, it doesn't work all that well against heavy rain. Eventually the seams will leak and the pores will plug with dirt and sweat. For this trip, we'd have to use Helly Hansen rain gear, the kind preferred by fishermen. It was the only way to stay dry when conditions were unforgiving. Underneath the rubber, we wore fleece underwear to wick perspiration away from our skin. Body heat would keep the underwear dry and comfortable.

We had purchased full rain suits for everyone; hooded coats, storm bibs, hats, and boots. I had asked a seamstress in Oregon to design and sew a rain jacket for the camera.

Alaskan wildlife photographer John Hyde had advised me that there was no way of keeping dry in a tent for months on end unless you kept the tent itself dry. This young man had once been a student of mine at the university and was now the very best wildlife photographer I had ever known. He had lived in the bush on and off for years.

John showed me his technique for pitching tents inside a water-free zone. We first stretched a waterproof tarp above the camp area to keep the rain off our campsite while we pitched our tent. We then stretched out another waterproof and dry tarp on the ground beneath the overhead tarp, to seal ourselves away from the wet soil. We then removed our boots and pitched our tents, the ones that don't use stakes, in the water-free zone between the tarps. Finally, Elaine bound the two tarps together at the edges to keep out any wind-blown, horizontal rainwater. When entering one of the tents, we first removed our rain gear and left it hanging outside under the overhead tarp. Nothing wet was ever allowed inside a tent.

The system worked amazingly well. No rain could reach the tent walls, and no ground water could seep from below. Best of all, the tents could still breathe as they were designed.

Dehydrated or freeze-dried food was to be carried in a plastic dry box. We would be working in the middle of bear country, so the food would have to be as scentless as possible. Everything that smelled like food would be slung between two trees at night, out of a bear's reach.

Once loaded, the canoes sat deep in the water. They were still within their design capacity but drew several inches of water. I worried that we might find some stretches of river too shallow to float the canoes, and dragging or lifting them around such places would be a real struggle.

"Boys, let's go," Elaine called out. Neither had caught anything, so they were eager to move on to more productive water upstream.

Elaine and I agreed that we wanted our sons to experience the natural world on its own terms. If we were going to go off into the wilderness on a canoe trip, the boys were going to need some basic canoe-handling skills. We had spent time back in Oregon introducing our boys to the canoes and had managed to show them what it would be like if a canoe overturned in fast water. For this trip, John was assigned the bow of my lead canoe. Elaine took the stern of the second canoe and Rob took its bow. Ted sat in the middle of the second canoe, unhappy about being forced to sit in the middle. I steadied my canoe and sent John scurrying over the top of the heavy load, his hands and feet on the gunwales in a crab walk. Then I stepped into the canoe and pushed off.

We were going to canoe through white water, but we would be paddling upstream for the first two days. There would be no coasting, no taking it easy. If you stopped paddling, your canoe would be caught by the current and washed back downriver. From the moment the canoes hit the water, everyone was going to have to struggle for every foot of forward progress. Luckily the Thorne River wasn't very high. The water was moving slowly that day. Nevertheless, it was hard work.

I didn't know if John could keep up his end of the canoe, but there really was only one way to find out. Two hours into the trip, everyone had the answer. The lead canoe was doing quite well. It was at least a hundred yards out in front.

The scenery was spectacular. Bald eagles perched around every corner. They were watching for trout or salmon that might come close to the surface. When they saw one, the eagles would drop down, scoop the fish up in their talons, and fly back to their nests to feed their young. There was also the occasional osprey. The river was teeming with fish. This wilderness was unlike anything I had seen before. Usually the natural world is diverse; wildlife is spread out. You rarely find great concentrations of any one species. Alaska was different. Here, the eagles, like everything else, had come to the river for the salmon.

Salmon runs represent one of the easiest and richest meals in nature. Every summer, millions of chum, pink, sockeye, king, and coho flood up these Alaskan streams. The salmon and steelhead trout live most of their lives at sea, where they grow fat. When they return to the streams in which they were hatched, they bring with them all the fat they accumulated at sea. The result is a tremendous loading of each stream with nutrients and protein. Once in the streams, salmon are vulnerable to all kinds of predators, including black bears and brown/grizzly bears, eagles, wolves, and even other fish. All these predators converge on the streams to feed on the salmon and steelhead. After the salmon spawn they promptly die, littering the riverbanks with their bodies.

The old trapper's cabin we were searching for was about ten miles up the river. It was known as the Hanson cabin because it had been built in the early 1900s by Jim Hanson. Jack Gustafson thought he'd better share the official state records on the cabin with me because the cabin was the site of what some claim to be the first documented North American wolf attack on a human being.

I had read it carefully . . .

According to the report, the tragedy had occurred in the winter of 1939 to a seasoned trapper by the name of Crist Kolby. He had been alone in the wilderness, as almost all trappers are, using the cabin as his base of operation. The attack occurred in the winter when food was scarce and wolves were desperate. According to the documents, Kolby carried a 357-magnum revolver for protection but otherwise roamed pretty much at will up and down the river tending his trap line. Kolby's plan was to spend February and March trapping, then to canoe downriver as soon as the weather broke and the ice melted.

Come spring, Kolby hadn't shown up in town as expected. The state commissioner eventually sent a search party, headed by W. R. Selfridge, upriver to investigate the disappearance. The Selfridge report was published in *The Alaska Book* (Chicago: J. G. Ferguson, 1960). It describes how investigators found Kolby's remains near the cabin, and in the remains, a .357 revolver. At first, they were puzzled how an experienced trapper could have let a pack of wolves get the better of him when he was armed. But on closer examination, they found that the revolver's mainspring was broken and the gun was useless to the cornered man.

From the report:

> We all left camp at eight the next morning—November 6th— and reached the fatal spot at about 10:30. Before our eyes lay mute evidence of the quick and dramatic death of a brave but unlucky man. From the scattered clothing and bones, we could easily reconstruct the scene which had taken place that day in early March.
>
> Crist was returning to his cabin, traveling on the ice of Thorne Lake. He knew his revolver was out of commission. Suddenly the wolves appeared. And Crist figured that, without his gun, his only hope was to run to the woods and climb the nearest tree.
>
> He threw down his knapsack on the ice, and made for the woods. But the wolves were too close. One met him at the edge of the ice, and seized his coat by the right shoulder. Crist struck at the murderous beast with his skinning knife, but lost the knife in the struggle. Somehow, too, his coat and the wristband of his shirt were torn off [and fell to the ground] right there.

Desperately, Crist ran for two trees about fifty feet [away]. If he could only make it! Just under the first tree, one wolf caught him this time its fierce fangs found their mark. . . .

We stood for some time as if watching the helpless man while that bloody drama was re-enacted before our eyes. . . . I thought of the panic, the desperate struggle, and the anguish of those few moments before a human soul was sent too soon to its maker.

The Selfridge report lays down in black and white a very rare event, a time when a wolf actually may have been responsible for the death of a human being. Rare or not, this sort of story has come to define Alaska.

While wolf attacks are exceedingly rare, bear attacks are not, and we were throwing ourselves directly into the middle of bear country. Taking no chances, we were well armed. I had checked and cleaned each of our guns one last time before leaving Oregon. A gun was located in each of the two canoes. I had a .357 revolver in a shoulder holster, and Rob had a 12-gauge shotgun standing vertically in front of him in his canoe.

"This will be a tricky landing," I warned John. I'll bring the bow in right behind that big old log." I pointed with my paddle. "Be ready to jump out with the bowline in hand. Don't worry about the canoe, just hold on to the rope and make sure you're ready for the pull of the canoe as it comes around in the current. Don't let it pull you back into the river."

"OK, when do I stop paddling?"

"Give me one reverse sweep and then stow your paddle . . . now!"

Two days in a canoe and John was already proficient. Like an expert, he jumped out of the canoe and braced himself against the line, waiting for the heavy current to pull the canoe downstream. With the bowline held taut, the canoe simply swung around and came in broadside to the shore. I climbed out, took the line from John, and tied it off around the nearest tree.

John went to help his mother bring in the second canoe. Rob threw him the bowline, and John pulled the canoe in.

The cabin was everything Jack and Jackie had said it would be, tiny, half buried in the ground, and covered with thick, green moss.

There was just barely enough headroom in the cabin to stand up in the middle. The A-frame roof rose to a little over six feet in the center but came down nearly to my waist on both sides. The builder must have wanted to conserve heat in winter. There was one tiny window low to the ground. The door rose only to about four and a half feet and was equipped with an ingenious, handmade wood locking system.

"Someone had a lot of time to dream this up," I remarked.

Opening the door, I was careful not to stick myself with one of the two hundred or more rusty nails that protruded outward, having been driven through from the inside. The nails were there to discourage bears from trying to force their way into the cabin.

Inside, the cabin looked as if Crist Kolby had just walked out the door. There was a small bed covered with dry grass, a wood stove, and a bench in front of the window. A few photographs of family members were on a shelf. The inside of the cabin couldn't have been any bigger than the smallest bathroom in our Oregon home. The floor was dirt, and I was struck by how dry everything was despite all the rain outside. Many of the dishes and tools dated back to the turn of the century. On a shelf above the bench there were a number of useful items, including a bottle of scotch and a mason jar filled with stick matches that were swimming in kerosene to keep out water.

The cabin was obviously built and used by one person. There was one plate, one cup, and one incomplete set of silverware. The cabin looked as if its owner had departed in a hurry. A stack of wood outside the cabin door was grown over with about a foot of rich green moss. "You know, I don't think anyone has visited this cabin in years . . . maybe not for a decade," I observed.

Mice were everywhere. Every corner, every pot and pan, and even the stove itself, had small nests of grass in them. There were more than a few blind baby mice in each of the nests. In fact, if you stopped for a moment and were very quiet, everything inside the entire cabin appeared to move. There were little scurrying sounds coming from every corner.

Elaine took one look and said, "I hope you didn't have any plans for us to sleep in here?" At first, I thought she was referring to the zoologic activity, but I was wrong. "I doubt we'd be able to fit more than one very small person in that bed" she continued.

"I'll bet we would have difficulty getting a volunteer to sleep in here with all the wildlife." I was right. The tents, even without the wood stove, were preferable to the piles of tiny mouse droppings.

But the cabin did have its uses. Once thoroughly cleaned and the mice cordially invited to find homes elsewhere, it became our drying hut. In the evening, when everyone returned from a day's work or play, we typically hung our wet clothes in the cabin and built a small fire in the stove. The counter space was given over to the camera equipment; when not otherwise in use, the cameras kept dry in the cabin.

It was apparent, right from the beginning, that Hanson had constructed his cabin with bears in mind. The nails in the door, the tiny windows. . . . I wondered just how much bear activity we could expect.

It turned out that we couldn't have picked a better spot to photograph bears, because Hanson had built his cabin on one of the island's most productive salmon rivers. In the summer, when salmon run up the river, bear congregate at the waterfall, where the food is most plentiful.

Logic dictates that you should avoid the areas where bears concentrate, because all bears are dangerous. If the bears are all down by the stream feeding, you should put your camp up in the hills. But wildlife photographers can't always do the safest thing. By choosing to use the old trapper's cabin as a drying hut and by putting our tents on the only flat dry spot near the doorway of that cabin, we were knowingly placing ourselves in the center of bear activity. Especially at night, bears were accustomed to walking along the riverbank, fishing. You just couldn't miss the well-worn trail and the piles of scat right in front of the cabin door. Some of the tracks in the mud were seven inches long—a clear sign of some very large bears.

The trick would be to get the bears to stop using their traditional trail, at least while the tents were pitched at the cabin site. It didn't sound like a big problem, but it turned out to be more complicated. That first night around the camp stove, I asked for ideas. "How do we keep the bears from walking through camp every night?"

The boys instantly had ideas. "Why don't we string a line across the trail and hang our pots and pans on the string?" John asked. "When the bear comes down the trail, he'll run into the string, and the pots and pans will bang together."

"That's a good idea," Elaine replied. "The important thing is to warn the bear that we're here so that no one is surprised, the bear or one of us."

I suggested we also use urine to "mark our territory." It was a technique used by almost all predators. "Maybe the bears will honor our scent posts, just as they would their own."

Everyone stayed awake as best they could that first night, listening and waiting for the bear to come. At a little past eleven, a big one showed up. The bear could be heard ambling down the trail perhaps fifty yards away. It was making no effort to be quiet. The wind was blowing up the river, so the bear was probably unaware that he was heading for a new campsite. Suddenly, he reached the pots and pans and our scent posts. The bear stopped in its tracks. There was a long period of silence followed by a low grunt.

Inside our tent, Ted's eyes jumped around with excitement. He giggled and covered his mouth with a hand so that the bear wouldn't hear him. We all waited for the first sign that the pots and pans had worked. I couldn't resist it any longer. I turned on my headlamp and poked my head out the tent flap, scanning downriver for any sign of the bear. At first, I saw nothing, just black. Then slowly, two bright shiny discs blinked back at me. My headlamp was reflecting back from the eyes of a big black bear.

A long minute passed. Abruptly, the bear turned toward the woods and slowly circled the camp, rejoining the trail on the other side of the cabin.

The idea had worked perfectly, so the boys had a job: each night after dinner for the next week, they would go out on their rounds, hanging the pots and pans and freshening the scent boundaries, just to make sure that the bear knew that we were still using a portion of her territory.

In the beginning, the bear honored the scent boundary, each night skirting the camp, giving her human neighbors plenty of room. After a week or so, she became bold and began walking past the scent posts, until one night she came to the very edge of the camp. In the morning, I found the bear's footprints in the mud less than ten feet from the tents. I was afraid a confrontation could not be put off much longer.

The next night, while everyone in the camp was sleeping, the big old mother bear walked up to the scent post, paid no attention, broke down the trip wire with all the pots and pans, and walked right into the middle of the camp. She was a big bear. I knew we had a problem when one of the bear's front feet softly landed on the ground just outside the thin nylon wall of the first tent, less than two feet from my head.

There was no doubt in my mind what the sound had been. There was a tent wall separating me from the bear, but it offered no protection. Both the bear and I could hear each other breathing.

Gently, so as not to startle her, I slid Elaine's head off my shoulder. Normally she would have just rolled over and continued sleeping, but this time she sensed my tension and came fully awake. I held her mouth so that she would not speak. The bear grunted very lightly, then slapped our water container with one of its forepaws. The container flew across the camp and struck the cabin with a loud bang.

Slowly, I reached for the sawed-off twelve-gauge shotgun that I kept along my right side, within easy reach. It was loaded with alternating rounds of buckshot and magnum slugs, a lethal combination for any animal. Yet so were a bear's claws. I kept the gun loaded, but for safety's sake, the chamber was empty. It was the trigger assembly that I felt first, but the gun was pointed down, toward my feet, while the bear was behind me near my head.

The bear snorted, sniffing the air. She could undoubtedly sense the humans inside the tent, moving around. I left the shotgun for a moment, pulled a pistol flare gun out of my day pack, and handed it to Elaine. With hand signals, I told her to wait for the count of three and then to fire the flare through the tent doorway toward the old trapper's cabin. I hoped the flare would bounce off the door and light up the area. If nothing else, the flare should startle the bear and maybe cause it to leave. At least it would give me some light so I would see the bear more clearly should I have to shoot it.

I picked up the shotgun and slowly rose into a crouching position. Ever so slowly, I edged toward the door. Luckily the tent was equipped with a plastic zipper on the mosquito netting, which made no noise when I eased it up and around, leaving an open doorway and just enough ambient light to see Elaine beside me.

I raised my left hand, showing Elaine a countdown. Rhythmically, I raised one finger, then a second, and finally a third finger. Elaine pulled the trigger.

The projectile roared out the tent door barely missing my shoulder, smashed into the side of the cabin, and bounced between the bear's legs, illuminating the entire camp with a brilliant red glow.

As soon as the flare cleared the tent door, I jumped out, hitting the ground on my feet, knees bent, back straight, and head up. I was well balanced but not sure what to expect. The shotgun was in a defensive position across my chest. I slammed a round into the chamber, and let out a war whoop to startle the bear. Maybe not a good idea, but I wasn't thinking all that clearly.

Luckily, the tactic worked—the bear was surprised. Before the scream settled in the trees, she bolted across the camp, crashed into the river, and half-swam, half-ran to the other side.

Ted woke up, stuck his head out our tent door to hear the last half of my scream. There was a brilliant but eerie red light bathing everything within a hundred feet, casting my bigger-than-life shadow against the wall of the cabin. Through the doorway, the boys could probably see my figure crouched in a no-nonsense position, cradling the shotgun. Only then did I realize that I was completely naked. Ted started laughing at me.

17

ANCIENT FORESTS

JUST AFTER DAWN THE NEXT MORNING, Elaine and I rose, fed the boys, left them and the shotgun in Rob's capable hands, and headed upstream.

Elaine and I had long wanted to immerse ourselves in an ancient forest. Now we had our chance. We soon found ourselves surrounded by the majestic, ancient primeval rainforest of North America, smelling hemlock all the while bathed in the cool, damp mist that shrouds these trees and drips from every branch. I wanted to carefully expose myself and my film to the great beauty that hides in the dim light of an old-growth forest.

We grew quiet for a moment, because the ancient forest demanded it. We let the forest wash over and invade our spirit. An impossibly old tree lay in repose at our feet, blocking the path. Before it came to rest here, it must have stood in this forest, a giant, for six hundred years, leaning into the forces that would ultimately tear it down—the winds and the heavy snows—resisting everything that Alaska could throw its way. This tree beat the odds for a long time, and then it could resist no longer.

Not even death could strip this tree of its majesty. Perhaps four feet and a few inches in diameter, probably 150 feet tall when it stood in the forest—now it was covered in heavy, green moss, looking as if it were draped with a thick fur cape. My head kept telling me this tree was dead, but my eyes kept telling me it was not. Perhaps an old tree has no less important a life after death. Certainly, the hundreds of little trees that grew from the old battered trunk, the millions of carpenter ants that slowly broke the tree into tiny morsels, the colorful red lichen that sent roots deep into the tree's core, were all living proof of life.

We worked our way upstream through the dense forest, stopping frequently to shoot film. It didn't take long to find what we were looking for. At the base of a small waterfall there were a number of shallow pools, each full of salmon. The waterfall wasn't an impassable barrier to the salmon migration, but it did slow the fish down, which was all a bear would need. It was clear that bears were using the pools; the ground was covered with dung, tracks, and broken vegetation. The thick smell of bear urine was heavy in the air.

I wanted to place the camera close to the action while being careful not to interfere with the feeding process. I chose a heavy berry bush on a small island in the middle of the stream, chopped a tunnel into the middle of the bush, and cleared a spot about eight feet in diameter. I set up our blind in that tiny clearing. The island was getting heavy use. In fact, bears were snacking on the berries in between salmon dinners.

The wind was consistently blowing downriver, so the blind was probably going to be hard for the bears to find. We settled in for the rest of the day, but we didn't have to wait long. Within an hour, a big old sow came out of the trees directly across the river from our blind and stood on a broken log, scanning the forest for anything out of the ordinary. The blind was well hidden, and the bear didn't notice it. The bear turned around and "spoke" to something behind her, and in an instant, an identical pair of black fur balls tumbled out of the forest. I began rolling film.

The cubs, born during the sow's winter hibernation, were tiny. The three bears were a study in contrasts. While the old sow stood guard, watching everything around, the cubs just played. They attacked each other, dove, rolled, and bounced. They chewed on a branch and swatted a mushroom through the air. The Arriflex camera was blimped, but silenced or not, the sow heard the camera and made a low *woof* sound. The two cubs did as they were told and scampered up the nearest tree.

The sow wasn't sure what she'd heard or from which direction the sound had come, so she waited. The cubs were still arguing about something even while up the tree, so she made another grunting sound and the two cubs instantly stopped fooling around. The sow listened carefully, but nothing seemed out of place. She looked directly at the blind and the camera lens, staring for a full minute. I tried not to move a muscle. We were well camouflaged, but movement was always a dead giveaway.

After another full minute the cubs, tired of hiding, jumped down from their perch in the tree and started chasing each other around. The sow finally tired, too, and let her young go on with their games. She climbed down the embankment and began fishing. She walked up to the side of the river, spotted a salmon in shallow water, slapped it silly with a mighty blow from her clawed paw, and then bit the fish just behind the head, severing the spinal cord. The attack was over in an instant.

Without ceremony, the three bears turned and disappeared into the forest carrying their four-pound dinner. I had a spectacular shot.

———————

Elaine and I practically lived in the blind for the next few weeks. Each morning before light, we climbed in carrying enough food and water for the entire day. We took turns watching for bear, staying at our post until dark.

On the second day of filming, we discovered the disadvantage of putting a blind so close to the action. A cinnamon boar bear came out of the woods, walked down to the river, and instead of stopping to fish from the far bank as all the other bears had done, he simply waded across the river, then climbed up on the island fifteen feet from our blind. Luckily, the wind was still flowing downriver with the water, so our human scent did not give away our position. I kept the camera focused on the young bear, cranking through a half roll.

As the bear continued to move toward us, the palms of my hands began to sweat. Soon, the bear walked inside the minimum focusing distance for my lens, which was a little less than ten feet. I couldn't risk changing the lens, so I was helpless. I couldn't risk breathing loudly. The bear probably weighed two hundred pounds, maybe a bit more. If it were to suddenly realize that humans were less than ten feet away, it might very well attack out of fright. Armed or not, the outcome of such an encounter would not have favored the weakling humans on that island.

Using the .357 magnum was the very last thing I wanted to do. I often carried the weapon when in close proximity to predators but had never felt the need to draw, much less use it. In fact, I'm not even sure what it would take to get me to use a lethal weapon against an animal I was photographing. It was a question I hoped never to have to answer. Elaine carried a can of pepper spray—an especially strong formula created just for bears in Alaska—which was our first line of defense. But I admit to not being terribly confident that a pepper spray would change the mind of a charging bear.

We waited.

I didn't dare turn around to see how Elaine was doing, but I could hear her rapid, shallow breathing behind me. The throbbing blood passing through my temples seemed louder than the river. The bear continued to move closer but remained unaware of our presence. Soon, I could see his individual hairs and a couple of salmon eggs stuck to his muzzle. When the bear got to within about four feet of our blind, he lifted his nose and sniffed the air, then ever so slowly turned his massive head and looked directly at me. I froze, not wanting to move or even breathe. For two minutes, we just looked at each other, separated by nothing at all. The bear worked its jaw and nose, trying to determine what scent was in the air. I didn't move; he didn't move. I didn't dare blink.

The stalemate continued until the bear finally looked away, then walked upstream, never having discovered our hiding place. It finally caught and bit a sockeye in the neck, tore out its gills, and waded back to the forest on the other side of the river. As quickly as it had begun, the encounter was over. I had on film another dramatic moment.

After the bear left the area, Elaine asked, "Did you see all that blood on his face?"

"Fish blood," I reassured her.

"Let's go back to camp and check on the boys."

For the next several days we worked underwater at the small waterfall. I wore my dry suit. The Arriflex was inside a watertight housing. Salmon were everywhere—some bright silver, others dark red, and still others decomposing. I swam among them, quietly pushing my camera into dark corners. The water was stained slightly orange by the tannin juices of the forest. Most every fish that swam around me weighed about five pounds, had a hooked nose, and was showing signs of decay. Most of these would die of natural causes within a few days.

As I swam from one section of the falls to another, thousands of fish were in front of me, behind me, and even between my legs. I could not walk through the water without stepping on a fish, so I swam everywhere. As I worked my way through an especially large school of fish, I came in contact with a monofilament line stretching through the water. I attached my camera to a D-ring on my dive belt so that it would not float away, freeing my hands. I grabbed hold of the line. To my surprise, a six-pound salmon was on the other end. I stood up, lifted the salmon into the air and turned to my sons, "Would you like salmon for dinner?"

John and Ted had been using hooks and lines, trying and failing to catch one of these prize salmon all morning, so the idea that their father had caught one by hand while shooting film underwater was more than the boys could take.

"You've got to be kidding," Ted yelled.

I pulled my dive knife from its leg holster, and because the hook was far down the fish's gullet, cut the line just in front of the salmon's lip. The giant fish dropped into the water and disappeared. "It needs to spawn," I said.

John looked at me in utter disbelief. "You are never going to make a very good fisherman," John chided. "You're supposed to keep the big ones!"

———————

When we left Prince of Wales Island, I could see and hear the saws relentlessly moving in on the Honker Divide, and I knew if our film was going to have any impact on the outcome, we would have to hurry with the postproduction process. My goal was to finish this film as quickly as possible and to get it into the hands of people who might be able to make a difference in Southeast Alaska.

Within days of returning to Oregon, I began assembling and screening the raw footage. The key would be to set the stage early in the film. We would need to establish visually the role forests play in the water cycle of Earth. I wanted to describe the rainforest as a vital component of the broader Earth biological system. Joe Cone and I also wanted to highlight the role forests play in producing breathable oxygen. Forests produce most of the Earth's oxygen and consume a significant percentage of its carbon dioxide. In this way, life could be shown to be actively maintaining the conditions for life on Earth.

Donald liked the rough cut of *Ancient Forests* as much as Elaine and I did. He became our greatest advocate within the National Geographic staff. Sid also liked the visual elements of the rough cut but remained concerned about the strong narration. I had the momentum here, so I pressed on. In the end we persuaded Sid to permit the film's message and to promote it widely.

By the end of 1991, we were wrapping up one of the most beautiful films of our careers, and I finally knew I belonged among those few photographers who call the National Geographic Society home. This film captured in picture, music, and narration the essence of an ancient, primeval forest. I believed the film was both beautiful and moving.

The release of *Ancient Forests* also capped off our most significant contributions to the emerging scientific understanding of the Earth as a global ecosystem. *The Living Ocean, The Living Earth,* and now *Ancient Forests* together made a compelling case that life actively transforms and regulates its own environment.

Of course, when our film was released we began receiving blowback, not only from the logging industry but also from shadowy groups and individuals who support resource extraction and dispute science. But this time, the opposition was especially intense.

I still remember the first death threat. Elaine answered the house phone that night and listened. The boys picked up on Elaine's anxiety from her body language.

"What's going on?" Ted asked me, but I didn't know.

John pressed his mom for an answer, but she remained quiet. Elaine simply said, "Nothing is wrong. Just an idiot."

When I mentioned the death threat to Jack Gustafson, he told me that he personally has received many such threats. "In fact," he said, "I had to replace a picture window in our Ketchikan home because some coward put a bullet through it in an attempt to intimidate either me or Jackie."

I have always been surprised by the lengths some people will go to deny science or prevent scientists from reporting their findings. When *Ancient Forests* was released, a group of logging firms in the Northwest hired an outside lobbyist and spent heavily to fight our film's message. Simultaneously, this same lobbyist started pushing to have me fired from the university and also muzzled at the National Geographic Society.

Once again, President Byrne stood his ground and did the right thing. He argued that faculty members are not bound by political interests but are free to express their own ideas and to present their own research without fear of being fired. Universities, as we know them today, could not exist without such academic freedom. Because the lobbyist could not point to a single factual or scientific error in the film's narration, the matter never gained traction within the university. But the death threats continued.

At the National Geographic Society, Donald Cooper volunteered to write a letter that would push back on the lobbyist's demands. The truth is, Donald was a far more articulate, brilliant writer and thinker than the lobbyist. A copy of the letter and Donald's response ended up in the hands of the executives at the Geographic, who stood by us and our film.

Even though we could not save the entire Honker Divide—parts of it had already been cut—we did play a small role in saving the core of the watershed from the saws. Jack Gustafson later told me that our film helped to jolt the US Forest Service and convince it to stop issuing cutting permits in the Honker Divide. Instead, faced with intense pressure from environmental groups, they designated the remaining forests in the Divide as an old-growth reserve.

Our film was also distributed widely in the lower forty-eight states and went on to help build basic understanding of our role as human beings in the complex ecosystem of which we are a part. It may even have played some small role in slowing the logging industry's momentum in Southeast Alaska. Two years after its release, the Bill Clinton administration convened a massive conference to deal with the Tongass and other northwestern forest management. Growing public support for conservation of these forests drove the conference. After long deliberation, the Tongass was given protected status. Much of the forest was ruled off-limits to new road building, which meant that clear-cutting on Forest Service lands dramatically declined.

The Clinton conference was the most comprehensive effort to date to address the wholesale harvest of trees in the Northwest. The new rule reduced the allowable cut from these forests from four billion board feet per year to just over one billion, which scientists thought was their approximate growth rate. The advocates for these new limits argued that this lower harvest level would be sustainable over time. The opponents argued the rules would strangle the economic activity of the region. Because the new rules gave voice to the long-term, sustainable conservation of forest and were based on the best available science, they have remained in effect ever since. So long as that new roadless rule stays in effect, some old-growth forests will remain out of reach to loggers.

After delivering the film to Sid, Elaine and I took about a month off and then began writing the treatment for our last film in the environmental series. By then, we had a title for this new, all-important film: *Diversity of Life.*

18

DIVERSITY OF LIFE

I ROSE EARLY, AS I ALWAYS DO, crawled out of our two-person tent, and stepped up to the edge of a four-foot bank overlooking Wyoming's Fire-hole River. Stars were still twinkling overhead. The eastern horizon was slowly brightening, first red, then orange, then yellow. Dawn was just minutes away. I hurried to set up my tripod, then pulled the Arriflex out of its foam backpack and mounted it atop the tripod. I could hear running water somewhere below my perch. In the distance, there was a splash and then a grunt. I could just barely see dark shadows moving across the river.

Suddenly, dawn flashed across the water. An intensely yellow light caught a giant bison up to its belly in the rushing river. Almost imme-diately, the heat of the sun began sucking curls of fog from the water's surface. Within just a few minutes, the entire river was blanketed in yellow backlit fog. A small herd of bison was now crossing the river, slowly emerging from the fog, coming my way. A tiny calf struggled in the current, trying to keep pace with its mother. Suddenly, the calf panicked and turned back toward shore. The cow let out a low grunt, and the calf turned back and fought its way through the current to its mother's side.

It was now fall 1992. Elaine and I both suspected this new film would be our most important ever. It would highlight the millions of species of plants, animals, fungi, microorganisms, genetic diversity, and the diversity of ecosystems themselves. Biological diversity is arguably the single most important characteristic of life on Earth. This diversity is the reason the biosphere appears stable, why it looks as it does.

But biodiversity is being threatened everywhere. The bison are just one example of man's impact on that diversity. This species once roamed throughout most of North America but was hunted and slaughtered for a century until the great herds were destroyed. They now live free in just a few parks and reserves in the West.

I wanted to tell the story of diversity by beginning with just this one endangered species in one of those parks. I had chosen bison because I knew that most everyone was familiar with the story of the decline of bison. I needed to open the film with something familiar because the film's concepts were going to be difficult to articulate.

I knew I would need help with the film. For that, I turned to a colleague at Oregon State University, Dr. Jane Lubchenco, because she was a world-renowned ecologist and leader in the study of biodiversity. While Elaine and I were in Yellowstone, she was busy making arrangements for us to film at the Missouri Botanical Garden in St. Louis. When Elaine and I finished filming the bison, we met Jane in Chicago and then flew on to meet Peter Raven, the director of the garden in St. Louis. Peter was responsible for maintaining an impressive collection of plant genetic material from all over the world. Some of the most important samples being housed at the center dated back to Charles Darwin himself.

While Jane got reacquainted with Peter, Elaine and I began setting up the camera and lights among the giant tropical ferns and palms in the garden. The humidity in the garden was oppressively high, and there were waterfalls everywhere. I had to be careful when running the electrical cables for the lights not to let them touch the many pools scattered around the garden. This place was so unique, so valuable. I didn't want to disrupt anything or leave a footprint. When we were ready, Jane began questioning Peter about the importance of diversity in plant and animal life. She asked him about his concern for the loss of biodiversity worldwide.

"We're losing biodiversity at a tremendous rate," Peter said. "Just since World War II, about half of all the tropical rainforests have been cut, about a fifth of all topsoil has been lost, and the characteristics of our very atmosphere are changing." He went on to explain that much of this damage was the result of out-of-control population growth. "The effects on forests and grasslands and coral reefs and waters all over the world are absolutely tremendous." These losses are a global phenomenon and problem, he told us. "Endangered species have come to symbolize what is wrong with the way we interact with the environment."

I was really happy. On-camera interviews rarely go so well. Usually, I have to tease things from people and shoot multiple takes just to get a coherent statement. Being on camera is difficult for anyone. But Jane did a wonderful job drawing Peter out, and between the two of them we had just what we needed—a clean statement and the importance of biodiversity. Elaine and I spent the rest of the day shooting film of all the tropical plants being housed at the garden and then moved on to the archive where Darwin's samples were held.

We lit the entire room and then asked one of the archive botanists to show us some of Darwin's seed collections. He pulled out some tropical plant specimens, handling the parchment with cotton gloves. He explained their significance as still-living remnants of a long-gone era. "This genetic material existed in a brief moment in time. Except for the samples held in this garden, these materials don't exist anywhere else in the world."

Genetic diversity in nature is the key to the maintenance of the world as we know it. If we lose a few species, the system will self-correct. But if we lose too much diversity, nature will not have the raw materials essential to restoring those ecosystems. I wanted our film to convey the need for diversity and the urgency of preventing its loss.

Three weeks later, we headed out again, this time driving to the World Center for Birds of Prey, located in Boise, Idaho. I wanted to portray how difficult and expensive it can be to restore any single species after it is lost from an ecosystem. The best example I could think of was the precipitous decline and slow recovery of the peregrine falcon.

During the 1950s and '60s, many bird populations were devastated by pollution. Throughout North America, the peregrine falcon populations had collapsed. It was shown conclusively that the problem was the widespread and indiscriminate use of the pesticide DDT. The pesticide interfered with normal calcium metabolism in just about anything that accidentally consumed it. Female birds were especially vulnerable because they have a high demand for calcium when producing eggshells. DDT caused peregrine to produce thin-shelled eggs that were easily broken during the normal incubation process. Survival of young peregrine falcons declined as a result.

By the early 1970s peregrine falcons were extinct in the entirety of the eastern half of North America, and there were just a few dozen breeding pairs left in the western states. Among the first to recognize the problem were Tom Cade, with the Laboratory of Ornithology at Cornell University, and Bill Burnham at Colorado State University, who went on to establish the Peregrine Fund and the World Center for Birds of Prey. This private, nonprofit organization, backed by falconers and bird-watchers across the country, launched an ambitious breeding program to keep the species from disappearing altogether.

The center was probably the best single example of a group of scientists stepping in to save an endangered species from extinction. Elaine and I started in Boise, Idaho, where the Peregrine Fund had established a captive breeding program. The birds were raised in protected aeries where their diets could be controlled and protected from DDT.

One particularly warm day in early June 1993, we set up our cameras in the laboratory. I replaced all the lights in the room with our temperature-controlled halogens. Elaine set up to record sound. A lab tech came in carrying a white tray covered with a light blue towel. The top of the towel was moving. Tiny squeaks and screams came from the tray. The tech came over to a bench in front of the camera, slowly raising the towel. Six little heads popped up, each with their mouths wide open. The chicks were flightless, having not yet developed the necessary feathers. They wore only down feathers and not many of them. They were helpless, just tiny feather balls not-so-patiently waiting to be fed. The tech was essentially the chicks' surrogate mom stuffing tiny morsels of meat into each of their gaping mouths. I could tell the hatching order by the relative sizes of the chicks. The oldest was also the biggest and he (or she—I really couldn't tell) was first to push his way forward and demand to be fed. You couldn't help but fall in love with the little ones as they frantically clamored for something to eat.

Once DDT had been banned in North America and environmental levels had declined, the Peregrine Fund began releasing adult birds into the wild in an effort to repopulate the species to its former range. At the time of our filming, the center had already released thirty-five hundred birds back into the wild, and for the first time in twenty years, peregrine numbers were on the rise throughout most of their former range. To complete this segment of the film, we followed the center's team to the mountains west of Fort Collins and filmed the release of four young birds.

The ecologists carried four big cardboard boxes from the bird transport van to a cliff edge overlooking some of the most pristine mountain habitat in the Rockies. A temporary home made of plywood and wire sat on a cliff face, ready for the young birds. Elaine and I set up at the cliff edge, strapping the camera in so that we could get the feel for the setting without endangering ourselves or the equipment.

Our guide explained, "We're going to place these four birds in that temporary nest box. They'll spend a week or so there before we open the door and release them. This way, the birds will grow accustomed to their new surroundings and, hopefully, stay in the area."

Everyone moved around slowly and carefully, just to make sure no one went over the side of the cliff. On a large blanket, each bird was fitted with a leg band so that biologists would be able to track them and measure survival rates. Each bird screamed at the biologists while being handled, but once inside their new home, they quieted down. We tore down our gear, slipped out the back, and left the birds to acclimate to their new surroundings.

Everyone at the two locations was quick to point out that the breeding program, although wildly successful, was also extremely expensive. So far, the peregrine rescue program had cost more than $50 million, about $15,000 per bird, all of which came from private bird lovers.

Jim Enderson, one of the founders of the program, told us that such a restoration effort simply could not be attempted for more than a few high-profile species. "If a whole ecosystem were to be endangered, there wouldn't be enough money in the world to save it," he pointed out.

———————

Not long after our trip to Denver, Elaine and I took our sons to the coast and placed them in Bruce and Mary Lou Mate's care. We hired their oldest daughter, Michelle, to care for the boys while we were on a ten-day trip to Central America. Neither Elaine or I fully grasped just how important leaving the boys with the Mates would turn out to be.

Donald joined us from Washington for this trip. He, Elaine, a graduate student of mine by the name of Aaron Ferster, and I took off for San José, Costa Rica, with eight camera cases and our jungle gear. It was clear right from the first day that Donald liked Aaron very much and, as a result, the fit was perfect. The two of them sat in the back of the airplane locked in conversations about their similar early childhoods. Elaine and I sat more toward the front of the airplane and talked about the Caribbean and the sky.

I was struck by the vast expanse of blue outside my window. The ocean below was blue; the sky above was blue. In fact, they were exactly the same cerulean shade, so I really could not tell where one ended and the other began. The horizon was lost in this vast expanse of unbroken color. There were tiny powder-puff clouds in the sky, some below and some above us. I couldn't tell up from down.

Looking out at that vast expanse, I could easily imagine why so many people have a hard time understanding the scale of the problem facing humankind. When you see so much empty space, it's hard to imagine that humans are so profoundly affecting the environment. From thirty thousand feet, the oceans look fine. The sky looks clean. The challenge we face as ecologists and as filmmakers was obvious: How do we convince people that the loss is real?

———————

When we finally arrived in San José, we were immediately struck by the vast array of colors. No longer surrounded by unbroken blue, we were now in the midst of a riot of red, yellow, and blue and all the mixtures in between. Everything was blooming; flowers hung from every tree and every building. The smells were overwhelming.

Our first stop was a small town on the outskirts of the capital city. We checked in at the Hotel Bougainvillea on June 13. It was a lovely place, fashioned from fine teak. Tropical flowers grew everywhere and covered much of the roof. Inside, the dinner tables were covered in white linens, accented with more tropical flowers.

The central mountains of Costa Rica are a paradise. The elevation, just over four thousand feet, keeps the temperature pleasant. It rains a lot because Costa Rica has oceans on either side. The humidity is always high, and everything is lush.

That first night we all sat around one of the Bougainvillea's tables, and the conversation shifted from subject to subject. Everyone was excited for the coming day's filming. But Donald wanted to know more about something Elaine had told him.

"Jim, this is not your first trip to Costa Rica?"

"Oh no, I was here as an exchange student back in the '60s."

"How old were you?"

"I spent my junior year as a high school student at the Liceo Jose Marti in Puntarenas on the west coast of Costa Rica. I was a Rotary International exchange student."

Donald kept probing, and eventually I opened up, telling everyone at the table about my final months there. About six weeks before I was to return home, I contracted what was ultimately diagnosed as paratyphoid fever. The doctor in San José told me he couldn't tell for sure whether I had typhoid or paratyphoid. If I survived the night, he would have his answer.

Well, I did survive, but it was a devastating disease. Every epithelial cell in my body died in the first twenty-four hours: skin, tongue, gut lining, even the surface of my eyeballs. It took nearly three months to recover while I lost one-third of my body weight.

I was not eager to repeat the experience.

After a very pleasant night at Bougainvillea, we all piled into the van and drove to the offices of the Costa Rican National Institute of Biodiversity. INBio, as it was known, had only been in existence for a few years, but already it had a worldwide reputation based on its distinct approach to conservation.

The INBio director, Dr. Rodrigo Gamez, explained it to us in an on-camera interview. "To adequately protect nature," he said, "one must have a vision of the future, and one must be willing to manage the Earth's limited resources so that they will last not only for our lifetimes but for our children's lifetimes and their children's lifetimes—in other words, forever."

It seemed Costa Ricans were far ahead of much of the rest of the world in this regard. They had already set aside more than a quarter of their land as national parks and preserves. Dr. Gamez explained that he and his colleagues believed that their forests are worth far more alive and standing than they would ever be if they were cut down, plowed under, or burned. Wilderness, he explained, is the Earth's *only* source of genetic diversity. Without it, we as a species will not survive.

Under Dr. Gamez's leadership, INBio trained scores of what they call para-taxonomists to explore its nature preserves and collect examples of Costa Rican life. Every year, these para-taxonomists bring back more than one hundred thousand specimens to INBio headquarters to be studied and cataloged.

The biologists at INBio want to learn more about Costa Rican bio-diversity, and they want to put that knowledge to work supporting their country's economy. They are betting that they will be able to find potentially valuable substances in the INBio samples.

"For example, most of today's life-saving drugs are not invented in a laboratory by human chemists," he explained. "They come from discoveries biologists have made in nature. We find an organism that has a particular valuable trait. We analyze the mechanisms and chemical compounds that make that trait so useful to the organism. And then we synthesize that compound and try to harness it for the good of mankind. If we didn't find the chemical in nature, we would never know to synthesize it in the lab."

The INBio operation faced a daunting task precisely because so little is known about what lives in the Costa Rican rainforest. Fewer than 20 percent of the organisms the taxonomists find have been previously catalogued or named.

Dr. Gamez had a profound impact on my thinking. His words would echo through my head for a long time after our interview. As we wrapped up our gear, I knew he was also going to have an effect on the way we put this film together.

———————

For the next two days, we moved around the rainforests north of San José filming para-taxonomists at work, hopping from one site to another from central Costa Rica to La Selva, Monteverde, Liberia, and Guanacaste in the north. Our goal was to show just how rich and diverse the rainforest of Costa Rica was and then to show how INBio treats those riches.

Our footage clearly showed how the people of the National Institute of Biodiversity had found ways of working with the wild lands of Costa Rica, taking only samples and knowledge, leaving behind intact ecosystems. From the specimens they collect, the scientists the world over learn how to construct new chemical compounds, grow new crops, and develop new medicines. "More important," Gamez said, "these benefits will flow from the Costa Rican forests for all time."

Much of our film work had to be done at night because that is when the rainforest is most alive. I spent my time searching for ways to portray the insects and small animals of the forest as they worked in the dark. One night we concentrated on a colony of ants as they worked as a coordinated team cutting leaves apart and moving those leaves hundreds of feet from the trees to their underground nests. The entire colony of leaf-cutters worked as a coordinated unit, all pursuing the same goal, all marching in single file down the tree trunks, across the forest floor, and into their underground nests.

Working in the jungle at night can be especially difficult because there are a lot of poisonous critters about after sunset. The INBio biologists advised us to wear heavy snake boots and long-sleeved shirts and to turn our baseball caps around so the bill would be in the back. Doing this simple thing helped prevent poisonous spiders and snakes from dropping out of trees, down our necks, and into our shirts.

One day a young man from INBio came running into the jungle waving a piece of paper in his hand trying to get my attention. He was carrying a cable from home. He handed it to me with an urgent look on his face and I read:

> To: Jim And Elaine Larison, National Institute of Biodiversity, San Jose, Costa Rica
> From: Mary Lou Mate
> Re: Ted
>
> Ted ill stop. High fever stop. Possibly serious stop. One of you needs to come home stop.

Elaine immediately began making plans for a speedy return to Oregon. I drove as fast as possible to the hotel, where Elaine called Christina Cooper, our travel agent, and told her the problem. Christina knew exactly what to do. She said, "Leave immediately for the airport in San José. Just get to the airport."

We drove to San José, quickly kissed as she grabbed her bag, and took off running. When she went through the doorway headed for the ticket counter, I could see she was still wearing her snake boots. I was left standing in the parking lot with a hollow feeling in the pit of my stomach.

Christina had done her job well. Elaine had a seat on the next flight to Dallas–Fort Worth. But even though the airplane must have been flying at nearly 600 miles an hour, it just wasn't fast enough. When Elaine arrived in Dallas, an airline employee was waiting for her with a US Customs agent at her side. They stamped her passport as they ran to an awaiting van, then the two of them drove Elaine across the tarmac, around immigration formalities, and straight to a United flight waiting for her arrival. Everyone else was already onboard. The passengers had been told that they were holding the flight for an emergency passenger coming over from the international terminal. When Elaine ran up the stairway, she was met by a flight attendant, who showed her to her seat. The aircraft main door closed immediately, and the plane headed for the end of the runway.

Elaine took a moment to breathe, then realized she was sitting with a young couple from Oregon. They were balancing a young toddler on their laps. The boy was giggling and laughing. The trauma of the moment hit her, and Elaine began to cry. The couple just sat in stunned silence.

Once on the ground in Oregon, Elaine took the shuttle out to long-term parking, picked up our car, and drove home, not knowing what she would find when she arrived.

Sometime while Elaine was on one or the other of the airplanes, Ted's fever had broken and the hospital determined that the emergency had passed. They discharged Ted and sent him home with Mary Lou, a registered intensive care nurse, with a couple of bottles of antibiotics.

Elaine ran through the door to find Ted asleep on the couch, with dark rings under his eyes but alive. The doctor had told Mary Lou that Ted had contracted toxic shock from a small scratch on his forearm—a freak accident.

Phone service to Central America in those days was impossible, so Elaine called Western Union and dictated the following message:

> To: Jim Larison, National Institute of Biodiversity, San Jose, Costa Rica
> From: Elaine Larison
> Re: Ted
>
> Ted recovering stop. All is well stop. Finish and come home stop.

For the next three days, I did everything I could to wrap things up so that I could get home. At the first possible moment, Donald headed back to Washington while Aaron and I headed for Oregon.

When I arrived home, Ted ran out across the driveway and jumped into my arms. From all appearances, he was a thoroughly recovered ball of energy.

"Tell me about the snakes. I want to hear about the snakes!" he said.

I carried him through the door and joined him on the floor for a little light wrestling.

We had about a month before we were to begin shooting the next portion of the *Diversity* film. Elaine had dropped the kids off at their school, come home, and put coffee on the stove. She was unusually quiet.

The moment the coffee was ready, she began, "Jim, this next trip is a big one, and it's all the way on the other side of the Earth. I don't know if it would be possible to pick a place that would be farther away from Oregon than Palau. I know you need my help, but I can't leave the kids so soon after Ted's close call."

She was right and I knew it. I took a moment to gather my thoughts and then surprised myself by saying, "I don't think you can or should. In fact, I've been thinking a lot about this while on the airplane coming back from Costa Rica. We have to figure out a way of doing the work as a family, with the kids going with us wherever and whenever possible."

Elaine's eyes began to brighten. "Are you saying we should take the kids with us to Palau?"

"Yes, I think so. Why not? They will love it."

"Are you thinking of taking a caregiver with us?"

"Yes, that is exactly what I mean."

Elaine was quiet for a moment, sipping her coffee. "What about Michelle Mate? She's certainly old and mature enough to handle the kids. She loves the kids, and the kids love her."

"I wonder if she could get free for two or three months."

Elaine immediately got on the phone and called her mother, Mary Lou. Michelle was our first choice. She was an experienced traveler, having gone with Bruce on a number of research expeditions. She was like our daughter already. After about an hour of intense and excited phone calls, it was decided: Michelle would be joining us on our next long assignment in the South Pacific.

19

PALAU

As our "Air Mike" turbo-prop commuter plane skimmed over the tops of the last of the tiny islands that make up the Republic of Palau, everyone was glued to the windows. Beneath us was an endless string of densely forested and mostly uninhabited islands, each connected to the next by a maze of colorful reefs and channels. The ocean was so clear that it looked almost black in places. The submerged reefs surrounding and connecting the islands were bathed in green, turquoise, and cobalt blue water. White-capped waves formed delicate sparkling necklaces that appeared to be draped around each of the coral reefs. All were in constant motion as continuous lines of breakers crept over the reefs and rolled toward shore.

"Heaven," Elaine whispered to me, as the Air Micronesia flight circled Koror City, the economic hub of the islands. I kissed the back of her hand, and then she ran her fingers through Ted's brown hair. This was the kind of assignment Elaine liked best, a steamy, tropical island. A peaceful place, away from everything. For the next two months, these islands would be our home away from home. Elaine was looking forward to sharing this experience with our children.

Our gear was stacked in the back of the commuter plane spilling into the passenger compartment. A curtain separated the baggage from the twenty passengers. Elaine and I were seated across from one another toward the rear of the airplane so that I could keep an eye on our camera gear. Michelle and the boys were in front of us talking a mile a minute, pointing at the reefs.

This trip was going to be challenging. Much of what we had to do would involve underwater work. It was important that this film show each of the major ecosystems on Earth, not just those on land. I needed footage that would help me say that all these ecosystems were not only diverse but fragile.

After searching the world for the most pristine and healthy coral reef system, I had settled on this remote set of tiny South Pacific islands, really a chain of more than four hundred undersea mountains stretching from Japan south almost to the shores of New Guinea. Some of these mountains stand as much as twenty-seven thousand feet above their bases on the seafloor. At the southernmost tip of this mountain chain sit Guam, Yap, and the Republic of Palau, a paradise among paradises. Palau's reefs were known for their rich life—seven hundred different species of coral and a thousand species of fish.

As I stared out the window, all I could think about was that amazingly beautiful water and our first dive. For this film, it was important that we show how reefs worldwide are among the most threatened of ecosystems. They are dying at alarming rates almost everywhere. This loss was especially troubling to me because life itself had begun in the sea, where those first forms of life were afforded some protection from lethal solar radiation. Partially as a result, the oceans have had an extra 2.5 billion years to develop complexity and diversity. My goal in coming to Palau was to show some of that complexity and to show how it was being threatened by human activities.

Coral reefs are especially susceptible to overfishing because they are what ecologists refer to as *closed systems*. Nutrients do not flow freely in or out of a reef because each reef is somewhat isolated from all other reefs by vast stretches of open, almost sterile ocean. Within a reef, nutrients are recycled endlessly by the organisms that live there. If too many fish or shellfish are harvested and removed from a reef, the entire ecosystem can become impoverished and, in worst-case scenarios, collapse.

I also wanted to show how a large proportion of the world's human population depends upon these reefs and their biological diversity for food. I believed strongly that Western society, North Americans in particular, had lost touch with nature. The vast majority of people in the developed world buy their food from supermarkets, failing to appreciate the links between what is on the store shelves and the environment from which that food comes. It would be important to show just how many people throughout the rest of the world still depend directly on wild plants and animals.

It was late afternoon as we circled Koror. As was common in the Western Pacific so near the equator, thunderstorms were beginning to build and drift among the island peaks. Every time the small airplane bumped its way through one of them, my window became streaked with drops of rainwater. Once again I was reminded of Alaska and the fragile nature of airplanes. I quickly put the matter aside. I didn't want anything to spoil this trip.

We were all tired, having flown nearly seventy-five hundred miles since leaving Oregon, passing first through Seattle, then Honolulu, and then the Philippines. We had spent nearly a week on Luzon filming the local population as they used nets to fish from the nearshore reefs. Now we were on final approach into the Koror airport.

The Republic of Palau was first settled by people living in what is now known as the Philippines and Indonesia. But for much of its recent history, Palau had been under Japanese influence. World War II changed everything in Palau. The islands were strategically located close to the Philippines and in the middle of some of the most important South Pacific shipping lanes, so the Americans wanted to control them. The native people of Palau were dragged into the war as their islands became stepping stones in the Pacific campaign. Two foreign powers fought viciously for control of the skies and seas around the islands. Twelve thousand people died in the struggle for Palau. The wreckage of that battle can still be found scattered in the island's jungles and across the seafloor.

Slowly our twin-engine turbo prop commuter began its descent. It dipped through the clouds, lowered its wheels, and gently touched down on the gravel runway. A crowd of the curious had gathered along the length of the fence to catch a glimpse of the outside world.

With a great whirring sound, the port engine cut out first; its propeller feathered back and abruptly stopped. The starboard engine cut out next. The copilot then worked his way from the cockpit back through the aisle, spun the locking mechanism, and pushed opened the rear door. A wall of humid, steamy air immediately flooded the cabin, giving us our first real taste of this tropical paradise. It was as if we were walking directly into a hot sauna with our clothes on. I could feel the moisture running down the middle of my back. My hands were wet, and it was clear we were all wearing the wrong clothes for this place.

As the other passengers began to stand in the airplane aisle, Elaine, Michelle, and I began gathering together our carry-on bags, but for some reason the boys stayed in their seats, their noses pressed against the windowpanes. They were most often the first to line up at the door of an airplane, impatient to experience a new place, but this time they were transfixed at their windows.

Elaine looked at John and Ted, and they glanced back at her. Without a word and ever so slowly, Ted raised his index finger and pointed at the people gathered along the fence. His mouth opened but he seemed incapable of speech. Elaine followed the end of his finger. The curious onlookers were mostly local women. A few children clung to their mother's legs. Each of the women stood with hands raised and fingers interwoven in the chain-link fence. Most wore full-length grass skirts and sandals, but above the waist, some of the women wore nothing at all.

Elaine turned to me and whispered, "You'll have to explain this to the boys."

But the boys were not shocked by the semi-nudity. "Mom, look at their teeth," Ted implored.

Elaine looked out of the airplane window and indeed, these women did look unusual. Even from a distance of more than fifty feet, we were immediately drawn to the distinctive color of these women's mouths. Their teeth and gums were fire-engine red. It was as if all the women had applied bright red lipstick to the inside of their mouths.

The people of Palau, it turned out, chewed a locally grown fruit known as betel nut. It was the island people's biggest vice. Most everyone used it for its stimulant effects, much like people in the rest of the world chew tobacco or drink coffee. The men of Palau carry around a purse with their day's supply of nuts, a bag of crushed coral, and a number of leaves from the betel nut tree. When they wanted a hit, they split a nut in half, poured a pinch of coral limestone over the nut's cherry red core, wrapped the mixture inside a leaf, and placed the entire package between their cheek and gum.

The chew had a powerful effect. The betel nut was known to improve alertness, increase a person's stamina, and foster a sense of well-being. A side effect was that it stained the user's mouth bright red, especially the gums.

It took us no time at all to settle into our new home in Palau. Charles Birkeland, a scientist with the University of Guam Marine Laboratory, had arranged for us to use an oceanside cottage owned by the university. A local dive-boat operator by the name of Winkler worked for the marine lab. He offered his boat and services to us for the filming. By the end of the second day, Elaine and I were ready to begin our underwater work.

Winkler was a likable, gentle giant. He was strong, extremely friendly, and helpful. He took immediately to our sons. For the next couple of months, he regularly took the boys on his boat fishing. He taught them how to fish for shark. When Ted caught his first one, Winkler stripped out the backbone, bent it into a necklace, and said, "Fishermen in Palau wear their first shark." Michelle went along on all the boat rides to watch out for the kids, but it was Winkler who took over the duties of mentor.

At Winkler's suggestion, Elaine and I began by diving at the base of a huge rock arch not far from our cottage. Once I had all my dive gear on, I slipped off the boat, then signaled for Winkler to hand me the underwater camera. I immediately checked to make sure that it was functioning properly and then signaled Elaine to begin preparing to join me.

By the time we reached Palau, we had grown quite accustomed to working underwater together. I dragged the fifty-pound camera housing around. Elaine had a twenty-five-pound battery pack strapped to her belly, and a set of wires protruded from each end of the battery, which ran down each arm and connected to two underwater lights, which she carried in her hands. On the surface, Elaine was too heavily loaded to stand, let alone walk. Her tank weighed about forty-five pounds, her weight belt added another twelve pounds, and the lights and battery pack added thirty more. Fully loaded, she carried close to one hundred pounds. She could hardly move.

Winkler had to dress Elaine while she sat on the edge of the boat, and when she was ready, he simply pushed her backward into the sea. Her gear weighed nothing in the water because it was designed to be neutrally buoyant and was not so impossible to manage. But every piece of equipment that she carried was essential for the job.

The problem with filming underwater is that most of the sun's rays are filtered out by the water. Just a few feet of saltwater can reduce the light level, dramatically altering the ambient color balance. As you go deeper, the reds are filtered out first, then the yellows, and finally the blues. The deeper a diver goes, the darker and the more colorless the world appears.

The battery-pack lights raised the light level underwater and reintroduced the colors filtered out by the overhead column of water. We communicated with each other with hand signals. A raised index finger meant that I wanted a light to be turned on. Lower, higher, closer . . . Elaine had done this so many times before that she knew what I wanted, often before I signaled for it.

On this first dive, we had been underwater for about twenty minutes; I was just beginning to set up what was to be a moving shot through the middle of the arch when an alarm began to sound. At first, neither I nor Elaine recognized the sound, but when finally we realized that it was the electronic water sensor that was located inside the camera housing, I panicked. The alarm could mean only one thing: the camera housing was leaking. I flipped the housing over and stared into the lens opening. A small amount of water washed across the inside of the glass.

The camera was located toward the back of the housing and the lens was up front, so I pointed the housing down. I could afford to lose a lens to saltwater but could not afford to lose the camera. With the housing held nose down, a lot of water would have to accumulate inside before it would reach the camera itself. When Rod Mesecar had delivered the housing to me almost ten years earlier, he had said, "It's very unlikely that this housing will ever leak, but if it does, the leak will be a slow one. You'll have time to get the camera out of the water." But I had no idea how much.

I turned to Elaine and signaled her to return to the surface. Without taking the time to explain, I turned and headed for the boat. I broke the surface and tore out my regulator.

"Winkler! I'm going to hand you the camera. There is a bit of water inside. Keep the lens pointed down. Do not turn the housing over."

Without losing a moment, he reached over the side of the boat and grasped the camera by its two handles. Luckily Winkler was very strong and could easily lift the camera over the gunwale into the boat without letting the housing shift from the nose-down position. He gently set the camera down on the floor of the boat, then helped me with my gear.

I ditched my tank, weight belt, and fins, handing each to Winkler, then climbed over the stern of the boat. Wasting no time, I popped the latches that held the lens port to the housing. Sure enough, a bit of water flowed out, and a sick feeling spread through my stomach. Judging from the amount of water that came out of the housing, my strategy of holding the camera lens down seemed like the right one. The camera had not been sitting in water, but I did not know if the leak had been more like a drip, drip, drip, or a spray. I feared the latter and had to assume that at least a little water might have come into contact with the camera itself. Any amount of salt on the electronics of the camera would be highly destructive.

The Arriflex camera inside was worth as much as a small American house; the lens was worth as much as a full-size sedan. I doubted that any insurance company would pay off on a camera that was intentionally taken beneath the surface of the ocean. I feared the worst; it was, after all, unlikely that any camera would survive a saltwater bath.

If there was any chance at all of saving the Arriflex, I had to act quickly. I stripped off the rest of my dive gear, poured a container of soapy water over the outside of the camera housing and washed my hands and arms, almost as if I were a doctor preparing for surgery.

As soon as Elaine came onboard, she, too, washed the salt from her hands, and without so much as a word between us, she and I began systematically disassembling the camera, piece by piece, working from the outside toward the center. As each piece came free, Elaine immersed it in alcohol. We worked as fast as we could, and within ten or twelve minutes, we had done all that was possible. The camera was in pieces, the largest of which was the motor assembly. I didn't dare open the motor housing for fear I would never get it back together again. As far as I could tell, no saltwater had penetrated into the camera, but I worried about the electronics package. The computer that controlled the camera was located on the bottom. If it had gotten even a single drop of saltwater on the motherboard, it would probably never work right again.

Only after every piece had been thoroughly washed in alcohol did I turn to Winkler and ask him to head for shore. "Go slowly. We don't want any salt spray on this equipment. We won't be working tomorrow. I'll be trying to find the leak." After that, everyone fell into silence. How was I going to fix this problem while in Palau?

Luckily, we had come on this trip with two identical Arriflex cameras and two identical super-wide-angle lenses suitable for underwater use, so the loss of one camera or one lens would not be a catastrophic blow to the trip. But the underwater housing was one of a kind—there was no choice but to find the leak and to plug it before risking the second camera to the same fate.

For the next two days, I worked on the problem. I first tried the obvious things, the O-rings, but the O-rings were intact and had no cuts or hairs across them. They were not the problem. I then tried the not-so-obvious, but still the housing leaked every time I plunged it into a bath of water. After two days of looking I had not found the source of the problem.

Finally, Elaine had an idea. "Why don't you put some paper inside the housing? You know, tape it around the inside so that it won't move. Then dunk the housing in water. The pattern of water on the paper inside should help you track down the leak."

"Elaine, you have earned your week's pay."

The idea worked, of course, and it turned out that water was coming through the electrical wire that extended from the outside handle through the wall of the housing to the camera's electronic on-off switch. This was the one hidden weakness. It was the one penetration of the outside housing wall not protected by an O-ring. Over the past few hundred dives, saltwater had dissolved the wire itself and was being channeled by the rubber tubing through the housing wall one drip at a time. The good news was that the wire was small, so the leak was small. But under pressure, at depth, even a small hole can funnel a lot of water.

I had no choice but to pull the wire out, seal the hole with epoxy, and rig a manual switch by using one of the lens control arms. Finally, when the housing was tested and found to be watertight, I was willing to risk the second camera. We had lost too many days of precious time.

But we hadn't exactly lost the week. When I wasn't working on the camera housing, I was fulfilling a long-standing promise made to my eldest son. John was fourteen, old enough to learn to scuba dive. The cottage in which we were living was perfectly located for the purpose. It was on the edge of the bay along a seawall. The wall had a set of stairs that led down to a landing that, during high tide, was awash.

John's first few lessons took place on that landing. He learned quickly, which should not have come as any great surprise to anyone; after all, John was an accomplished swimmer and had been skin diving for several years now. Plus, he was highly motivated.

I began by teaching the basics of the aqualung and its regulators. John made a few controlled, shallow dives along the seawall, but within a few days he was ready for his first full-fledged free dive. I had decided to make that first dive in twenty-five feet of water. John and I made a slow circle around a large coral outcrop. We began at ten feet and worked our way down to the bay floor, then back up around the coral on the far side, ultimately returning to the landing on the seawall.

For the first time, John saw the full complement of reef fish, and it was an eye-opening experience for the young boy.

A few days later, on a second no-camera dive, John, Elaine, and I visited the wreckage of a Japanese fighter aircraft that had been shot down and had crashed in shallow water. The Japanese Zero was not far from our cottage. The fighter was sitting in bright white sand, some of which had worked its way into the cockpit itself. The paint had been eaten away and the engine was mostly gone, but amazingly, the aluminum superstructure was well preserved. The propeller stood vertically, its base encased in coral.

John crawled into the cockpit half expecting, I think, to find the pilot's bones, but of course they were not there. John immediately swam into the airplane and sat where there was once a pilot's seat. I wondered if the Japanese pilot had bailed out before the airplane hit the water.

Sitting in the warplane must have made the history books seem more real for John. It sure had that effect on me. Someone really flew this plane, fought in the sky above Palau, and probably died trying to defend these islands and himself. I wondered if the man who had flown and very likely died in this airplane was much older than my son.

———————

Over the next four weeks, Elaine and I dove every day, filming in detail the living organisms that made up the reef ecosystem. And there was a lot to film. The coral reefs around Palau were vibrant, colorful, and full of life. There were at least ten times as many fish swimming around as there had been in the Caymans. Everywhere we looked, there was another surprise, another species to film, another interaction between different species. There were hard corals, coral polyps, soft corals, emperor angelfish, grey reef sharks, schools of barracuda, jellyfish, and enormous sea fans. Some of the most spectacular images I obtained were of the tiny delicate yellow tentacles of tube corals as they fished the surrounding water. In some places, clown triggerfish were abundant. The giant white spots on their bellies stood in striking contrast to their nearly black backs. On every section of the reef, I could see tiny, orange clown fish poking their heads out from their hiding places among the tentacles of poisonous anemones.

On an especially calm day, Elaine, I, and Winkler headed off for what is known in Palau as the Blue Corner. This was one of the most spectacular dive sites I'd ever seen. Winkler told us it was the richest part of the reef. The "corner" refers to the southwesternmost tip of the barrier reef that surrounds the islands. To the west is the deep abyss of the Pacific. When we swam out to the edge of the corner, we found ourselves looking down into bottomless, inky purple depths. On an incoming tide, a massive flow of water causes an upwelling of nutrient-rich water along the barrier reef. As a result, millions of reef fish feed on the algae and zooplankton in the water. When the reef fish come out to feed, pelagic predators rush in to prey on the reef fish. Not far behind are the sharks. In a silent but constant procession, the sharks prowl along the edge of the barrier reef, looking for dinner.

To film in this location, we had to fight the incoming rush of water. We wedged ourselves to the bottom to keep from being swept away by the current. We could set up our camera at the edge of the reef, but if we reached out over the edge by even a few inches, the current would drive us back. More than once the current struck me in the face and ripped my mask half off. From our semi-protected position just behind the edge of the wall, we watched as sharks swam by in an endless procession less than three feet from our lens.

It was a marvelous experience. There were schools of iridescent blue fusiliers, scores of pyramid fish, uncountable numbers of jacks, snappers, and fish species I could not identify. There were scores of black-tip and white-tip sharks, and dozens of grey reef sharks. There was a school of barracuda too numerous to count. They blocked out the sunlight when they moved above us.

A few days later, Michelle, the boys, Elaine, and I left Koror and flew to Yap, where we all dove together on Miil Channel along one of the many mangroves that surround the Micronesian island. We had come to shoot film of manta ray. Michelle and the boys put on masks and snorkels and stayed close to the surface, while Elaine and I dove to nearly eighty feet to get beneath the giant mantas to silhouette their enormous wing-like bodies against the sunlight coming from the surface above.

Visibility in the rich water was low due to the density of plankton found there. We could just make out the boys floating above us on the surface when suddenly a manta swooped in over our heads between us and Ted. The manta weighed close to a ton and had a "wingspan" of nearly twenty feet. She had her mouth wide open as she swooped in to feed on the plankton. Another manta was hanging off to our right. I moved in to film tiny wrasses cleaning parasites off her gill plates.

Elaine and I drank our tanks dry in an attempt to stay with the mantas for as long as we could, but my pressure gauge eventually ran well into the red. I was forced to turn to Elaine and point toward the waiting boat. She looked at her gauge, reluctantly agreeing. We let go of the bottom and were immediately swept away with the current and headed back toward our awaiting boat.

On the way home from Palau, we needed to hop back across the Pacific from island to island. When we reached the ticket counter, just before our second hop, the agent said the airplane we were scheduled to take was experiencing engine trouble and the flight had been canceled. My eyebrows shot up as I imagined taking my family on an airplane that was not airworthy. I suddenly felt a lump in my throat and an ache in my gut.

The agent saw that I was worried and said, "No problem. We have rebooked you on an alternate carrier. We'll get you to Hawaii in plenty of time." Then she said, "Don't worry."

But I couldn't shake the feeling in the pit of my stomach. I headed back to tell Elaine and the boys about the change, all the while experiencing heightened anxiety.

We flew onward aboard an older 737. The flight was not full, so we spread out. John and I sat on the left side of the airplane in an exit row; I always picked exit rows for obvious reasons. John took the window seat, and I took the aisle. Elaine and Ted were on the right side of the airplane in the same row. As the airplane taxied, took off, and headed south, John had his nose pressed up against the window.

About fifteen minutes into the flight, there was a muffled bang. Emotional shock waves spread through the cabin and a few people gasped as the left wing of the airplane abruptly dipped toward the ocean. John spun around, looked at me, and pointed out the window. There was a thin line of smoke trailing out from the underside of the wing. That could mean only one thing: the engine was on fire.

Somewhere behind me, a child began to cry. Most everyone else was stunned and silent. John and Ted were both getting nervous. Their eyes turned to Elaine and me for explanation, but I had none to give.

In an exceptionally calm, understated voice, the copilot said, "Ladies and gentlemen, we have experienced a small electrical problem here in the cockpit. Please buckle your seat belts. We will be returning to the airport."

While his words were meant to convey calm, his pitch conveyed something else entirely. He was obviously trying to do at least two things at once—talking to us in a calm voice while simultaneously straining on the yoke in an attempt to regain control over the stricken airplane. Over top of his voice, I could hear the alarms blaring in the cockpit and the pilot making a distress call to the tower.

"Mayday. Mayday. Mayday."

"Flight attendants, TAKE YOUR SEATS." Now the copilot was beginning to sound a little more desperate.

We were losing altitude rapidly. I turned to Elaine and made eye contact. She knew this was serious. In a hushed voice, I said, "You take care of Ted. I've got John."

To myself, I said, *MY GOD, THIS IS HAPPENING AGAIN.*

The airplane was losing altitude very fast. I grabbed the loose end of John's seat belt and gave it a terrific pull.

"Dad, are we going to crash?" he asked.

"No. We are all going to be all right. I will take care of you," I reassured him. But I had no idea if I was going to be able to make good on that promise.

"Look at that door beside you," I said. "See the handle above the window. If the pilot tells us to use the emergency exits, we will have to open that door. If I can't do it for some reason, I want you to pull that handle out first. OK? That will be our way out."

I looked out the window and could see the engine was still streaming black smoke, but I could not see any fire. Somehow, the smell of smoke began finding its way into the cabin, accumulating at the ceiling, making my eyes burn. Someone behind me began to cough.

I glanced to my right and again caught Elaine's eyes. She had Ted wrapped up tight in her arms. I mouthed, "I love you."

When we got down below five thousand feet, the airplane entered thicker air and the pilots seemed finally to be winning the battle for control of the airplane. At least the left wing was beginning to come up and was pointed more normally toward the horizon. The nose of the airplane was now almost level. But we were skimming across the sea at an unusually low altitude. The water was little more than a blur.

"Ladies and gentlemen." This time it was a male flight attendant on the PA system. "We may have a hard landing. When I tell you to brace, grab the seat in front of you and steady yourselves."

The minutes ticked by as we flew on a straight line, skimming over top of the water toward the nearest runway. The passengers were stunned. Some were praying, others crying.

John's eyes were wide open, and he was clearly afraid.

I tried to reassure him that things would be OK. "The pilots have control of this. Don't worry."

Just then, a commanding voice came over the PA system, "BRACE! BRACE! BRACE!" We all did as we were told and raised our arms against the seat backs in front of us. Elaine was still holding Ted tightly against her body.

I glanced out John's window just as we passed over the end of the runway. There was a line of fire trucks and ambulances waiting for us on the ground. All my efforts to calm John were wiped away in an instant when he saw those emergency vehicles.

As we passed overhead, the lead truck took off in hot pursuit, followed by the entire department, lights flashing. They were paralleling us down the side taxiway. When our wheels hit the tarmac, the pilots stomped on the braking system. Without the use of both engines or the reverse thrusters, they had limited control of the airplane. Like a drunken sailor, we careened down the runway. It was all the pilots could do to keep the airplane on the asphalt.

Eventually, the airplane slowed and came to a stop in the middle of the runway, but before the pilot could shut down the one good engine, a fire truck flew around the left wing. Men in head-to-toe silver fire gear and oxygen tanks jumped out before the truck even came to a halt and immediately dragged their hoses into position around the hot engine. They then just stood there, guarding against a resurgence of fire.

"Are you OK?" I asked, but John didn't answer. He was staring at my hands. They were shaking. I couldn't hide them. I was being reminded of just how much was at stake this time.

I looked to the front of the cabin expecting someone to tell me to open the emergency exit. But the order never came. This time the pilot came on the PA system and said, "Thank you all for your patience. I'm sorry for the bumpy ride. They're going to be sending out a staircase for us to use to exit the airplane."

As quickly as the emergency started, it was over. When we exited the airplane, the pilot stood in the cockpit doorway trying to act as if nothing at all had happened. He was actually pretty good at it, but he wasn't fooling anyone; his face was still just a little bit pale and I suddenly realized I had seen that expression before—in Alaska.

20

EGEGIK REVISITED

The flight home from Palau caused a lot of long-buried memories to resurface. Reluctantly, I was forced to acknowledge that those memories still haunted me. Nightmares often played out in the half-light of the Alaskan midnight sun, icy arctic water mixed with jet fuel, flushing through my clothes. The torn and crushed wreckage of that airplane sitting abandoned in shallow water, its twin tails protruding above the sea surface, shuddering under the weight of each new Bering Sea wave.

One night, not long after returning, I woke, feeling pain radiating from every muscle, every bone, from inside my head, and from my lungs. I laid there in bed fully awake, soaking wet, feeling as if I were breathing pure oxygen. Phantom blood flowed down the palm of my hand, worked its way to the tips of my fingers, then dripped into an imaginary sea. I was cold. I remember being colder that night in Alaska than I had ever been before in my life. In the silence of our bedroom, I rolled over, seeking my wife's comfort and warmth.

That next morning, I rose early and headed down to the kitchen, convinced that I would have to confront this trauma. I could not continue to pretend that these things had never happened. When Elaine joined me, I already had the kitchen counter covered with the raw materials for breakfast. The coffee pot was just finishing its job. As Elaine threw the eggs and pancakes into two separate pans, I told her about the nightmare I had just had. She said she knew I was reliving something because I kicked her in bed while asleep.

"I have something I need to ask."

"Okaaayyy . . ." She drew out her response, waiting to hear what I had to say.

"I'd like to revisit the plane crash site in Alaska."

Elaine cast a surprised look my way but didn't say anything.

There was a long silence, so I continued, "I think I should go back to Alaska, crawl through the airplane wreck if it still exists, relive it, and that might take some of its power away. I am haunted still by what happened up there. Our last flight has just made it all that much worse."

"You sure you want to confront the past?"

"It's an open, festering wound. I need closure."

Elaine got on the phone immediately to ask Jim and Peggy Colman if they might take the boys for a few days. I didn't want to subject them to another trauma so soon after the engine fire. I booked the necessary flights to Alaska, and on July 5 we headed out the door with one small carry-on and a single Leica slung from my neck. I felt liberated without all the camera gear. I couldn't remember the last time I had gotten on a plane with only one bag.

Together we flew from Portland to Anchorage onboard an Alaska Airlines commercial flight and then hopped a commuter to King Salmon. We stayed that first night in a bar, store, and motel all rolled into one. The noise blasting from the bar that night made it impossible to sleep, but I didn't feel much like sleeping anyway.

The next morning we walked over to the airport, where a couple of tail-dragging DC-3s and an older C-119, like the one that had crashed that night, sat on the apron. This one had been retrofitted with a jet engine over the top of the fuselage to provide extra boost on takeoff. "If only we'd had that mounted on the plane in 1979," I mused.

We walked into the general aviation office and found a slightly balding, heavyset fellow with grease under his fingernails and dark lines of dirty oil buildup in the creases of his hands. He seemed to be in charge, so I asked if he had a bush pilot free to take us out to Big Creek. He pulled a rag from his back pocket to wipe his hands and asked why we wanted to go. I told him we wanted to have a look at whatever was left of the C-119 that crashed there some years back.

I was surprised he didn't ask why we wanted to see the wreck. Instead, he promptly slipped out of his oil-stained coveralls, saying he would be our pilot. He led us out to a Cessna 182, removed the tie-down ropes, and opened the right-side door, inviting us to climb in.

He asked if we were ready, then primed the engine and turned the ignition switch to "Start" and punched the starter. The prop spun up to speed and we lifted off, headed southwest.

We flew out toward the coast, then circled the area. There, in the sand, about seven-and-a-half miles north of Egegik, I could see the broken Fairchild. It looked fragile and lonely and forgotten.

As soon as the pilot put the Cessna down a couple hundred yards west of the wreckage, Elaine and I climbed out and began walking toward the twisted pile of aluminum. The wind was blowing just as it had been that night, and the gulls were standing strong with their heads pointed into the wind. Once again, the place smelled of rotting fish and salt air. The closer we got to the wreck, the more intense my memories became. It was as if the plane was pushing me away, its force increasing with every step I took.

Someone had gone to a lot of trouble and expense to winch the wreck back from the water. It was leaning forward with its nose—what was left of it—buried in the sand dune, its twin tails protruding precariously into the air.

I began crawling through what was left of the plane explaining everything in detail to Elaine. I touched the cold metal fuselage and pried a piece of metal from the wreck as a souvenir. The two-by-three-inch piece had the words NO STEP printed on its face. I looked but could not find the shattered seat I had once occupied.

After a half hour, I turned around to find a stranger standing behind Elaine, staring at the two of us. He was wearing muck boots, heavy rain gear, and fingerless wool gloves. He looked like a fisherman, deeply weathered, dark from the sun, a full unkept beard, and a wool stocking cap.

When the man saw I was looking his way, he hollered above the wind, "What you doing in there?"

Without moving my eyes from the wreck, I replied, "Staring into the darkness."

He ran his eyes over the twisted metal, as if it was his old friend, and said, "She's a mess, ain't she."

"I have some history here," I offered. "Just needed to see this wreck one more time."

"Do you know what happened here?" the fisherman asked, as if he had given this history lesson many times before to curious visitors and was just a little bit bored with having to explain it all again.

"Indeed, I do." I said, "I was in this thing when it went down."

Suddenly, his eyes popped wide. He looked at me suspiciously, glanced down at the camera around my neck, and it hit him. "Oh my God," he exclaimed. "Are you the photographer who went down with this crate?"

"Indeed."

"Well, Jesus." He briskly stepped around Elaine, pulling his fingerless glove off his right hand and offering it to me. "I was there that night. I pulled you out of the ocean."

I thought he must be kidding, but his eyes told me he was not.

"You all were lying in the water right over there," and he turned to point toward the beach. "I was sure you were dead. My friend and I picked you up and took you to our hut over there." He spun around and pointed at the roof of a shack, half-buried in the sand. "You were out of it."

There was an awkward silence as we exchanged looks. I was trying to come to terms with how I felt, meeting the man who pulled me out of the sea. He, too, didn't seem to know how to react. Elaine's eyes were widening with shock.

"We radioed for help and they sent a plane to pick you up." He went on to say, "I worried about your condition for a long time afterward but never heard back. What happened to you after you left here?"

Before I could answer, he hit his forehead with the palm of his hand and said, "My God! I have something of yours."

"What do you mean?" I asked.

"Well, come with me."

He led Elaine and me a hundred feet to his hut in the sand, then gave the door a swift kick before pushing it open. Elaine and I stooped down to enter the hut through the short doorway. We dodged around a clothesline hung low with wet shirts and underwear. There were three very sharp filleting knives on a rough table in a corner, a skillet with half-eaten beans, and a lever-action .30-30 standing in a corner.

The fisherman made his way past the stove to the back wall, reached up, and roughly pushed a cardboard box to the side to get at something. He turned back around and blew dust off the surface of my Arriflex motion picture camera—the one I had lost in the crash. He proudly but delicately handed it to me saying, "I think this might belong to you."

I gingerly took the camera, turned it over in my hands as if it were a rare, fragile flower, and a flood of memories came back. The last time I saw this camera, it shattered my hand and disappeared into a mangled mess of metal.

The fisherman's voice brought me back from my memories. "I always wondered if someone would come back looking for that."

"My God," I whispered. The camera appeared to be in excellent condition, but of course it was not. It was now little more than a twenty-pound chunk of rusted, salt-encrusted steel.

The fisherman noticed I was trying to open the camera and apologetically said, "That night, I cleaned it up as best I could, but when no one ever came back for it, I just threw it up there on that shelf."

"I can't thank you enough for this. And for everything you must have done for me that night." I glanced at his weather-beaten face and he just shrugged as if it was all in a day's work. But it wasn't and I knew it.

Eventually, the fisherman saw that I was overwhelmed. "Can I make you some tea?"

Elaine said yes. We sat down and asked our host about that night. He said he bandaged my wounds. As he talked he threw a piece of wood in the stove and told us the younger pilot was not seriously injured. "His Dad was pretty beat up. So was the boy who flew along to help with the loading process. Lost most of his teeth that night."

As he was working his way through what had happened, there was a knock at the door. It was our bush pilot coming to retrieve us. I had nearly forgotten about him.

"I need to get going. I've got a charter waiting for me back in King Salmon. Are you ready to go?"

Reluctantly, Elaine and I pried ourselves out of our chairs and thanked our host for everything. Elaine threw her arms around the man, thanking him for all he had done for me that night.

Twenty minutes later, when we arrived at the King Salmon airport, I asked the bush pilot about the best way to get back to Anchorage. He said there were no more passenger flights scheduled for that night. "But if you look right over there, that plane is headed back to the interior. Maybe you can hitch a ride with them."

My eyes tracked his finger across the tarmac and I noticed a cargo plane, not unlike the C-119 Flying Boxcar, preparing to take off. I hesitated only for a moment, weighing the options.

I glanced over at Elaine and she raised her shoulders just slightly. "It's up to you."

I said something about there being no time like the present. Just as I had done on the night in 1979, I walked up to the pilot. "Hi, my name is Jim Larison. This is my wife, Elaine. We work for the National Geographic Society and we would greatly appreciate a ride out of here. If you don't mind."

He hesitated, looking at me, then at Elaine. "What are you doing out here?"

I explained why we had come and what we'd seen out on the beach. He reached up to run his fingers through his beard and then quickly agreed to provide us with a hop over the mountains. "I'm not going to Anchorage, but I'll take you as far as Kodiak. You probably can hitch a ride out of there almost as easily as Anchorage."

The aircraft he was prepping for flight was a four-engine prop version of the DC-7. It was already loaded with sockeye salmon and was headed back to a processing facility.

As the plane warmed up and the load was secured, I talked more with the pilot. At first he was curious about our job working for the National Geographic Society. But shortly, the conversation turned to the plane crash on the beach at Big Creek, and I began to understand why he had agreed so easily to my request to fly along. He had seen the wreckage, flown over it many times, even landed on that same beach a time or two.

"I have to tell you—I'm surprised to hear that you survived that crash. That airplane was torn to shreds. I'd heard no one survived."

"Well, you know how rumors get started," I said.

"But the cockpit. When I first saw the plane, it was under the fuse-lage in ten feet of water," he insisted. "How could anyone survive such a crash?"

"Just dumb luck, I guess."

"What a mess," he observed.

As he continued readying the airplane for takeoff, the pilot contin-ued to ask a lot more questions. People always want to be assured that such an accident could never happen to them.

After a while, his flight preparation duties got in the way of our talk. He offered me the flight engineer's seat directly behind him in the cock-pit. Elaine went back into the aircraft and sat on a bench about a dozen feet behind me. History was repeating itself; I was offered the same seat I had been given that night on the beach—the engineer's jump seat. If I really wanted to face my fears, what better way than to sit right there in the cockpit of this gray, aluminum cargo plane loaded with sockeye salmon and fly once again. I sat down, strapped in, checked to see that Elaine was using her seat belt, and we took off.

For a while, I was overwhelmed by the sounds reverberating through the aluminum shell of the cargo plane. But I knew I had to deal with this, and so I started asking the pilot about the DC-7 he was flying, its size, lift capabilities, and its stall speed; I was curious about its four propeller-driven, piston Wright engines and how he managed to balance them one against the other. I was just occupying my mind with details, trying to suppress emotion.

The pilot told me the engines each produce about thirty-two hun-dred horsepower in thrust. The airplane carries as much as thirty thou-sand pounds of cargo. "Don't worry, we have less than half that on at the moment," he continued.

I asked him about the range and max speed and ceiling. "What did you say about this plane's stall speed?" I just couldn't stop asking ques-tions. Somewhere along the line, the pilot got the wrong impression.

"Are you a pilot yourself?"

I felt self-conscious. "No. I'm curious about everything to do with flying."

"But you know a good deal about aircraft," he observed.

"I might just be trying to get a better handle on what happened that night." I told him about the little bit of flight experience I had. "My job puts me in airplanes a lot. I have even taken the controls of a number of those airplanes when I wasn't filming. In my life, I have flown Cessna 172s and 182s. I also once took the controls of a twin-engine Beechcraft. Always with a real pilot sitting beside me," I assured him.

"Would you like to take the controls of this one?"

"This one looks a little complicated for me."

"I'll teach you."

The pilot motioned to his copilot, who promptly slipped out of his seat and I slipped in. For about half an hour, the pilot gave me a free lesson in managing the yoke and throttles. With the pilot's constant feedback, I flew the airplane starting somewhere just outside of King Salmon toward Kodiak. The pilot showed me how to manage the trim wheel and balance the four throttles. I adjusted the fuel until I had a three-hundred-feet-per-minute climb rate on the vertical speed indicator, the so-called VSI. And slowly, the big, four-engine aircraft lifted out of the Alaskan coastal region and flew through a mountain pass in the Katmai National Park on the way to Kodiak.

We cleared the snowcapped mountains with about five hundred feet to spare at midnight, just as the sun was reaching its low point in the summer sky. The engines hummed with unbroken precision as we started down the other side of the mountains, and the DC-7 began to pick up airspeed, topping off at just over three hundred knots on our way to the sea. The pilot showed me how to use the gyro compass and turn indicator to assist while I adjusted the aircraft heading, slowly turning to the right to line up with the runway on Kodiak.

The pilot then asked for the controls back. As he placed his hands on the yoke and I slipped mine off, he said, "You know, you take to this like a natural. If you ever want to leave your National Geographic gig, you'd have a future in the left seat of some aircraft."

"It's been a real joy to fly along with you guys," I said. I turned to the copilot, who was just slipping back into his seat, and thanked him for giving up his seat.

"Well, I'm just glad to see that you survived that mess back there on the beach."

As we approached Kodiak, I moved back and sat with Elaine in the rear of the cockpit. I put a set of headphones over my ears and the pilot broke in to ask how we were doing back there.

"Can't thank you enough. It's been great fun."

"Nothing quite like throwing yourself back into the teeth of the thing that scares you the most," he said, and then shifted his attention to his duties as pilot.

I turned to Elaine. She just smiled. "Did it help?"

"Maybe," I said.

She put her head on my shoulder and said, "I love you."

PART V

WOUNDS THAT WILL NOT HEAL

21

A WORLD OF WOUNDS

ELAINE AND I WOULD GO ON TRAVELING AND EXPLORING, making many more films for the National Geographic and a few more for the Public Broadcasting Service. Most of these dealt with environmental issues we thought important. Our job, as I saw it, was to stimulate discussion about important environmental issues and feed those conversations with an ecosystem perspective. This would, I hoped, affect the direction and outcome of such conversations and help people see the importance of wild places and ecosystem stability. My goal was to make our audience care about wilderness and the natural world. To do that, I knew I had to communicate clearly and vividly the importance of natural systems and processes. There simply was no better tool for doing that than film.

But as we crisscrossed the planet, camera in hand, we became increasingly concerned about what we were witnessing and capturing on film. Our films show in graphic detail the steady decline of nature, the loss of biodiversity, and the destabilization of Earth's life support system—the very system that supports human beings.

Elaine and I spent years walking and climbing on ice that is now gone. We shot footage of forests that no longer exist and photographed the expansion of deserts and the beginnings of a mega-drought across the American West. We photographed complex reef ecosystems that are now little more than white skeletons. We were stunned by the speed with which humans were destroying the ecosystems that sustain us all.

Without fully appreciating it at the time, our films also documented the leading edge of what is now commonly referred to as human-caused climate change. On Mauna Loa, on the Big Island of Hawaii, as far back as 1989, we filmed the raw data as it came in to the National Oceanic and Atmospheric Administration sensors, showing the proximate cause of this warming, the steady accumulation of carbon dioxide in the atmosphere, largely a result of burning fossil fuels. NOAA scientists provided this critical information to the public at the time. We, and other documentary filmmakers and journalists, picked that information up and broadcast it to the world, but precious little changed. Society moved on without taking meaningful action to curb the emissions of harmful carbon dioxide. When it became clear that the science was consistently pointing toward a worldwide serious threat, the oil and gas industry began to mount a public relations campaign to prevent meaningful regulation. Science itself came under withering attack, as if muzzling truth would somehow make it go away.

Conservationist Aldo Leopold once warned his students they would be living "alone in a world of wounds" and suggested we would either harden ourselves against what we were going to see or we would suffer with each mark of environmental death. As an undergraduate at Cornell University, I read his book but never fully appreciated what Leopold meant. Now, sadly, I do understand.

After an eventful career in ecology, I must admit to occasionally being just a little frustrated. I ask myself: How much impact did our films really have? Why do people continue to make such obviously bad decisions? I'm sure the answers are complex, but one thing seems clear to me: many people believe that we humans exist outside of nature—that we are bigger, better, smarter, and more important—and hence independent of natural processes, natural ecosystems, and the laws of nature. We think of nature as something we need to conquer.

As an ecologist, I can tell you with absolute certainty we are not outside of nature; we are a *product* and *constituent part* of nature. We do not so much need to tame nature as we need to learn to live in harmony with it—for our own sakes.

———————

Eventually, Elaine and I put down our cameras and retired from both the National Geographic Society and the university. Perhaps, not surprisingly, when that day came, we headed for the mountains. If I had learned anything while exploring and photographing wild places, it was that I am most at home in the mountains. Only in their presence can I truly find myself. The mountains we climbed and the pristine forests we lived in were the tapestry upon which we constructed our lives. We drew strength from these places and found peace in nature's silence.

We eventually found a place little more than a stone's throw from the Eagle Cap Wilderness area in northeast Oregon where we could relax. Fifty feet above one of Oregon's most pristine wild and scenic rivers, I built a bench for my wife. It was a retirement gift to the woman who had shared her life with me, traveled a million miles, and shared every struggle, never once complaining. Everything within view from that bench we have preserved, doing our part to ensure that at least this small piece of forest would remain wild and undisturbed for as long as we own it. At this particular spot, high in the Wallowa Mountains, the river is not much more than a clear mountain creek, about forty feet wide, running over top of well-worn boulders, cutting its way under rock ledges. Snowmelt from the mountains feeds this river with a steady supply of cold, pure, life-giving water. The roar of water carving rock reverberates through the canyon. Old-growth ponderosa pine, larch, and spruce, some of which have fallen into the river, provide shelter for rainbow trout. Bald eagles and ospreys fly by at eye level almost every day, sometimes stopping long enough to fish. In the spring, ruffed grouse drum in the woods. And in the fall, elk call from the surrounding mountains, frequently coming down behind our cabin to drink at the river's edge.

One day I walked up the short trail to that bench to join Elaine. She was quietly meditating. I tried not to disturb her. She seemed at peace.

Just then, a young cinnamon-colored black bear came out of the forest in front of us, ordered her two reluctant puffball cubs to swim the river, and came up the bank ten feet behind where we were sitting. Elaine turned around, was surprised to see such a large animal so close and said, "Why . . . you're a bear." The sow looked straight at her, decided we were no threat, and continued on her way up the mountain.

Ted came out to our Eagle Creek property shortly after we bought the place to help build an off-grid cabin. John joined us when we needed help putting on a metal roof. It has been a family project involving our kids, their wives, and our five grandchildren. We all regularly assemble at our cabin in the woods to share in each other's lives, to enjoy wilderness together. While we stay at our off-grid cabin, we can, to one degree or another push the "wounds" that Aldo Leopold wrote about out of our minds.

I think Elaine likes the bench and the cabin so much because they are stationary. No airplanes, no travel, no mountains of gear to haul around. She was happy just to sit and soak up the beauty of wilderness.

That day, we sat for hours not talking, just enjoying the peace and quiet. I reached out, put my arm around my wife's small shoulders, pulled her to me, and gently whispered in her ear, "Thank you."

EPILOGUE

HOW FILMS WERE MADE

OF COURSE, EVERYTHING ABOUT THE way we made films back then has changed. It will therefore sound odd, or perhaps even unbelievable to those who have grown up in the age of computers and gigabits of data stored on tiny thumb drives, but in those days television shows and films were not made digitally. Rather, they were produced with chemistry and light-sensitive film coatings of silver halide crystals. This film had to be kept cool and in the dark. Film magazines had to be loaded in the dark, no matter where you were filming. This meant that you had to carry a portable darkroom—a changing bag—around with you everywhere you went so that you could change film rolls on the fly. It also meant that we would have to carry a minimum of fifty pounds of film in a lead-lined suitcase. The airlines were, then as now, fond of X-raying baggage, so the lead lining was designed to protect the film from the destructive X-rays.

We used negative 16 mm film that was usually made by Kodak and was just over a half inch wide, with sprocket holes on either side. This light-sensitive emulsion was then run through exquisitely crafted German Arriflex 16SR II cameras at exactly twenty-four frames per second. In other words, twenty-four individual still images were made by the camera every second. When viewed in rapid succession, the images captured the illusion of motion. This negative film was copied, producing what we called a "workprint." This workprint could then be cut and manipulated without compromising the original negative, which was kept in a climate-controlled vault.

Sounds were laid down separately on continuous analogue acetate tape. The sound tape was one-quarter inch wide and had no mechanical sprockets to pull it along or to regulate its speed. Instead, the tape was run over electronic heads in a twenty-pound Nagra tape recorder that had an electronic method for keeping the tape running at a predictable and regular speed.

To keep the camera and sound recorder synchronized, one had only to create a visual and audible start mark at the beginning of each shot. This was done with what was called a *clapboard*. The sound engineer would stand in front of the camera and say something like, "Roll camera. Roll recorder. Film title, *Ancient Forests*, roll 10, tape 3, take 5." He would then slam the clapboard arm down to create a visual and audible start mark printed on both the film and tape. The tape would later be transferred to a magnetic film complete with its own sprocket holes. The Steenbeck editing table was designed to mechanically link this sound track to the workprint using the start mark as a reference so that the two could be held in sync. The Steenbeck could handle one visual track—the workprint—and two sound tracks at a time.

Once all the film was edited and cut together to make a rough cut of the final show, then the magnetic sound tracks were laid out and matched to the picture. Sometimes I would use as many as ten sound tracks: one narrator track, one or two music tracks, and three to seven sound tracks, to make up a finished film. In a sound studio, the sound tracks would then be mixed. The original negative could then be matched to the workprint by using consecutive numbers printed on the edge of the film. A single, composite internegative would be produced marrying the photographic images to that single sound track. Release prints, suitable for projection or conversion to video tape, could then be made from the internegative.

This entire method of making films is almost completely extinct, having been replaced by computers and digital data storage. The advantage once enjoyed by film—its ability to capture fine detail—have been completely erased by high-definition digital imaging. HD cameras are less than half the size and cost of their film counterparts, and they record far more data, yielding a sharper, cleaner image than was possible with silver halide crystals and chemical reactions.

In addition, today's digital systems permit far more flexibility and allow the filmmaker to view what the camera has captured in real time, rather than having to wait two or more weeks for the film to be processed and printed in some far-away laboratory.

Despite the advantages of the digital world, I somehow miss the good old days of film and smelly chemical developers. I think it was a simpler time, though I guess it doesn't sound very simple when I describe it.

I used the chemistry, the film emulsion, the characteristics of the camera, and above all, the light, to capture that all-important moment in time—to immortalize that perfect shot. But as I look back at the miles of film we accumulated, I see the Kodak colors beginning to fade, celluloid growing brittle. Projectors and film cameras are now dinosaurs.

It occurs to me that even our record of ecosystems past, so meticulously stored in climate-controlled vaults, will one day be gone. Not only will we have lost the old-growth forests and the reefs and so much of the ice but even this last film record of such pristine places will be gone, and we will be so much poorer for that loss.

ACKNOWLEDGMENTS

A FEW YEARS AFTER LEAVING OUR FILMMAKING LIVES, our oldest grand-daughter, Navah, asked me to tell her a story. She was just a little girl and she was curious.

"About what, honey?"

"About you and Nana."

I told her one story, which led to another and another. Her glistening eyes would bounce around and she would beg for just one more story. Her enthusiasm is what led to me write this book. I want to thank Navah, because without her insistence, I might never have tackled this years-long project. In fact, I want to thank all of my grandchildren, Navah, Naomi, Reed, Rhone, and Maggie, for being so supportive and curious.

I also want to thank my oldest son, John, an excellent English instructor and a bestselling author in his own right. Among many other things, he taught me the difference between telling a story and letting the story reveal itself. Without his guidance, this book would have been little more than a family travel log.

I want to thank my youngest son, Ted, who taught me the meaning of enthusiasm and what true grit really looks like.

In addition, I owe much to the people who read and critiqued this book before I sent if off to a publishing house; among these are Ellie Larison, Mary Lou Mate, and Yvonne Granados.

Filmmaking is, by no means, a solitary venture. Whenever any-one makes a film, countless numbers of people contribute to the process. I would like to specifically mention a few of the ones who made major contributions to our films over the years. These include, from the National Geographic Society staff: Dennis Kane, Sid Platt, Donald Cooper, Carl Ziebe, Susan Poole, Jean Berthold, Frances Ingram, Louise Millikan, and Nancy Rosenthal; Joe Cone, Pat Kight, Jim Hicks, Rob Phillips, Linda Weimer, and Sandy Ridlington all contributed immeasurably to the writing of these films; Jane Lubchenco, Elen Cutrim, Jack Gustafson, and Bruce Mate provided invaluable subject matter, advice, and counsel; Aaron Ferster, John Hyde, Jeff Anderson, Rob Schulze, and Michael Dun worked long and hard in the field with me as assistant cameramen and talent; Marti Keltner and Gene Griswold taught Elaine and me to climb mountains; Steve Adams taught us to dive. Bill Wick, Dick Tubb, and John Byrne had much to do with my ability to maintain my faculty position at Oregon State University while also functioning as a National Geographic filmmaker; Rod Mesecar designed and built much of our underwater gear; and I would like to also thank Fritz Albert for helping me to see and appreciate light and showing me how to become all that I could be as a filmmaker.

Especially, I want to thank my good friend Jim Hicks for sharing in this life and supporting me unconditionally—especially for being there that night in Alaska when I needed him the most.

And finally, I want to thank my dear wife, Elaine, without whom this book—indeed this life—would never have been possible. I especially appreciate the fact that she ignored her friends' advice and said yes when I asked her to marry me. I hope she has never regretted that consequential decision. There is simply no person to whom I owe more.

THE FILMS OF JAMES
AND ELAINE LARISON

Films Produced by Jim and Elaine Larison for the National Geographic Society

The Mountain States (1983)

Riches from the Sea (1984)

DNA: Laboratory of Life (1985)

The Robotic Revolution (1986)

The Living Ocean (1988)

The Living Earth (1989)

The Rocky Mountains (1989)

The Fire Station (1990)

The Hospital (1990)

The Police Station (1990)

Ancient Forests (1992)

Your Town: Communications (1992)

Your Town: Transportation (1992)

Diversity of Life (1993)

The Scientific Method (1993)

Simple Machines (1993)

Latitude and Longitude (1994)

9-1-1 (1994)

Where Do Animals Go in Winter? (1994)

What Is the Earth Made Of? (1995)
Signs of Nature (1996)

Films produced by Jim and Elaine Larison for the Public Broadcasting Service, the Discovery Channel, and various state and federal agencies:
The Solid Waste Problem (1973)
Runoff (1978)
Mammals of the Sea (1980)
Estuary (1982)
The Gray Whale (1982)
Farmers of the Sea (1984)
Identifying Canada Geese (1985)
Sagebrush Country (1987)
Oregon's Ocean (1992)
Saving the Great Whales (2001)

ABOUT THE AUTHOR

JAMES R. LARISON IS AN ecologist by training and a filmmaker by vocation.

Together with his wife, Elaine, Dr. Larison produced and photographed thirty-one films and television shows about wildlife and nature, most for the National Geographic Society. Their films won more than forty national and international awards, including the Izaak Walton Conservation Award, the Wildlife Conservation Education Award, the Grand Award from the Council for the Advancement and Support of Education, four individual awards from the Outdoor Writers Association of America, a Gold Ahre and two Silver Ahres at the Berlin International Film Festival, the Silver Tusker from the International Wildlife Film Festival, and the Albrecht Dürer Bronze at the Budapest Independent Film Festival.

Jim Larison grew up in upstate New York, earning a doctorate in ecology and a bachelor's degree in wildlife ecology, both from Cornell University, and a master's in journalism and filmmaking from the University of Wisconsin–Madison. He also served as a captain in the US Army and as a professor on the faculty of Oregon State University. He has a fondness for, and spent much of his life studying, alpine ecosystems and has written extensively on the effects of heavy metals on white-tailed ptarmigan populations in the Rocky Mountains.

In retirement, the Larisons live quietly in Oregon's Coast Range, surrounded by a grove of old-growth trees.